CRISIS AND CROSSFIRE

Issues in the History of American Foreign Relations

Series Editor: Robert J. McMahon, The Ohio State University

In this series

ⲥ

CRISIS AND CROSSFIRE

The United States and the
Middle East Since 1945

Peter L. Hahn

Potomac Books, Inc.
Washington, D.C.

Library of Congress Cataloging-in-Publication Data
Hahn, Peter L.
  Crisis and crossfire : the United States and the Middle East since 1945 / Peter L. Hahn.— 1st ed.
    p. cm.
  Includes bibliographical references and index.
  ISBN 1-57488-819-6 (hardcover : alk. paper) — ISBN 1-57488-820-X (pbk. : alk. paper)
  1. Middle East—Foreign relations—United States. 2. United States—Foreign relations—Middle East. 3. National security—United States. 4. Arab-Israeli conflict—Diplomatic history. 5. Middle East—Foreign relations—20th century. 6. United States—Foreign relations—20th century I. Title.
  DS63.2.U5H347 2005
  327.73056'09'045—dc22

                                                                              2005016525

Printed in Canada on acid-free paper that meets the
American National Standards Institute Z39-48 Standard.

Maps by Jay Karamales, copyright © 2005 by Potomac Books, Inc.

Potomac Books, Inc.
22841 Quicksilver Drive
Dulles, Virginia 20166

First Edition

10 9 8 7 6 5 4 3 2 1

For Anna Jane, Benjamin, Paul, and Mark

CONTENTS

ILLUSTRATIONS

Maps

Photographs and Drawings

SERIES EDITOR'S NOTE

FROM THE BIRTH OF THE AMERICAN Republic in the late eighteenth century to the emergence of the United States as a fledgling world power at the end of the nineteenth century, the place of the United States within the broader international system of nation-states posed fundamental challenges to American and foreign statesmen alike. What role would—and could—a non-European power play in a Eurocentric world order? The combination of America's stunning economic transformation and two devastating world wars helped shatter the old European order, catapulting the United States into a position of global preeminence by the middle decades of the twentieth century. Since the mid-1940s, it has become common to refer to the United States as a superpower. Since the collapse of the Soviet Union, its only serious rival, and the concomitant end of the Cold War, it has become common to label the United States as the world's lone superpower, or "hyperpower," as a French diplomat labeled it in the late-1990s.

By any standard of measurement, the United States has long been, as it remains today, the dominant force in world affairs—economically, politically, militarily, and culturally.

The United States has placed, and continues to place, its own indelible stamp on the international system while shaping the aspirations, mores, tastes, living standards, and sometimes resentments and hatreds of hundreds of millions of ordinary people across the globe. Few subjects, consequently, loom larger in the history of the modern world than the often uneasy encounter between the United States and the nations and peoples beyond its shores.

This series, *Issues in the History of American Foreign Relations*, aims to provide students and general readers alike with a wide range of books, written by some of the outstanding scholarly experts of this generation, that elucidate key issues, themes, topics, and individuals in the nearly 250-year history of U.S. foreign relations. The series will cover an array of diverse subjects spanning from the era of the founding fathers to the present. Each book will offer a concise, accessible narrative, based upon the latest scholarship, followed by a careful selection of relevant primary documents. Primary sources enable a reader to immerse himself or herself in the raw material of history, thereby facilitating the formation of informed, independent judgments about the subject at hand. To capitalize upon the unprecedented amount of non-American archival sources and materials currently available, most books will feature foreign as well as American material in the documentary section. A broad, international perspective on the external behavior of the United States, one of the major trends of recent scholarship, will be a prominent feature of the books in this series.

It is my fondest hope that this series will contribute to a greater engagement with and understanding of the complexities of this fascinating—and critical—subject.

Robert J. McMahon
Ohio State University

ACKNOWLEDGMENTS

I AM GRATEFUL TO SEVERAL PEOPLE who assisted me in the publication of this book. Paul Chamberlin, my graduate student at Ohio State University, served exceedingly well as research assistant and was particularly helpful at tracking down documents and photographs. Robert McMahon, the editor of the *Issues in the History of American Foreign Relations* series, initially recruited me to write this book and helped me conceptualize it. I appreciate the excellent advice of Douglas Little, who peer-reviewed the manuscript and made several wise recommendations on how to improve it. Don Jacobs, acquisitions editor at Potomac Books, provided superb counsel at all stages of my work. I am grateful to Potomac's staff for their first-rate service in producing maps, arranging photographs, copyediting text, and bringing my words to print.

As always, I am deeply grateful to my wife and our children for their encouragement as I wrote this book. Cathy provided her usual sturdy foundation of support for my professional aspirations. Anna, Ben, Paul, and Mark endured, and I daresay occasionally enjoyed, many dinnertime discussions on the intricacies of American foreign policy in the Middle East. Their thinking has matured enough that I have found it helpful to listen to their insights and evaluations. They also helped me select the photographs and voted their approval of the cover design. In appreciation of their enthusiasm for learning and their respect for my research, I dedicate this book to them.

Peter L. Hahn
Columbus, Ohio
March 2005

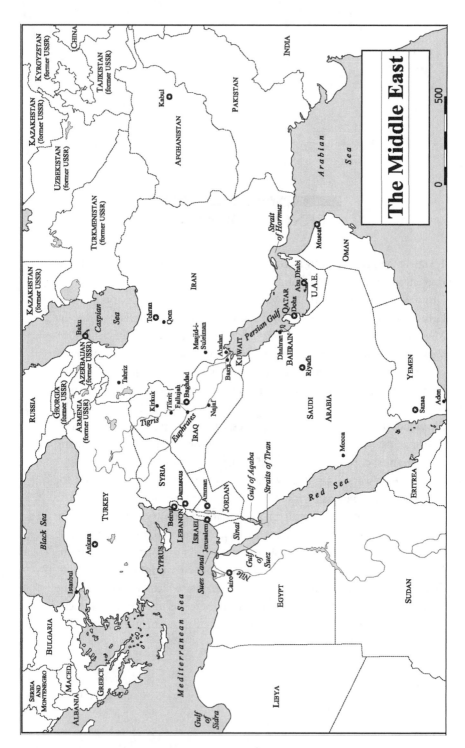

The Middle East

INTRODUCTION

FROM THE PERSPECTIVE OF THE UNITED States, the Middle East ranked as the most troublesome and dangerous region of the world in the early 2000s. A low-intensity battle with terrorists that had escalated through the 1990s exploded dramatically when the al-Qaeda terrorist network attacked the United States on September 11, 2001, and the United States responded by invading Afghanistan in pursuit of al-Qaeda members and leaders. Then, President George W. Bush ordered an invasion of Iraq to remove its dictator Saddam Hussein, but a widespread insurgency soon contested the American occupation of that country. Meanwhile, Palestinian-Israeli violence in the West Bank and Gaza that had erupted in 2000 stoked passions and extremism on both sides of that dispute and prevented a resumption of the deadlocked peace process.

This book explains and analyzes the broad contours of U.S. policy in the Middle East since the 1940s and in so doing it develops four major themes. First, it explores U.S. policy toward the Middle East in the context of the Cold War (and, briefly, the post–Cold War era). It examines the U.S. responses, in terms of both declared doctrines and erected security systems, to the perceived Soviet challenge to the region. It also assesses U.S. efforts to preserve strategic interests, such as oil and military bases, deemed necessary to the containment of the Soviet Union and other adversaries.

Second, this book examines the U.S. reaction to Arab and Iranian nationalism. It explains how the United States tried to curtail, modify, and channel nationalist movements to serve U.S. interests, and it assesses the degree of success in such endeavors. The book also studies U.S. relations with specific nationalist leaders and U.S. efforts to preserve conservative, pro-Western governments in the Middle East.

Third, this book examines U.S. policy toward the Arab-Israeli conflict. It explores U.S. policy toward the origins of the conflict and the U.S. position in the various Arab-Israeli wars. It also examines efforts by officials in Washington to make peace in the 1950s, 1970s, and 1990s. In the process, the narrative explains U.S. bilateral relations with Israel and its Arab neighbors.

Finally, this book stresses the rising level of U.S. involvement in the Middle East. Noting the absence of official U.S. involvement in the region before World War II, this study details the growing responsibility

for regional stability that the United States accepted in the postwar period and stresses the centrality of the region to U.S. policy in recent decades.

The book is divided into seven chapters. Chapter 1 analyzes the origins of U.S. involvement in the Middle East as a response to world war and cold war in the 1940s and 1950s. Chapters 2, 4, and 6 examine U.S. policy toward the Arab-Israeli conflict in 1945–61, 1961–82, and 1982–2005, respectively. Chapters 3, 5, and 7 analyze American efforts to promote stability and enhance other Western interests across the region in the 1950s–60s, the 1970s–80s, and the period since 1990.

CHAPTER 1

NATIONAL SECURITY

The Genesis of U.S. Involvement in the Middle East

A LTHOUGH RELATIVELY UNINVOLVED IN THE MIDDLE East before World War II, the United States began to assume responsibility as the region's protector in the aftermath of the global conflagration. Several factors drew U.S. policymakers to the region. The dynamics of World War II alerted them to the vast strategic importance of the Middle East, in particular its geographic location, its military bases, and its natural resources. The onset of the Cold War after 1945 stoked fears that Soviet power would sweep into the region in the absence of American commitments there. Intra-regional confrontations such as inter-Arab rivalry and Arab-Israeli conflicts also seemed to demand U.S. involvement lest the region experience internal instability that would undermine Western interests. World war and cold war, in short, resulted in the arrival of the United States on the Middle East stage.

Pre-World War II Antecedents

Prior to World War II, the United States took relatively little official interest in the Middle East. Although European empires had long engaged in the so-called Eastern Question—a diplomatic rivalry for dominance in the Middle East (as well as South Asia)—the government in Washington identified no strategic or political interests in the area and thus avoided entanglement in the imperial rivalry there. President Woodrow Wilson contemplated governing a mandate in the region after World War I, but the U.S. Senate's rejection of the Treaty of Versailles ended the scheme. Once Britain and France assumed political prominence in the Middle East after World War I, U.S. officials tended to defer to them. "Egypt is a charming place to be stationed," William J. Jardine, the American minister in Cairo, wrote in 1932. "As I see it there is not much going on here of tremendous consequence to my government. . . . It appears to me to be quite a sideshow."[1]

In the realm of culture, by contrast, the United States became increasingly involved in the Middle East after the early nineteenth century. Acting on an evangelical impulse to convert non-Christians in foreign lands, thousands of American missionaries flocked to the region in the middle and late 1800s. Those missionaries and other philanthropists promoted education as well, founding such institutions of enduring prestige as Robert College in Constantinople (opened in 1863), Syrian Protestant College (later renamed the American University of Beirut, opened in 1866), and the American University of Cairo (opened in 1919). By 1900, scores of U.S.-organized primary and secondary schools, hospitals, and orphanages also dotted the Middle East landscape. American field research in ancient history, archaeology, and Biblical studies attracted scholarly and popular attention to the region.[2]

In the early twentieth century, moreover, private American corporations accumulated commercial interests in the Middle East, especially in the emerging petroleum industry. Western officials first began to consider Middle East oil an important commodity in the 1910s, when their navies, followed by other components of their military forces, converted from coal to oil as their chief source of energy. Within the United States, the automobile, trucking, and highway booms of the 1920s tied the consumer economy to petroleum. Although the United States remained the world's greatest oil producer into the early 1940s, forward-looking businessmen calculated that the commercial development of Middle East oil resources would prove immensely profitable. The government in Washington increasingly protested European colonialism and endorsed nationalist independence movements in the Middle East, both to honor America's anti-colonial legacy and to gain new economic interests.[3]

Such inclinations touched off a wave of competition between American and British firms for oil concessions in the region, a competition in which the two Western governments took an active interest. Britain held the early upper hand. It completely denied U.S. oil interests in Iran, where it had organized the Anglo-Persian Oil Company after a major oil discovery at Masjid-i-Suleiman in 1908. The government in London also used its political leverage among Arab leaders to block oil concessions to American firms through the late 1920s, when complaints from the State Department and other factors convinced it to end the practice.

Gradually, U.S. firms captured a growing share of the Middle East oil industry. In the early 1920s, a consortium of U.S. firms secured a 23.75 percent share in the Iraq Petroleum Company, which struck it rich with a massive oil discovery near Kirkuk in 1927. Standard Oil of California (SOCAL) acquired an oil concession on Bahrain Island and struck oil there in 1932. After years of intense competition for a concession in Kuwait, the U.S.-owned Gulf Oil Corporation and the Anglo-Persian Oil Company formed a joint venture known as the Kuwait Oil Company, which in 1934 secured a seventy-five-year oil concession from Sheikh Ahmad. Four years later, the firm discovered a massive reserve in southeastern Kuwait.

Ultimately, Saudi Arabia would emerge as the most significant U.S. oil interest. After unifying most of the Arabian Peninsula through a series of wars and political initiatives, Abdel Aziz Ibn Saud established the Kingdom of Saudi Arabia in 1932. The next year, desperate for capital, King Ibn Saud gave SOCAL a sixty-year oil concession in exchange for 16 percent of the company's revenues. In 1936, SOCAL formed a joint venture with Texaco, alternatively known as Caltex or the California-Arabian Standard Oil Company (CASOC), and the new firm struck a major oil find at Dhahran in 1938. In May 1939, CASOC exported its first oil shipment from Ras Tanura, a new port it had built on the Persian Gulf, and the company's operations grew quickly as World War II generated enormous demand for its products. In 1944, CASOC was renamed the Arabian-American Oil Company (ARAMCO).[4]

The War Years

The dynamics of World War II compelled the U.S. government to take an abiding interest in the Middle East. As Germany ravaged most of Europe, it eyed the Middle East as a route to link up with its Japanese ally in south Asia and thereby consolidate its hold on the Eastern Hemisphere. A German advance through the Middle East would also capture or at least deny to the Western Allies the Suez Canal and the oil fields of the Persian Gulf region. Driven by such ambitions, German and Italian forces occupied North Africa and contested Britain's position in Egypt in 1941–42. Britain neutralized the Axis threat to the Middle East by stopping a German advance in the Battle of El Alamein, in western Egypt, in October 1942.[5]

Given the severity of the Axis threat to its interests, the United States extended its prewar tendency to defer to Britain in the Middle East during the period of maximum danger to the region. On April 2, 1941, for instance, pro-German Iraqi nationalist Rashid Ali al-Gaylani staged a coup in Baghdad and appealed to Adolf Hitler for assistance. Bracing for the German invasions of Greece and Yugoslavia, Britain quickly reinforced the port at Basra and the airfield at Habbaniya, fifty miles west of Baghdad, and from those bases advanced to Baghdad and deposed Gaylani, who fled to Berlin. The government in London also dispatched a force of British, Indian, Australian, and Free French forces to liberate Syria from the Vichy regime that had endorsed Gaylani's move in Baghdad. The Allied army occupied Damascus on June 21 and Beirut on July 10. Despite the legacy of U.S. anti-colonialism, the Franklin D. Roosevelt administration approved Britain's flexing of imperial muscle in these cases.[6]

The United States also endorsed Britain's imperial presence in Egypt during the peak of the Axis threat. In the so-called February 4, 1942, incident, Britain used military troops to force King Farouk to appoint a prime minister favorable to Britain rather than one sympathetic to Germany. President Roosevelt rejected Farouk's pleas for political support during the showdown. In addition, the Pentagon supplied the British army with tanks that proved crucial to the victory at El Alamein, and it constructed air bases needed to support British power in the country.[7]

The United States demonstrated a similar disposition in other situations in the region. Roosevelt refrained from protesting the joint Anglo-Soviet occupation of Iran in August 1941, undertaken to purge Nazi influence from that country, and he even sent some thirty thousand U.S. soldiers to the country to build transportation systems needed to deliver Lend-Lease supplies to the Soviet Union. The president authorized participation in Britain's Middle East Supply Centre (MESC), an agency established in 1941 to coordinate trade and delivery of war commodities in the region, even though some of his advisers suspected that the Centre would favor British over American commercial interests. Despite pressure from American citizens to endorse Jewish immigration to Palestine, moreover, the Roosevelt administration refrained from contesting Britain's prohibition of such immigration. "Disorder in Palestine," Acting Secretary of War Robert P. Patterson cautioned, "would adversely affect the situation in the whole area and possibly even the course of the entire war."[8]

Once the Axis threat to the Middle East was vanquished, by contrast, the United States began to contest certain aspects of European colonialism in the region. After the Battle of El Alamein, Roosevelt declared that the United States would pursue an open door policy of equal economic opportunity in the Middle East. He rejected a British suggestion of extending the MESC into the postwar era and he endorsed in principle the independence of Middle East states from European imperialism. President Harry S. Truman, who assumed the presidency upon Roosevelt's death in April 1945, reiterated these ideals.[9]

The Roosevelt and Truman governments also flexed their political muscle against French imperialism in Syria. Charles de Gaulle, leader of the Free French government-in-exile, reclaimed sovereignty in Syria after Allied armies liberated it from Vichy control in 1941, but the re-emergence of nascent independence movements among Lebanese and Syrian subjects, dormant since the late 1930s, caught Roosevelt's attention. Determined to assert America's will as a great power, to check French pretensions, and to curb any Soviet inroads into the territory, Roosevelt pressured France to surrender its mandate. The United States recognized the independence of Lebanon in September 1944 and that of Syria in April 1946.[10]

The Cold War in the Middle East

The Cold War emerged in the aftermath of World War II as the United States and the Soviet Union vied for political influence in the postwar era. Confrontations developed over the postwar political orientation of Poland, Germany, and other regions formerly dominated by Axis powers, with flashpoints flaring in the Berlin crisis of 1948–49 and the Korean War of 1950–53. Once diplomacy failed to establish international control over atomic energy, an atomic and nuclear arms race ensued. The Communist victory in the Chinese civil war in 1949 added to the tension by raising in U.S. minds the fear of a global communist menace. Controversies over economic aid, including the Soviet Union's exclusion from the Marshall Plan (the U.S. initiative to rebuild the economies of Europe), exacerbated the conflict.

The Middle East was the scene of some of the earliest Cold War conflicts. U.S.-Soviet tension rose in 1945–46 over the departure of Allied forces from Iran, ruled since 1941 by Shah Mohammed Reza Pahlavi. Under wartime agreements regarding the joint occupation of that kingdom, the United States, Britain, and the Soviet Union had pledged to withdraw their occupation forces within six months of the end of the world war (a date that turned out to be March 2, 1946). U.S. forces left Iran ahead of deadline and British troops pulled out on schedule. Soviet units, however, seeking oil concessions on a par with those gained by the Western powers, remained in the northern province of Azerbaijan, where they protected a secessionist movement led by local Communists. After

U.S. and British officials strongly protested this Soviet action at the United Nations and in other diplomatic venues, Soviet Premier Joseph Stalin ordered a withdrawal of his forces from Iran in May 1946. The secessionist movement collapsed as the Shah restored his sovereignty in Azerbaijan. Western leaders concluded from the episode that the Soviet Union had expansionist designs but would retreat in the face of firm Western resistance.[11]

A similar great-power controversy erupted over Turkey. As Allied armies marched to victory over Berlin in 1945, Soviet leaders issued a series of demands that Turkey grant them certain naval base rights in the Dardanelles, the strategic waterway linking the Black Sea to the Mediterranean Sea. Recalling that German navy ships had penetrated the Black Sea in wartime, the Soviets demanded these rights to safeguard the security of their homeland. U.S. leaders, however, bolstered Turkey in its stalwart refusal of Soviet demands and established a new naval command in the Eastern Mediterranean as a show of support. Intent on erecting an anti-Soviet security system around the world, the United States sought to deny the Soviets the ability to project power into the region.[12]

A more complicated conflict developed in Greece after retreating German forces abandoned that country in 1944. Greek Resistance fighters, many of whom had communist inclinations, battled invading British forces seeking to reimpose their authority in the country. By January 1945, the British had sufficient strength to erect a pro-Western regime. Yet civil war flared again in early 1946, when Communists backed by Yugoslavia (but apparently not by the Soviet Union) challenged the government. Suffering from a postwar economic recession, Britain informed the United States in February 1947 that it would curtail its anticommunist policy in Greece, as well as its fiscal aid to the government of Turkey, on April 1.[13]

Worried by the prospect of communist expansionism in Greece and Turkey, Truman moved quickly to assume Britain's traditional role of protector of Western interests in those two countries. To secure an appropriation of funds from an economy-minded, Republican-controlled Congress, the president alarmed the American people about the situation in Greece. Rather than portray the conflict as a civil war, he characterized it as a conspiracy by foreign Communists to undermine a friendly government. "I believe that it must be the policy of the United States," Truman declared to Congress on March 12, 1947, in words that would become known as the Truman Doctrine, "to support free peoples who are resisting attempted subjugation by armed minorities or by outside pressures."

The ploy worked: Congress appropriated $400 million in aid for Greece and Turkey, the government in Athens defeated the Greek communist insurgency, and Turkey continued to resist Soviet encroachment.[14]

U.S. Cold War Interests in the Middle East

As U.S. leaders undertook to contain Soviet power in Europe and Asia, they came to view the Middle East as a region of critical strategic importance. The Arab states possessed special value because of their oil resources, military facilities, and close proximity to the Soviet Union. It also seemed crucial to align the Arab Middle East with the West for economic, cultural, and political reasons. Israel assumed strategic importance because of its location at the center of the region and its internal political complexion. Accentuating the evidence that the Soviet Union had expansionist ambitions in the Middle East, U.S. leaders resolved to pursue an anti-Soviet policy in the region by becoming involved there, initially as a partner of Britain.

In light of the Cold War, the United States assigned vast importance to the petroleum resources of the Middle East. The region boasted the world's largest proven oil reserves, and U.S. officials considered it vital to deny that resource to Soviet Russia in peace or war, to use it to fuel the economic reconstruction and revitalization of Europe and Japan, and to preserve Western Hemisphere oil reserves for periods of international emergency. In 1947, Arab states supplied half of the oil consumed by U.S. armed forces and most of that fueling the Marshall Plan. The Central Intelligence Agency (CIA) deemed Middle East oil "essential to the security of the US." U.S. capital investments in the oil industry, the State Department added, generated "substantial revenue" in federal taxes.[15]

Access to Middle East oil remained a vital U.S. interest in the 1950s. By 1955, proven oil reserves in Middle East states totaled 100 billion to 150 billion barrels, three to five times more than U.S. reserves. Middle East states produced some three million barrels per day, including one million each from Saudi Arabia and Kuwait and 600,000 from Iraq, and supplied 90 percent of the oil consumed in Western Europe. "The uninterrupted supply of oil from the Middle East is so vital," the Pentagon observed in 1956, "that nothing should be allowed to threaten its continuance."[16]

Because of the Cold War, U.S. officials also deemed it essential to exclude Soviet influence from the Middle East for broader security reasons. According to contingency war plans devised in the late 1940s by strategists in Washington and London, military bases in Arab states would prove essential to victory in any armed conflict with the Soviet Union. Possession of bases in Arab states would enable the Western allies to conduct a punishing aerial offensive against the Soviet industrial heartland, to concentrate armored forces for offensive ground action, and to position intelligence gathering, propaganda, and covert action operations close to the enemy's frontier. The Suez Canal, interregional air routes, and other communications facilities gave the Middle East additional security importance in peace and war.[17]

U.S. policymakers repeatedly affirmed the strategic importance of the Middle East in their secret policy papers. "If a hostile Power secured control of this area," U.S. and British officials agreed in 1947, "not only would we lose very important resources and facilities but it would acquire a position of such dominating strategic and economic power that it would be fatal to our security. It is therefore vital that we must retain a firm hold on the Middle East." The Arab states, the CIA reasoned in 1949, were "of critical importance to the security of the United States." Should the Arab states "fall under the control of the Soviet Union" by war or subversion, State Department officials added in 1952, "the immediate as well as the ultimate cost to the United States would be incalculable."[18]

U.S. officials also recognized the commercial importance of the Arab states. In 1947, 2,813 U.S. ships transited the Suez Canal, and U.S. investors and corporations had substantial stakes in the region's oil industry. U.S. trade with Syria, Lebanon, Palestine, and Jordan increased sixfold between 1939 and 1948. While commercial assets in the Middle East were modest relative to other regions of the world, they were deemed important to U.S. officials who shared the Atlantic Charter's vision of a global capitalist system of free trade. The "prosperity of the Western World," State Department officials summarized in 1950, seemed "closely linked with the fate of the Near Eastern countries."[19]

Cultural and political factors in the Middle East also seemed important to U.S. officials. The region contained the holy sites of Islam, a religion with 300 million believers in Africa and Asia. A century of philanthropic and missionary activity by U.S. citizens, officials in Washington estimated, had created a reservoir of goodwill between the United States and Middle East Muslims. Such friendliness would quickly erode if the West followed policies that Muslim states deemed inimical. Any hostile power dominating the region, State Department officials reasoned, "would be in a position to extend cultural and political penetration to the remainder of the vast Moslem area, now generally friendly to us."[20]

Determined to protect Western interests in the Middle East, U.S. officials assigned great value to certain Arab states. The Suez Canal, operated by a British-owned firm, gave Egypt commercial importance, and Britain's sprawling military base complex in northeastern Egypt featured prominently in U.S. and British contingency plans for war against the Soviet Union. "There is *no substitute for Egypt* as a base," G. Lewis Jones of the State Department's Office of Near Eastern and African Affairs wrote in 1950. Two British airbases in Iraq, secured through a treaty signed in 1930, gave that country military importance as well. Iraq occupied a position near "major communications lines for three continents," State Department officials noted in 1952, and provided "a base in close proximity to the Soviet border."[21]

Saudi Arabia figured even more prominently in U.S. thinking about the Middle East during the early Cold War. To protect access to the kingdom's vast oil resources during World War II, President Roosevelt

Following World War II, U. S. concerns about Soviet expansion, regional instability, and oil supplies led to a policy of active involvement in the Middle East. This was a departure from the country's prewar detachment from the affairs of the region. Here, President Franklin D. Roosevelt (right) meets with King Ibn Saud of Saudi Arabia at Great Bitter Lake in Egypt on February 14, 1945. The U.S. guaranteed Saudi Arabia's security in exchange for access to Saudi oil. The three men standing are unidentified. Franklin D. Roosevelt Library

had negotiated a security partnership with the kingdom. In 1943, he officially declared that Saudi Arabia was a vital interest, making it eligible for
Lend-Lease assistance. Soon, U.S. military advisers ventured to the kingdom and the Pentagon constructed an airbase at Dhahran. As Roosevelt
returned home from the Yalta Conference in February 1945, he welcomed
Ibn Saud aboard a U.S. naval vessel for a meeting designed to promote
the commercial ties and political amity between their two countries.[22]

The Truman administration advanced the strategic partnership
with Saudi Arabia. Minister to Jidda J. Rives Childs likened Saudi Arabia
to "an immense aircraft carrier lying athwart a number of the principal
air traffic lanes of the world" as well as the sea-lanes of the Indian Ocean,
Persian Gulf, and Suez Canal. In 1950, the State Department offered an
assurance that the United States "will take most immediate action at any
time that the integrity and independence of Saudi Arabia is threatened."
In 1951, King Ibn Saud signed a five-year, renewable base agreement
granting the United States access to the Dhahran airbase in exchange for
military aid. U.S. officials also relished Ibn Saud's political orientation.
"If you could find a Communist in Saudi Arabia," the king mentioned to
a U.S. Air Force general, "I will hand you his head."[23]

U.S. officials also protected the flow of Saudi oil by meeting
King Ibn Saud's demands for a greater share of ARAMCO's revenues.
As ARAMCO profits soared in the late 1940s, the king pressed the firm
for a share of royalties well above the 16 percent provided in the 1933
concession. The United States favored increasing the revenue stream to
the king as a means of stabilizing his regime and securing base rights
from it, while ARAMCO feared that resistance might stimulate a move
toward Saudi nationalization of the industry.[24]

These dynamics set the stage for the so-called 50-50 deal, an
innovative financial agreement approved in 1950. In the arrangement,
ARAMCO conceded 50 percent of oil revenues to the kingdom, and the
U.S. Treasury considered such payments as income tax paid to a foreign
state (even though the kingdom had no formal income tax). This provision enabled ARAMCO to claim a major tax deduction. Between 1949
and 1951, ARAMCO reduced its annual tax liability to the U.S. Treasury
by $37 million, while Saudi oil revenues climbed from $39 million to
$110 million. For a loss of $37 million per year in tax revenues, the U.S.
government sealed its emerging partnership with Saudi Arabia.[25]

In addition to such official relations, close unofficial ties emerged
between the United States and the Saudi kingdom. In 1946, King Ibn
Saud hired Americans to engineer a ten-year plan to modernize his

country's infrastructure. By 1946, ARAMCO had invested $100 million in the country, and by 1949, it produced 550,000 barrels of oil per day, claimed $350 million in investments, and employed 5,000 Americans in the country. U.S. investors owned half of the Saudi Mining Syndicate. Trans World Airlines depended on servicing facilities at Dhahran for its flights between Cairo and India, making Saudi Arabia, in the words of one U.S. official, "an important way station on this great commercial international air route."[26]

After 1949, the Pentagon also assigned strategic importance to Israel. Across the Jewish state ran oil pipelines from Iraq to the Mediterranean and roads and railroads that had once linked Egypt with Lebanon, Syria, and Jordan. Israel's network of air bases would provide crucial tactical advantages to whichever power controlled them in a world war. In the event of global conflict, Western access to Israeli territory would prove essential to the defense of the region against a Soviet assault. Once Israel established a stable democratic system in 1949 and shed its lingering neutralism in 1950–51, U.S. military planners eyed it as a crucial strategic factor.[27]

As they ascribed greater importance to the Middle East, U.S. security experts feared that the Soviet Union had postwar designs on the region. In hindsight, it appears that Soviet Premier Joseph Stalin considered the Middle East less important than Europe or East Asia in his ideological quest to promote socialism and in his preparations for conflict with the capitalist world. Lacking the strength to contest Anglo-American dominance in the Middle East, Stalin remained cold to Arab leaders, whom he considered reactionary pawns of British imperialism. Rather than nurturing Israeli neutralism, he adopted an anti-Semitic orientation that contributed to the suspension of Soviet-Israeli diplomatic relations in February 1953. U.S. officials suspected, however, that Stalin had inherited the traditional tsarist quest for warm-water ports and friendly regimes in states along Russia's southern border. Stalin's attempt to project his influence in Turkey and Iran in 1945–46, although foiled by Western resistance, thus signified in U.S. minds a Soviet threat to the Middle East. Although Stalin appeared uninterested, the CIA estimated that the Soviet Union "desires to achieve eventual control" of the region.[28]

After 1953, by contrast, U.S. officials had better reason to fear Soviet influence in the Middle East. Nikita Khrushchev, who emerged as Soviet leader after a brief power struggle following Stalin's death, promoted peaceful coexistence with the West on European issues but welcomed political competition in the Third World. In 1954–55, the Soviet

Union sought political and economic ties with Third World leaders and promoted nonalignment of their states in order to undermine Western imperial assets. Elevating pragmatism over ideology, Khrushchev nurtured closer relations with Egypt, which Stalin had eschewed, on the reasoning that Premier Gamal Abdel Nasser's nationalism might provide a vehicle for contesting Anglo-American hegemony in the region.[29]

U.S. officials monitored the increasing Soviet interest in the Middle East. They interpreted Soviet broadcasts in Middle East media, trade agreements, industrial fairs, public declarations, UN diplomacy, and support for a labor strike among oil workers in Dhahran as bids to impress Arab audiences. The Soviet-Egyptian arms deal of September 1955 seemed doubly troubling because it signaled new departures both in Soviet assertiveness in the region and in the receptivity of an Arab state to Soviet aid. Syrian leaders also seemed open to Soviet overtures. The Soviet Union, the Dwight D. Eisenhower administration noted in 1956, was engaged in "an extensive economic and diplomatic effort which seriously threatens the British and American position in the area."[30]

U.S. officials also feared that internal problems threatened the region. Inequality of wealth and power caused revolutionary tendencies and resentment against Western nations. Decolonization generated a wave of nationalism conducive to Soviet exploitation and intra-regional conflict. Rivalries between the Saudi monarchy, the Egyptian crown, and the Hashemite kingdoms of Iraq and Jordan added to the volatility. U.S. support of the creation of Israel (discussed in chapter 2) antagonized the Arab states. These factors, the State Department estimated in 1953, made the region "tinder for Communist conflagrations." Soon thereafter, Nasser emerged as an outspoken advocate of neutralism and a critic of Western dominance of the region.[31]

To safeguard their vital interests in the Middle East, U.S. officials formulated three important policy principles. First, they frequently clarified that the United States favored Middle East stability, which meant establishing a democratic, pro-Western, and anticommunist sociopolitical framework. "It is our policy," the State Department clarified in one typical statement, "to assist the Near Eastern countries in maintaining their independence, to strengthen their orientation towards the West, and to discourage any tendencies towards the development of authoritarian and unrepresentative forms of government." Stable political regimes would facilitate economic development, which would in turn further stabilize the region.[32]

Second, U.S. officials resolved to replace their prewar aloofness from the Middle East with involvement in the region. "It is extremely important that the influence of the United States should increase rather than decrease during the next few critical years in the Near and Middle East," Assistant Secretary of State Loy Henderson advised in September 1945. U.S. officials must abandon "the comfortable old pre-war era when we felt it unnecessary to trouble ourselves with the trend of events in distant lands." Consonant with such thinking, U.S. officials frequently resolved in succeeding years to become more involved in the Middle East.[33]

Third, the United States built a partnership with Britain to secure American interests in the Middle East. Before 1945, the two powers had competed against one another for commercial interests in the region, and after 1945, they occasionally quarreled about policy in Palestine and other places around the globe. The onset of the Cold War, however, compelled the two states to renew the special relationship they had developed during World War II. As they cooperatively bolstered West Germany; shored up Greece, Turkey, and Iran; implemented the Marshall Plan; challenged the Soviet blockade of Berlin; and signed the North Atlantic Treaty Organization (NATO) alliance, they also aligned their fundamental policies toward the Middle East. "There is no question of attempting to replace British by U.S. influence, or vice versa," U.S. and British diplomats agreed in 1947. The two powers would "strengthen and improve our mutual position by lending each other all possible influence and support." Given U.S. commitments to West Europe and East Asia, the Truman administration favored Britain's traditional dominance in the Middle East.[34]

Security Systems

To protect its strategic interests in the Middle East against the perceived Soviet challenge, the United States erected a series of security systems in the region during the early Cold War. The first formal U.S. commitment to the security and stability of the Middle East—the Tripartite Declaration of May 1950—was the product of an intense debate among U.S. leaders about the propriety of supplying arms to local powers. State and Defense Department officials, determined to bolster Arab partners to resist Soviet communism, endorsed Britain's policy of arming Arab states in the aftermath of the Arab-Israeli war of 1948–49. Members of Congress and the White House staff, by contrast, predicted that such a policy would imperil Israel while contributing little to regional security. Buffeted by conflicting advice from both quarters, President Truman ordered the State Department to conceive of a policy that protected Israeli interests.

Under such a directive, the State Department resourcefully conceived the Tripartite Declaration. In it, the United States, Britain, and France agreed to condition arms supply to any Middle East state on its willingness to pledge nonaggression. The declaration authorized arms supply to Middle East states "for the purposes of assuring their internal security and their legitimate self-defense and to permit them to play their part in the defense of the area as a whole." If any state broke its nonaggression pledge, then the three Western powers would "immediately take action, both within and outside the United Nations, to prevent such violation." While established to resolve a debate over arms supply, the Tripartite Declaration represented the first explicit U.S. commitment to Middle East security.[35]

Second, the United States integrated Turkey and Greece into the European alliance system. The Truman Doctrine had enabled the Greek government to crush its communist rebellion by 1949. U.S. strategists had come to see Turkey as an anti-Soviet bulwark at the intersection of Europe and the Middle East, and its emerging democracy and credible military force made the notion of a formal alliance politically palatable and tactically desirable. Both Greece and Turkey dispatched troops to fight with the United States in Korea. To reward their assistance, bolster their conservative rulers, and discourage the emergence of neutralism, the United States arranged for Greece and Turkey to join NATO in February 1952. Turkey thereafter provided a critical outpost for electronic and aerial espionage and weapons monitoring against the Soviet Union, for staging U.S. forces that interceded in Lebanon in 1958, and for deploying nuclear-tipped Jupiter missiles in 1959–61.[36]

Third, the Truman administration tried to erect a mutual defense system in the Middle East in 1950–52. After the outbreak of the Korean War in June 1950, U.S. officials assumed that the Soviet Union would try to expand into the Middle East. They felt simultaneously empowered by the rearmament under NSC-68, the global anticommunist strategy paper approved by Truman in mid-1950; concerned by a perceptible decline in British capabilities to protect the Middle East; and alarmed at mounting evidence that Arab states were ambivalent toward the West. The combination of these factors overpowered the traditional American reluctance to incur security commitments in the Middle East.

To safeguard the Middle East against the Soviets and to assuage Arab leaders, U.S. planners resolved to erect a security pact on an Arab foundation. Inspired by the NATO alliance, they conceived of an integrated command structure, called the Middle East Command (MEC), that would enlist Arab states as partners of the West. By basing MEC in Egypt, they also hoped to solve an Anglo-Egyptian dispute over military bases in the Suez Canal Zone and to settle an Anglo-U.S. disagreement over allied naval commands. In light of Israeli neutralism and Arab-Israeli dynamics, U.S. and British planners decided to exclude Israel from MEC. By October 1951, the United States and Britain enlisted France and Turkey to cosponsor MEC and agreed to invite Egypt to join the pact and to base it in Cairo.[37]

Egypt, however, inflicted a severe blow on MEC in October 1951. When approached by the four Western sponsors, Egyptian leaders not only rejected the MEC proposal but also abrogated their defense treaty with Britain and demanded that British forces withdraw from Egypt. The United States and Britain then invited other Arab governments to join the command, but they declined because of widespread approval of Egypt's action by their peoples. Only Syrian Prime Minister Hassan Abdel Razzak el Hakim openly endorsed MEC, provoking a crisis that led to his resignation. Worse, as U.S. officials sought to promote the MEC concept among Arab states in 1952, they came to realize that the British and Turkish forces slated to provide the backbone of MEC's combat forces were wholly inadequate to stop a major Soviet thrust against the region.[38]

In a futile effort to overcome its shortcomings, U.S. and British officials modified MEC in June 1952. To dilute Arab opposition, they renamed it the Middle East Defense Organization (MEDO), called it a planning board rather than a command, and tried to sell the idea to Arab military officers rather than the politicians who seemed preoccupied by Israel. But Egypt remained hostile to any defense arrangement prior to British evacuation of the Canal Zone, and other Arab states remained reluctant to defy Egypt. The failure of the MEC-MEDO concept convinced State Department officials that "it is no longer safe to assume, automatically, that Britain can and should be considered the principal protector of western interests in the Middle East." Even if Britain felt "great resentment," Secretary of State Dean G. Acheson noted, "we had the responsibility in the Middle East and had to do something about it." The United States stood ready to take charge in the Middle East.[39]

Finally, the Eisenhower administration continued the quest for a Middle East security system, focusing on the states along the so-called northern tier of the Middle East. President Eisenhower and Secretary of State John Foster Dulles concluded that a MEDO based in Egypt was impossible to establish given the intensity of Egyptian nationalism against Britain, stemming from the ongoing base dispute, and against the United States, owing to the conflict over Israel. By contrast, Turkey, Pakistan, and Iraq felt "the hot breath of the Soviet Union on their necks," Dulles told the National Security Council in spring 1953, and they were "less preoccupied with strictly internal problems or with British and French imperialism." The overthrow of Iranian Premier Mohammed Mossadegh in August 1953 (discussed in chapter 3), moreover, made Iran another prospective partner. Because Turkey had joined NATO in 1952 and Pakistan was slated to join the Southeast Asia Treaty Organization (SEATO) in 1954, a northern tier pact promised to extend the cordon of anti-Soviet pacts from northern Europe to the Pacific Ocean.[40]

Certain military and strategic factors also underscored the appeal of a northern tier alliance. The concentrated British base in Egypt seemed increasingly vulnerable as Soviet nuclear strike capabilities improved in the early 1950s. At the same time, development of the Atlas, Thor, and Jupiter missiles, which could deliver thermonuclear warheads but only at short ranges, made it imperative for the United States to have access to base sites relatively close to Soviet territory. Pentagon strategists came to favor a series of Western air and missile bases dispersed along the Soviets' southern frontier. A northern tier pact would provide such assets.[41]

U.S. officials breathed life into the northern tier concept by encouraging area states and Britain to form a defense alliance. The United States extended military aid to induce Turkey and Pakistan to sign an agreement on April 2, 1954, pledging cooperation and consultation in defense matters. After months of painstaking diplomacy, Iraq and Turkey signed a more formal mutual defense pact at Baghdad on February 24, 1955. Britain adhered to the pact in April, Pakistan in September, and Iran in October. Although the United States refrained from joining the pact, its support was crucial to the pact's formulation.[42]

From the beginning, the Baghdad Pact displayed several serious flaws. First, the combat forces of Baghdad Pact members, including British forces in the region, were deemed incapable of even slowing a Soviet invasion, and the northern tier states lacked the infrastructure needed for the United States to offer a credible nuclear deterrent. As Iraq's political rival, moreover, Egypt directed a chorus of Arab protests against the pact, charging that it divided the Arab community, undermined Arab League defense arrangements, and served European colonial and Israeli interests. Denouncing Iraqi premier Nuri Said as an "Anglo-American stooge," Nasser waged an intense political campaign to dissuade other Arab states from acceding to the pact. In addition, Israel opposed the pact because it funneled weapons to Iraq and encouraged Turkey to mollify Arab states at the expense of Turkish-Israeli amity.[43]

The problems besetting the Baghdad Pact left Eisenhower facing a dilemma. The Pentagon endorsed the demands of the member states that the United States join the pact formally and thereby bring it military and political integrity. Dulles and other political advisers, by contrast, cautioned that formal U.S. membership might provoke a Soviet counterstroke, attract Egyptian wrath, and prompt Israeli demands for a compensatory defense commitment (demands likely to gain favorable support in Congress). In the end, Eisenhower declined to accept formal membership in the Baghdad Pact, but he wove the United States into its structure by designating Pentagon officers to participate in the pact's military planning, directing diplomats to attend pact meetings, and paying one-sixth of the pact's annual budget. Eisenhower took such steps both to bolster the pact and to deflect allied and Pentagon pressure to join.[44]

Badly flawed from its inception, the Baghdad Pact collapsed precipitously in 1958–59. On July 14, 1958, Iraqi nationalists violently deposed their country's Hashimite monarchy and Nuri Said's government. The new government of General Abdul Karim Qassim withdrew Iraq from the Baghdad Pact in March 1959. The remaining pact members changed its name to the Central Treaty Organization (CENTO) and relocated its headquarters to Ankara, while the United States negotiated bilateral defense treaties with Turkey, Iran, and Pakistan. These alterations could not offset the impact of Iraqi withdrawal, however, and CENTO lost much of its stature long before it was officially abolished in 1979.[45]

Conclusion

The United States passed several major watersheds in the Middle East in the 1940s and 1950s. The threat of Nazi conquest drew the attention of U.S. foreign policy officials to the region during World War II, and the emergent fear of Soviet designs on the region held their attention in subsequent years. As a result, the United States began practicing a fundamental policy of anticommunist containment that remained a bedrock objective through the remainder of the Cold War.

Consonant with such concerns, U.S. officials also resolved to stabilize the Middle East against internal turmoil that would render it vulnerable to Soviet machinations and to nurture a strategic partnership with Britain that would safeguard the mutual interests of both countries. In the process of resisting external communism, promoting internal stability, and partnering with the British government, the United States became deeply and inextricably involved in the affairs of the Middle East.

CHAPTER 2

INTO THE
MIDDLE OF A FIGHT

The United States and the Arab-Israeli Conflict to 1961

THE ARAB-ISRAELI CONFLICT OF THE late 1940s and the 1950s threatened U.S. interests in the Cold War. Because the dispute destabilized the Middle East and seemingly opened the region to Soviet influence, U.S. officials desired in principle to end or minimize the conflict. Such officials were pulled, however, by competing and inconsistent impulses: domestic political and cultural values that dictated sympathy toward Zionist/Israeli ambitions, on the one hand, and national security concerns that favored amity with the Arab states, on the other. The Harry S. Truman and Dwight D. Eisenhower administrations found it impossible to resolve the conflict on terms consistent with U.S. strategic, diplomatic, and domestic political and cultural values.

Origins of the Conflict

The Arab-Israeli conflict originated in a complicated dispute over Palestine. At the dawn of the twentieth century, the territory was officially under the control of the moribund Ottoman Empire. Inspired by the Zionist dream of restoring a community in the ancient homeland of the Jewish people, European Jews had flocked to Palestine in the late 1800s and early 1900s. By 1914, some 66,000 Jews resided there. Arab Palestinians, who numbered some 570,000 in 1914, by contrast, gradually developed a national identity and embraced a vision of political independence from Ottoman authority. They warily eyed the Jewish community as it increased in physical size and economic strength.[1]

During World War I, Britain stepped into and complicated the emerging Palestine dispute. Preoccupied by the war in Europe, British officials

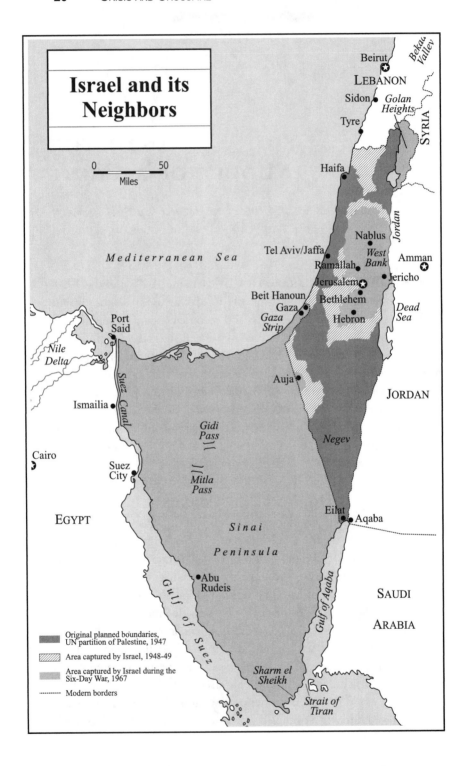

Israel and its Neighbors

0 ——— 50
Miles

Beirut
LEBANON
Sidon
Tyre
Golan Heights
SYRIA
Bekaa Valley

Haifa

Mediterranean Sea

Nablus
Tel Aviv/Jaffa
Ramallah
Jerusalem
Beit Hanoun
Gaza
Gaza Strip
Bethlehem
Hebron
West Bank
Amman
Jericho
Dead Sea
Jordan

Port Said

Nile Delta

Ismailia

Cairo

Suez City

Auja

JORDAN

Gidi Pass

Negev

Mitla Pass

Eilat
Aqaba

EGYPT

Sinai Peninsula

Abu Rudeis

SAUDI

ARABIA

Gulf of Suez

Gulf of Aqaba

Sharm el Sheikh

Strait of Tiran

Original planned boundaries,
UN partition of Palestine, 1947

Area captured by Israel, 1948-49

Area captured by Israel during the
Six-Day War, 1967

---------- Modern borders

issued a series of uncoordinated and inherently contradictory diplomatic declarations regarding the disposition of territories expected to be stripped from Ottoman control. In the Sykes-Picot Agreement (1916), officials in London secured France's recognition of their postwar control of Palestine. In the Husayn-McMahon Correspondence (1915–16), Britain implicitly promised support of Arab independence in Palestine in exchange for an Arab revolt against the Ottoman Empire. To serve certain domestic political and diplomatic objectives, Britain also pledged in the Balfour Declaration (1917) to "view with favour the establishment in Palestine of a national home for the Jewish people." The conquest of Jerusalem in December 1917 positioned Britain to demand postwar control of Palestine. By 1922, London established a League of Nations mandate over Palestine and established Transjordan as a separate territory.[2]

The decades following World War I witnessed a triangular clash in Palestine. The Jews and Palestinians battled each other for political, economic, and cultural interests in the territory and increasingly sought independence from British imperialism. Britain aimed to maintain law and order in its mandate and to find terms of a permanent settlement of the internal conflict. Outbursts of Arab-Jewish violence in 1919–21, 1929, and 1933 left hundreds of Jews and Palestinians dead. In the Arab Revolt of 1936–39, Palestinians who worried about rising Jewish immigration organized a massive labor strike that triggered rioting and violence against Jews and British officials as well as reprisals by both groups on the Palestinians. To appease the Arabs and stabilize the mandate on the eve of World War II, Britain issued the White Paper of 1939 that curtailed Jewish immigration and land purchases and pledged statehood to Palestinian Arabs within ten years.[3]

The White Paper of 1939 stabilized Palestine for the war but did not prevent serious postwar conflict. Although supportive of Britain's anti-Nazi war aims in Europe, the mainstream Jewish community of Palestine routinely violated the White Paper's immigration restrictions. Jewish extremist groups used violence to sap Britain's willingness to remain in Palestine. Leaders of the Palestinian community discredited themselves in British eyes by cavorting with the Nazis and failing to develop a viable political system in the country. As World War II ended, Jewish-Arab tensions in Palestine escalated as British capacity to govern the land waned.[4]

By 1947, British officials found the situation in Palestine unmanageable. They searched in vain for a political solution to the Jewish-Palestinian conflict and realized that the strategic advantages of controlling Palestine did not justify the costs. They proved unable to stem unauthorized Jewish immigration, to halt the Arab-Jewish violence, or to avoid becoming the targets of attacks. In 1947, Britain notified the United Nations that it would abandon the mandate, and it set a target date of May 15, 1948, for its final withdrawal from Palestine. In November 1947, the United Nations adopted a plan to partition Palestine into a Jewish state and a Palestinian state.[5]

Truman's Policy and Motives

Before World War II, U.S. government officials counted few political interests in Palestine. They took episodic interest in protecting the fortunes of U.S. merchants and missionaries and occasionally endorsed Zionism to serve their domestic political interests, but they never seriously challenged Britain's hegemony in the mandate. Privileging national security considerations during World War II, President Franklin D. Roosevelt avoided any step in Palestine that would undermine the Anglo-U.S. alliance, weaken the prospect of victory over the Axis, or imperil Western strategic, commercial, or petroleum interests in the Middle East. He pledged to anti-Zionist Arab rulers that he would consult with them before deciding U.S. postwar policy in Palestine.[6]

Despite such official detachment, by contrast, many U.S. citizens embraced Zionism in the 1930s and early 1940s. Stimulated by the plight of European Jewry, American Jews formed an activist Zionist lobby that demanded immediate termination of the British mandate and establishment of a Jewish state in Palestine between the Mediterranean and the Jordan River. Non-Jewish U.S. citizens also sympathized with Zionism. They pitied the victims of Nazi persecution, identified with Jewish settlers seemingly repeating the U.S. frontier experience, predicted that Jews would make Palestine prosper, and looked down upon Muslims and Arabs. Many evangelical Christians favored the establishment of a Jewish state as a fulfillment of Biblical prophecy. Sensitive to the domestic political culture, members of Congress embraced Zionism and both the Republican and Democratic parties declared pro-Zionist planks in their 1944 platforms.[7]

The clash between national security interests in the Arab states and domestic political sympathy for Zionism buffeted the policymaking of Harry S. Truman, who assumed the presidency near the end of World War II. The State Department and Pentagon warned the president that supporting Zionism would undermine vital national interests in the Arab world, whose political loyalty seemed essential to prevailing over the Soviet Union in the emerging Cold War. Yet several of Truman's personal advisers encouraged him to endorse Zionist ambitions for moral and political reasons. Torn by the conflicting advice of his professional and personal advisers, Truman made key policy decisions that significantly contributed to the fulfillment of the Zionist dream in Palestine.[8]

Several factors bred an innate sympathy for Zionism in Truman's mind. Raised in an evangelical Christian tradition, he had been exposed to the religious belief that Jews deserved special status and that a Jewish return to Palestine was part of Biblical prophecy. A political liberal, Truman was profoundly disturbed by the news of the Holocaust and pitied the hundreds of thousands of Jewish displaced persons who remained confined to refugee camps in Europe after the war. The president counted several Jewish friends who retained access to him in the Oval Office, and no such acquaintances with Arab roots. Truman's populist distrust of eastern elites, manifest in his derogation of State Department officials as "tea hounds" and "striped pants conspirators," left him suspicious of the department's advice. Perhaps Truman was also motivated, ironically, by a subtle form of anti-Semitism, common among white Missourians of the early twentieth century, that favored settlement of Jews in Palestine over their admission to the United States.[9]

Political and cultural factors contributed to the president's pro-Zionist proclivities. An embattled politician, Truman remained sensitive to the voting strength of Jews, especially in key electoral states such as New York and Illinois. "There is a large and aggressive element in public opinion which not only wholeheartedly endorses the Zionist position, but even criticizes the Administration for not going far enough in following a pro-Zionist line," State Department officials noted in 1946. By contrast, anti-Zionism, "if it exists, has not been articulate." In addition, U.S. news media, Christian churches, and other cultural mediators shaped a powerful anti-Arab bias in U.S. culture and thereby created an anti-Arab frame of reference in the minds of U.S. leaders.[10]

Such factors impelled Truman to advance Zionist ambitions over the objections of his national security advisers. In 1945–46, he publicly endorsed Zionist demands that Britain issue 100,000 immigration permits to Jews seeking entry to Palestine. In October 1946, on the eve of the Jewish Yom Kippur holiday and a month before U.S. midterm elections, Truman publicly endorsed the Zionist goal of partition of Palestine into a Jewish state and a Palestinian state. In 1947, he supported the United Nations partition resolution, and in subsequent months he halted a State Department initiative to replace the partition plan with a UN trusteeship scheme. Truman's actions flew in the face of warnings from his national security advisers. "We are not only forfeiting the friendship of the Arab world," Assistant Secretary of State Loy Henderson cautioned on one occasion, "but we are incurring long-term Arab hostility towards us."[11]

Perhaps the most dramatic manifestation of Truman's pro-Zionism was his prompt recognition of the State of Israel. In May 1948, leaders of the Jewish community of Palestine declared the independence of Israel at the moment that Britain formally terminated the mandate. Eleven minutes later, Truman extended to the new country de facto recognition by the United States. That step provided a major boost to Israel's claims to national sovereignty and territorial integrity, and it electrified the morale of the Israeli government and people. By overturning the State Department's trusteeship initiative, Truman's action angered his national security advisers. By following immediately upon the declaration of statehood, it also convinced Arab leaders that the United States was the protector of the Zionists. "Our prestige and influence in the Middle East," Director of Navy Intelligence E. T. Wooldridge noted, "has suffered what may be irreparable damage."[12]

To be sure, there were limits to Truman's pro-Zionist disposition. The president privately articulated disquiet over the situation in Palestine and regret that domestic political pressures influenced foreign policy (even as he submitted to such pressures). Earlier, after calling for immigration of 100,000 Jews, Truman refused Zionist entreaties to endorse a higher number. He registered distaste for the assertive style of certain Zionist leaders, such as Rabbi Abba Hillel Silver of Cleveland, whom Truman banned from the White House after the rabbi pounded on Truman's desk while making a point during a meeting in July 1946. The unofficial meddling in the partition vote at the United Nations, especially, angered Truman. Although his actions appeared pro-Zionist, Truman also harbored anti-Zionist impulses.[13]

The simultaneous expiration of the British mandate, declaration of Israeli statehood, and U.S. recognition of Israel drastically changed the situation in Palestine. As Arab armies invaded Palestine to crush Israeli independence, undeclared civil war among inhabitants of a British mandate suddenly became an international war. Issues that had monopolized U.S. attention since 1946—partition and trusteeship—became moot points. In warfare that raged between May 15 and July 18 (interrupted only by a ceasefire from June 8 to July 8), Israelis scored a series of battlefield victories that ensured the survival of their state and gained land beyond the partition lines.[14]

The United States took a relatively passive posture during the early fighting. Truman focused on his reelection campaign and departed Washington for three weeks in June. The Soviet blockade of Berlin on June 24 absorbed the attention of top officials. Dispirited by the sudden widening of the conflict and by Truman's recognition of Israel, State Department officials merely endorsed the appointment on May 20 of Count Folke Bernadotte of Sweden as UN Mediator, encouraged the belligerents to honor the ceasefire resolutions passed by the Security Council on May 22 and July 15, and maintained an arms embargo on both sides of the conflict. The Pentagon dispatched officers to serve as UN observers but refused Bernadotte's request for combat troops to enforce the ceasefire.[15]

In contrast to their passivity during the early months of war, U.S. officials became involved in a plan for a permanent settlement in Palestine formulated by Bernadotte in September 1948. The Bernadotte plan proposed that Arab states acquiesce in the existence of Israel, that Jordan

President Harry Truman (left) receives gifts from David Ben-Gurion (right, seated) and Abba Soloman Eban (standing) of Israel, May 8, 1951. Due to both public opinion and personal inclination, Truman espoused pro-Zionist policies, including the prompt recognition of the new state of Israel in 1948. His advisers warned against such policies, perceptively predicting long-lasting Arab disaffection with the United States. Abbie Rowe, photographer, National Park Service Photograph. Courtesy of Harry S. Truman Library annex the portions of Palestine not designated to Israel, that all powers approve border alterations, that Israel repatriate Palestinian refugees, and that an international regime govern Jerusalem. Although the Arab states and Israel showed little enthusiasm for the plan, the State Department, with Truman's blessing, promoted it vigorously. But the department made little headway against Arab and Israeli opposition before Israeli extremists murdered Bernadotte in Jerusalem on September 17.[16]

State Department leaders sought, fruitlessly, to advance the Bernadotte plan by capitalizing on worldwide remorse—and outrage against Israel—over the assassination. Truman authorized Secretary of State George Marshall publicly to endorse the plan on September 20–21. But such efforts to make peace on compromise terms were stymied by three factors. First, neither Israel nor its Arab adversaries indicated any willingness to make peace on the basis of the plan. Second, U.S. pressure on Israel to yield control of the Negev to Egypt, which had occupied the region in the early weeks of the war, prompted an Israeli offensive on October 15–21 that captured Beersheba and secured the northern Negev.[17]

Third, the plan was mortally wounded during the U.S. presidential election campaign. Israeli officials and domestic supporters of Israel exerted enormous pressure on Democratic and Republican Party leaders to repudiate the Bernadotte plan. On October 22, Republican nominee Thomas Dewey criticized the plan, and Truman followed suit two days later by declaring that he would oppose any territorial changes that lacked Israeli consent. By December, State Department officials realized that Israel would not concede any territory and thus they laid the Bernadotte plan to rest.[18]

The Truman administration reverted to passivity in late 1948 when Israel triggered hostilities to secure the southern Negev. Emboldened by the decline of the Bernadotte plan, Israeli leaders attacked Egyptian units in the southern Negev on December 22 on the pretext that Egypt refused to make peace. Truman authorized the State Department to secure a UN ceasefire resolution that took effect on January 7, 1949. But he prohibited the department from pressuring Israel to relinquish the territorial gains of its October or December offensives. Rather, the department endorsed the efforts of Ralph Bunche, a U.S. diplomat working on the staff of the UN Secretary General, to negotiate a series of bilateral armistices between Israel and its Arab adversaries. Armistices were signed between Israel and Egypt (February 24), Lebanon (March 23), Jordan (April 3), and Syria (July 20). Iraq agreed simply to withdraw its forces from the battlefield.[19]

U.S. officials hoped that the armistices would enable the belligerent states to negotiate treaties that would officially end the Arab-Israeli War, establish permanent borders around Israel, and restore stability to the Middle East, but the dream of peace proved fleeting. U.S. envoys participated in UN-organized peace conferences in Lausanne, New York, Geneva, and Jerusalem in 1949–50, but all such talks deadlocked amid the stubborn refusal of both sides to make any concessions or compromises. U.S. officials also encouraged Israeli-Jordanian and Israeli-Egyptian bilateral deals, but these efforts proved equally futile. U.S. diplomats worked assiduously in 1951 to contain a crisis over land and water rights along the Israeli-Syrian border, but the underlying tension persisted. They also attempted to promote resolutions of specific points of controversy such as the disposition of Palestinian refugees, the control of Jerusalem, and the closure of the Suez Canal to Israeli ships, but their efforts proved in vain.

Several reasons account for the failure of peacemaking. First, political conditions in the Middle East were simply not conducive to any settlement. Emboldened by victory, Israeli leaders rested their security on their military prowess rather than compromises with the Arab states, and they categorically refused to yield any territory occupied in the war. Embittered by defeat, most Arab leaders and peoples desired to disable Israel, prevent it from expanding, and gain territory at its expense. Intra-Arab rivalries encouraged firmness toward Israel, as signified by the assassination in 1951 of the moderate King Abdallah of Jordan by a disaffected Palestinian.

Second, the United States offered limited and ineffective leadership in peacemaking. To be sure, U.S. officials supported the peace process in myriad ways, but in the face of intense Arab-Israeli animosity, they refrained from taking major initiatives. Moreover, they privileged their Cold War interests over Arab-Israeli settlement when the two conflicted. Thus they refused to consider any peace plan that would involve the Soviet Union in the region, and they discouraged Egyptian-Israeli negotiations that might have weakened the regime of Mohammed Naguib in Cairo, upon which Western security seemed to rest.

Third, the Truman administration's deep internal divisions with respect to Israel also compromised its peacemaking capability. Perhaps still regretting the creation of Israel over their objections, State Department officials advised Truman that Israel must make substantial concessions to accomplish a peace treaty. Mobilized by the Israeli embassy, by contrast, certain officials and private citizens encouraged Truman to reject such advice. Such internal divisions within his administration neutralized the president's ability to lead.[20]

Eisenhower's Approach

The Dwight D. Eisenhower administration could not avoid confronting the Arab-Israeli conflict. The dispute provoked anti-Western sentiment in Arab states, hindered the establishment of a regional defense scheme, limited economic and social development, and created opportunities for Soviet meddling in the region. Soon after taking office, President Eisenhower and Secretary of State John Foster Dulles concluded that solving the problem would serve U.S. interests in the Middle East.

Eisenhower and Dulles applied three basic principles to the Arab-Israeli conflict. First, in light of apparent Soviet activism in the Middle East, they affirmed the importance of settling the conflict. Arab-Israeli tension, one Pentagon officer warned, "offers the Communist Bloc a troubled water in which to fish." Second, Eisenhower and Dulles became determined, in Dulles's words, "to convince the Arab World that the United States is operating upon a policy of *true* impartiality." Third, Eisenhower approved in principle a plan to promote settlements of major Arab-Israeli controversies actively and to seek full and final peace treaties between the two sides.[21]

Yet peacemaking by the Eisenhower administration faced enormous obstacles. Arab leaders showed little interest in any peace schemes that would require them to recognize the legitimacy of Israel. "The Jewish state is regarded as a cancer on the body of the Arab Middle East," the State Department observed. "Quite frankly, the Arabs want it removed." Nor did the Israelis seem anxious to settle. Prime Minister David Ben-Gurion and Foreign Minister Moshe Sharett, Israel's two most eminent founders and early statesmen, claimed to desire peace but refused to make any concessions or compromises on behalf of a settlement. In light of such obstacles, the Eisenhower administration initially refrained from promoting Arab-Israeli peace. But in the absence of peacemaking, low-intensity violence flared along Israel's borders and the parties to the dispute sparred over such issues as the closure of the Suez Canal to Israel, the control of Jerusalem, the disposition of Jordan River water, and the fate of the nearly one million Palestinian refugees.[22]

By early 1955, several factors converged to galvanize the Eisenhower administration to become more active in peacemaking. First, U.S. leaders perceived growing Soviet interest in the Middle East, a danger made acute by the persistence of the Arab-Israeli conflict. Second, despite the obstacles to peace, NEA officials saw "a glimmer of hope here and there" in improved U.S. relations with certain Arab leaders, in Egyptian Premier Gamal Abdel Nasser's pledge to consider peacemaking once he settled a military base issue with Britain in 1954, and in the relative tranquility along Israel's borders in late 1954 through January 1955. Third, Eisenhower and Dulles realized that they must advance peacemaking before the U.S. election campaign of 1956, when domestic political conditions would prevent them from acting impartially toward Israel. That British officials offered to collaborate in Middle East peacemaking further sweetened the prospect.[23]

In early 1955, U.S. and British officials outlined a comprehensive peace plan code-named "Alpha." It proposed a permanent Arab-Israeli peace settlement featuring specific terms on several points of controversy. Israel would repatriate a fixed number of refugees and the Arab states would absorb the remainder. The states of the region would share water resources on an equitable basis and agree to border adjustments that would establish contiguity between Egypt and Jordan. The Arab states would terminate their economic sanctions on Israel, including the Suez Canal blockade. A United Nations entity would oversee Jerusalem. As an incentive to accept the plan, the United States would dispense more than $1 billion over five years, and Britain and the United States would guarantee the revised Arab-Israeli borders against violent changes.[24]

Unfortunately for Eisenhower and Dulles, the Alpha plan fell flat, a victim of rising tensions within the Middle East. Nasser first learned the terms of Alpha in February 1955, only days before Israel launched a devastating raid against an Egyptian army post at Gaza. That event embittered Nasser against Israel and triggered a crescendo of Egyptian-Israeli border violence. The establishment of the Baghdad Pact, which included Egypt's political rival Iraq, soured Nasser toward the West and impelled him to seek weapons from China and the Soviet bloc. To pressure Israel and Egypt to accept the terms of Alpha, Dulles publicized the plan in August 1955. Within days, however, a major Egyptian-Israeli border incident nearly triggered another regional war. The Soviet-Egyptian arms deal of September further aggravated Israeli mistrust of Nasser, and persistent violence along Israel's borders threatened to escalate into general hostilities. Alpha gained no legitimacy in such a context, and by the end of 1955, the plan had clearly failed.[25]

Faced with the prospect of war in the Middle East, Eisenhower and Dulles tried in early 1956 not only to deter hostilities but also to achieve a permanent peace. The president dispatched a special emissary,

Undersecretary of Defense Robert Anderson, to arbitrate an Egyptian-Israeli settlement, but Anderson proved unable to broker agreements on any of the major issues. Dulles then arranged a United Nations peace mission headed by Secretary General Dag Hammarskjöld, but during his visit to the Middle East in April, Israel and Egypt fought a series of border skirmishes and nearly started a full-scale war. In a bid to deter hostilities, Eisenhower dispatched the U.S. Navy to the region and hinted that he would defend any victim of aggression in the theater. But tensions continued to rise, and U.S. officials realized that political conditions in the region were simply not conducive to peace. Eisenhower braced for a war.[26]

The Suez-Sinai War and After

The Arab-Israeli conflict took a new and unexpected turn after Nasser nationalized the Suez Canal Company in July 1956. Nasser took over the British- and French-owned firm to demonstrate his independence from the European colonial powers, to avenge an Anglo-U.S. denial of economic aid, and to garner the profits the company earned in his country. The deed touched off an international crisis during which Britain and France prepared to use military force against Egypt unless Nasser relented. The crisis eventually provoked a war that proved to be one of the most perilous events of the Cold War.

Consonant with his ambition to stabilize the Middle East, Eisenhower approached the canal crisis on three basic and interrelated premises. First, although he sympathized with Britain's and France's desire to recover the canal company, he sought to avert a military clash and settle the canal dispute with diplomacy before the Soviet Union exploited the situation for political gain. Eisenhower directed Dulles to defuse the crisis on terms acceptable to Britain and France, through public statements, negotiations, two international conferences at London, establishment of a Suez Canal Users Association (SCUA), and deliberations at the United Nations. By late October, however, these efforts proved fruitless, and Anglo-French preparations for war continued.[27]

Second, Eisenhower aimed to avoid alienating Arab nationalism and included Arab statesmen in his diplomacy to end the crisis. His refusal to endorse Anglo-French force against Egypt resulted in part from the realization that Nasser's seizure of the canal company was widely popular among his own and other Arab peoples. Indeed, the surge in Nasser's popularity in Arab states short-circuited Eisenhower's efforts to settle the canal crisis in partnership with Arab leaders. Saudi and Iraqi leaders declined U.S. suggestions that they challenge Nasser's prestige.[28]

Third, Eisenhower sought to isolate Israel from the canal controversy in the fear that a mixture of the volatile Arab-Israeli and Anglo-French-Egyptian conflicts would ignite the Middle East. "Any action which would put the Israelis out in front in the Suez situation," Dulles warned, "would solidify the Arab world." Accordingly, Dulles denied Israel a voice in the diplomatic conferences summoned to resolve the crisis and prevented discussion of Israel's grievances about the Suez Canal blockade during the proceedings at the United Nations. Sensing a spike in Israeli bellicosity toward Egypt in August and September, Eisenhower arranged limited arms supplies from the United States, France, and Canada in the hope of easing Israeli insecurity and thereby averting Egyptian-Israeli war.[29]

Eisenhower's quest to resolve the Suez Crisis peacefully was seriously complicated by the threat of a war in Jordan. In September, a series of hostile incidents along the Israel-Jordan border threatened to trigger a full-scale war. To defend his territory, King Hussein invited Iraq to station troops in his country, a step that Israel vowed to contest. Meanwhile, political turmoil inside Jordan raised the prospect that King Hussein's regime might collapse. In October, the Joint Chiefs of Staff (JCS) observed that Jordan was vulnerable to "serious internal disorder, military intervention by neighboring states, or both." Bracing for trouble, Eisenhower predicted that "we are going to have a donnybrook in this area."[30]

As Eisenhower anticipated, a donnybrook quickly enveloped the Middle East. The melee erupted on October 29 when the Israeli army invaded Egypt. Israel attacked under an elaborate collusion scheme hatched in the preceding weeks with Britain and France. Under the ruse, Israel would invade the Sinai; Britain and France would issue ultimatums ordering Egyptian and Israeli troops to withdraw from the Suez Canal Zone; and, when Nasser (as expected) rejected the ultimatums, the European powers would bomb Egyptian airfields within forty-eight hours, occupy the canal zone, and depose Nasser. The collusion between Britain, France, and Israel to attack Egypt completely melded the canal controversy and the Arab-Israeli conflict, adding a new dimension of complexity to the situation facing U.S. officials.[31]

Caught off guard by the start of hostilities, Eisenhower and Dulles took a series of steps to end the war quickly. Angered that his close allies in London and Paris had deceived him in the collusion scheme, Eisenhower worried that the war would drive Arab states into Soviet dependence. To stop the fighting even as British and French warplanes bombed Egyptian targets, he imposed sanctions on the colluding powers, achieved a United Nations ceasefire resolution, and organized a United Nations Emergency Force (UNEF) to disengage the combatants. On November 5, however, Britain and France landed paratroopers along the Suez Canal; the Soviet Union, in a ploy to distract attention from its brutal repression of a revolutionary movement in Hungary, threatened to intervene in the hostilities and perhaps even retaliate with "atom and hydrogen weapons" against London and Paris. Despite Eisenhower's efforts to segregate the Arab-Israeli conflict from the canal crisis, the two problems intersected, with portentous consequences.[32]

The events of November 5 sent the 1956 war into its most dangerous phase. "The Soviets are scared and furious," Eisenhower observed, and ready "to take any wild adventure." As intelligence officials monitored reports of Soviet forces concentrating in Syria, the president ordered the Pentagon to prepare for a world war. Shaken by the sudden prospect of global conflict, he also moved quickly to avert it. He applied political and financial pressures on the belligerents to accept a UN ceasefire deal on November 6 that took effect the next day, and he endorsed efforts by UN officials to deploy UNEF to Egypt at once. Tensions gradually eased. British and French forces departed Egypt in December, and following complex negotiations, Israeli forces withdrew from the Sinai by March 1957.[33]

In the aftermath of the Suez War, Eisenhower approached the Arab-Israeli conflict more passively than he had in his first term as president. In principle, the president considered Arab-Israeli peace a foundation of a stable and noncommunist Middle East, but in the late 1950s he found the Arab states and Israel unprepared to make the concessions required by a comprehensive peace plan. Thus he decided to suspend peacemaking initiatives until the local states became more prepared to cooperate. Convinced that peace initiatives doomed to failure would only aggravate Arab-Israeli tensions, in fact, Dulles even hindered such initiatives by other countries. In 1957–61, the United States put comprehensive peacemaking to rest.[34]

The United States also adopted a passive approach to the specific points of contention between Israel and the Arab states. On several occasions, the State Department helped contain border violence between Israel and Jordan, Egypt, and Syria, but it refrained from promoting a general settlement of the underlying issues. Nor, despite its interest in solving the refugee crisis and promoting water development, did the department actively address either issue. U.S. diplomats passively tolerated the status quo on the disputes over canal transit, the Gulf of Aqaba, Jerusalem, Jewish immigration to Israel, and the Arab boycott against Israel because the chances of settlement seemed remote. They concluded that because the Arab states and Israel were simply unprepared to settle, peacemaking would prove futile.[35]

Even when they avoided the role of peacemaker, U.S. leaders found themselves the target of anger and reproach by the parties to the Arab-Israeli conflict. To please Nasser, the State Department downplayed Israeli transit rights on the Suez Canal, but Nasser remained recalcitrant and Israel became angry in the process. Arab states criticized the U.S. implicit acceptance of Israel's positions on such issues as refugee resettlement, Jerusalem, and Gulf of Aqaba transit rights. Israel complained of U.S. arms supply to Arab states and its rapprochement with Nasser. "The U.S. wants to be friends with all countries in the Middle East," Eisenhower told Nasser in September 1960. But it could not avoid backlash from either side against its amity with the other.[36]

Conclusion

The Arab-Israeli conflict posed a difficult impediment to the U.S. goal of a stable and noncommunist Middle East. The conflict bred tensions within the region, encouraged extremism among rulers of the area, and offered opportunities for Soviet meddling. In principle, U.S. officials of the 1940s and 1950s favored resolution of the conflict and sought permanent peace treaties built on the foundations of the armistice agreements of 1949.

The U.S. hope of a peaceful Middle East proved futile for several reasons. First, conditions in the region were simply not conducive to peace: passions, animosity, and mistrust among the principals were sufficient to derail any prospective peace plans based on compromise and concession. In effect, both sides to the dispute calculated that they could better preserve their own interests through war rather than peace.

Second, U.S. leaders offered limited leadership in resolving the Arab-Israeli conflict. In 1945–53, deep divisions among officials who favored close relations with Israel and those who favored close relations with the Arab states produced a national policy that was prone to inconsistency and passivity. On several occasions, moreover, the prospect of making peace conflicted with the pursuit of the anti-Soviet containment policy, and officials in Washington consistently favored their anti-Soviet objectives over their commitment to conflict resolution. Eisenhower attempted a bold, comprehensive peace plan in his first term in the White House. But his plan failed, and he encountered such monumental obstacles that he settled into a passive posture for the remainder of his presidency. The Arab-Israeli conflict, and the difficulty it caused U.S. officials, would persist for many decades.

CHAPTER 3

TUMULTUOUS DECADES

Nationalism and Counterrevolution, 1950s–1960s

IN ADDITION TO SOVIET EXPANSIONISM AND Arab-Israeli conflict, the United States faced the problem of revolutionary unrest in the Middle East in the shadow of World War II. The global conflagration undermined the ability of European powers to maintain their colonial empires and stoked the determination of colonized peoples to achieve national independence. As a result, political turmoil swept much of the Middle East. Intent on stabilizing the region on behalf of their anti-Soviet objectives, U.S. officials displayed a tendency to suppress revolutionary movements and leaders in Iran, Egypt, and elsewhere.

Confronting Revolutionary Nationalism

The situation in Palestine was part of a worldwide wave of decolonization that crested after World War II. Encouraged by the wartime exhaustion of European powers, numerous revolutionary and nationalist movements sought to create independent nation-states in territories that the British, French, Dutch, Belgian, and Japanese empires had colonized in previous eras. From 1946 to 1960, thirty-seven new countries declared independence, including eighteen in 1960 alone. The United States, although focused primarily on the communist threats posed by the Soviet Union and China, confronted a wave of unrest and instability in this so-called Third World. American leaders attributed momentous importance to that situation because of the Third World's vast human and physical resources, its strategic assets and proximity to the Soviet Union, and its commercial value to the development of global capitalism.[1]

Certain characteristics of the independence movements rendered

35

them especially troublesome to the United States. First, many of the movements tended toward a leftist political orientation, because Marxism-Leninism attributed Third World poverty to capitalist exploitation, offered a model for rapid industrialization, and vaguely promised liberation from foreign control. Second, in their rebellion against Western imperialism, revolutionary leaders took such actions as confiscating property, denying civil liberties, disallowing political dissent, practicing neutralism in the Cold War, and otherwise rejecting Western political culture. Many revolutionary movements also seemed laced with anti-Americanism, a reaction to America's ostentatious wealth, cultural insensitivity, and racial discrimination against persons of color. Having used force to oust the imperialists, moreover, many revolutionary regimes adhered to a militarist foundation.[2]

In general, the United States embraced a counterrevolution policy toward the Third World. Because many revolutionary movements threatened the traditional order in the Third World and opened the door to communist expansion, the United States aimed to limit or reverse revolutionary tendencies in the Third World and to maintain a sense of order and stability that would serve U.S. interests in the Cold War. Counterrevolution became manifest in a variety of American actions in the Third World, including support for colonial powers, support of indigenous conservatives, negotiation of defense alliances, military and covert intervention, and economic aid.[3]

In the Arab Middle East in particular, U.S. officials monitored a disturbing tendency toward revolutionary nationalism in the 1945–61 period. At the end of World War II, the Arab states appeared to be tied loosely to the West through commercial and security arrangements with Britain and cultural and business ties to the United States. But Western observers viewed with alarm the overthrow of pro-Western regimes in Syria in 1949, Egypt in 1952, and Iraq in 1958, a near-collapse of Lebanon in 1958, and a series of challenges to the pro-Western throne in Jordan. Worse, in American calculations, the revolutionary movements and governments tended to espouse anti-Western nationalism and neutralism in the Cold War.

The radicalization of Arab states provoked an American reaction. The U.S. government bolstered conservative governments against apparent radical intrigues by issuing arms supply and political support. It avoided formal membership in the Baghdad Pact to avoid angering radical leaders, and it engaged in covert operations to unseat a radical regime in Damascus. The Eisenhower Doctrine offered protection to the conservative rulers of Saudi Arabia, Lebanon, Iraq, and Jordan and, as implemented, seemed more a weapon against Arab radicalism than communism. Presidents Dwight D. Eisenhower and John F. Kennedy sought a rapprochement with Egypt in hope of slowing the rise of communism in Syria and Iraq. U.S. officials avoided Arab-Israeli peacemaking in the late 1950s and early 1960s because it promised to encourage Arab radicalism.

While U.S. officials realized that the Arab-U.S. estrangement stemmed from many causes, they sensed that the presence of Israel aggravated it. Arab nationalism, galvanized by Israel's presence, targeted the United States because it had supported Israel. While U.S. officials differentiated between nationalism and communism and recognized that anticommunism permeated Arab culture, moreover, they feared that anti-Israelism exceeded anticommunism in Arab states and that Arab governments might accept Soviet assistance in attacking Israel. They also feared that the Soviet Union would promote anti-Israel and anti-Western extremist leaders in Arab states as a means of eradicating Western influence and projecting Soviet influence in the Arab community. The existence of Israel remained a source of contention in U.S. relations with Arab states, especially the ones that seemed most likely to open the Middle East to the Soviet Union.[4]

Counterrevolution in Iran

Iran provided the scene of one of the earliest U.S. struggles against revolutionary nationalism. The drama in Iran originated in the late 1940s, when nationalists led by Mohammed Mossadegh challenged the Anglo-Iranian Oil Company (AIOC), the British-owned firm that had dominated the country's lucrative oil industry since the early 1900s. Iranian nationalists demanded a greater portion of the AIOC's revenues than the 20 percent provided in the concession of 1933, and news of the 50-50 deal in Saudi Arabia (discussed in chapter 1) galvanized them to action. As the AIOC rejected such demands, Mossadegh emerged as premier and enacted nationalization of the British firm in 1951. Recalcitrant British leaders planned to wage a war to unseat Mossadegh and secure their oil interests, but President Harry S. Truman talked them out of it. Britain instead shut down the AIOC's massive refinery at Abadan and organized a Western embargo of Iranian oil that brought the country's industry to a virtual standstill. But Mossadegh refused to yield, gathering a political following in Tehran that challenged the authority of pro-Western Shah Mohammed Reza Pahlavi.[5]

Taking office in 1953, President Eisenhower inherited the

showdown in Iran and moved quickly to resolve it. As the embargo brought the country to a financial breaking point in May 1953, Mossadegh appealed to the U.S. president for financial assistance, suggesting that otherwise he might be forced to seek Soviet aid. In June, Eisenhower rejected Mossadegh's appeal on the pretext that American taxpayers would not endorse aid to Iran. Even before he sent his reply to Mossadegh, Eisenhower authorized U.S. and British intelligence officers to overthrow the Iranian premier covertly.[6]

Eisenhower authorized clandestine operations against Mossadegh for several reasons. Although the Iranian leader was not a Communist, the president reasoned, Mossadegh was apparently becoming dependent on the local Communist (Tudeh) Party for political support, making his threat to turn to Moscow for aid troubling. Mossadegh's nationalization of the AIOC undermined Britain's prestige and set a precedent for similar action against other Western firms in the developing world. Instability in Iran impeded the president's quest to establish an anti-Soviet pact among states on the Soviet Union's southern border. As long as the situation remained unresolved, Eisenhower also reasoned, the chance of Anglo-Iranian war loomed. Covert action seemed to offer the best escape from an irresolvable and destabilizing deadlock. As Mary Ann Heiss has suggested, vast cultural differences between Mossadegh and his American interlocutors discouraged U.S. officials from seeking an amicable resolution of the crisis.[7]

The U.S.-British covert operation took place in August 1953. Following a brief showdown with Mossadegh, the Shah fled the country on August 15. When Mossadegh's antiroyalist forces split between Tudeh members and Muslim nationalists, however, Western intelligence officers exploited the schism by raising an anti-Mossadegh mob in Tehran and recruiting key units of the armed forces to support the Shah. On August 20, Mossadegh was arrested by forces loyal to the Shah, and by August 31, the Shah returned to his throne in Tehran. Although some of the unrest in Iran was indigenous and spontaneous, U.S. influence was decisive in determining the timing and results of these developments.[8]

In the aftermath of the coup, Eisenhower quickly bolstered the Shah, who became a staunch ally of the United States. The United States extended an economic aid package worth $45 million and, with Britain, lifted the economic embargo. The question of oil ownership was resolved through complex negotiations. The British accepted the principle of nationalization and yielded the AIOC's original concession to a consortium of Western corporations, in which a 40 percent share was held by British

Petroleum (the heir to the AIOC); a 40 percent share by U.S. firms; a 14 percent share by a Dutch firm; and a 6 percent share by a French firm. The National Iranian Oil Company, a creation of Mossadegh, gained recognition as the owner of all local production facilities, and through complicated financial terms the government of Iran gained 50 percent of oil revenues.[9] Iran would remain ensconced in the Western orbit for a generation.

Dealing with the Revolution in Egypt

Of all the Arab states experiencing revolutionary nationalism, Egypt presented U.S. officials with the most complicated challenge. Egypt entered the post-1945 era as a semicolonized part of the British Empire. In the late nineteenth century, Britain had militarily occupied the country and gained ownership of the Suez Canal Company as well as major banks, railroads, and public utilities. Britain quashed a nationalist rebellion in 1919, and in 1936, it gained treaty rights to develop a major military base in the Suez Canal Zone. During World War II, tens of thousands of British troops poured into Egypt to defend the canal and the oil fields to its east from Axis conquest. British strategists deemed Egypt a valuable strategic asset for the postwar period.[10]

Domestically, Egypt became ripe for revolution in the 1940s. King Farouk, who had occupied the throne in 1936 at age 16, lost favor with his people because of his ostentatious wealth, corruption, and inability to challenge British rule. The Wafd political party—formed as a revolutionary movement during the World War I era—grew complacent with British imperialism, tolerated the corruption of the royalist regime, and spent its energy perpetuating its hold on power. Meanwhile, Egypt's burgeoning population lived in semifeudal conditions, with millions of landless peasants toiling on the vast estates of wealthy elites. Political unrest stirred in fringe movements, such as the Muslim Brotherhood, and in the Egyptian army, where officers such as Mohammed Naguib and Gamal Abdel Nasser began to dream about leading Egypt into a new era.[11]

The situation in Egypt after World War II confronted U.S. officials with a dilemma. As shown in chapter 1, national security officials who warily eyed the Soviet Union emphasized the importance of preserving the Anglo-American alliance and of perpetuating Britain's military occupation of Egypt. Yet certain diplomats recognized the wisdom of embracing Arab nationalism. "The whole Arab world is in ferment . . . [and] its peoples are on the threshold of a new renaissance," Ambassador to Lebanon George Wadsworth told Truman in November 1945. "If the United States fails them, they will turn to Russia and will be lost to our civilization." U.S. officials had to decide whether protecting security imperatives or promoting anti-imperialism would best advance U.S. interests in the Cold War.[12]

With regard to Egypt, this dilemma soon became acute. Egyptian nationalism increased in reaction to Britain's demand for a perpetuation of its base rights in the Suez Canal Zone and as a result of the Palestine War of 1948–49 and the Egyptian-Israeli quarrels that followed it. Egyptian nationalists became suspicious of the United States in light of U.S. friendship with Britain and support of Israel. In October 1951, the United States proposed the Middle East Command (MEC) as a vehicle to preserve a Western strategic presence in the Middle East on terms acceptable to Egyptian nationalism. But Egypt refused to cooperate with the scheme because the United States had recently alienated it by siding with Britain (and indirectly with Israel) in a dispute over transit rights on the Suez Canal.[13]

Egypt's refusal of the MEC opened a period of instability in Egyptian politics that led to a revolution in July 1952. Prime Minister Mustapha Nahas not only rejected the MEC but also unilaterally repudiated the 1936 Anglo-Egyptian treaty. Within weeks, violence erupted in the Suez Canal Zone between British soldiers and Egyptian guerrillas. The unrest peaked in January 1952, when insurgents killed two British soldiers in Ismailia; British troops occupied the city at a cost of scores of Egyptians dead; and an angry mob killed eleven British nationals and burned down dozens of structures in Cairo identified with the Western powers. This turmoil gravely undermined the stature and legitimacy of King Farouk's regime in the eyes of Egyptian nationalists.[14]

Revolution swept Egypt on July 23, 1952. The "Free Officers," a network of nationalistic army officers who had plotted to take over the government, seized control of Cairo, exiled King Farouk, and established the Revolutionary Command Council (RCC) to govern the country. The Free Officers appointed General Mohammed Naguib as prime minister, but Colonel Gamal Abdel Nasser was soon recognized as the driving force behind the revolution and the power broker in Cairo.[15]

For about two years, U.S. officials were upbeat about the revolution. Naguib appeared to be a moderate leader who might cooperate with Western security plans for the Middle East. Although some U.S. officials worried about the radicalism manifest in the RCC's land reforms and cancellation of elections, they were relieved that the regime stabilized

Cairo and prevented the spread of communism there. To bolster Naguib, the Eisenhower administration refrained from pressuring him to make peace with Israel even when conditions seemed conducive to settlement. U.S. officials also encouraged negotiation of the Anglo-Egyptian treaty of October 1954, in which Britain pledged to depart the Suez Canal Zone base by summer 1956.[16]

Despite this promising beginning, the U.S.-Egyptian relationship began to sour in late 1954. After a brief power struggle, Nasser ousted Naguib and took over as prime minister. U.S. officials became concerned in August 1954 when Nasser published *Egypt's Liberation: The Philosophy of the Revolution*, a treatise announcing that Egypt would seek to replicate its revolutionary experience in the Arab world, the Muslim world, and the African continent. U.S. concern deepened in 1955, when Nasser refused to cooperate with the Alpha peace plan, shunned participation in the anti-Soviet Baghdad Pact, signaled his intention to practice a neutralist foreign policy by attending the conference of nonaligned states at Bandung, Indonesia, and purchased a major quantity of Soviet weapons.[17]

The year 1956 marked the nadir of U.S.-Egyptian relations. In December 1955, the Eisenhower administration tried to alter the direction of Nasser's diplomacy by offering (together with Britain) an aid package of $200 million for construction of the Aswan dam, the centerpiece of Egypt's domestic reform package. But Nasser resisted Western requests to make peace with Israel and to split with the Soviets, he recognized Communist China, and he fomented a revolt in Jordan against King Hussein, a pro-Western monarch who had taken power in 1953. In March 1956, British and American officials agreed on the so-called Omega initiative of isolating and confining Nasser through subtle political means, and in July, Secretary of State John Foster Dulles abruptly terminated the Aswan aid offer. Nasser reacted by denouncing the Western powers and nationalizing the Suez Canal Company, thereby sparking the Suez Crisis and War of July–November 1956.[18]

The Suez imbroglio further complicated the U.S. response to Egyptian nationalism. As described in chapter 2, U.S. officials approached the crisis determined not to aggravate Arab nationalism. Thus they encouraged Britain and France to settle the dispute peacefully, deployed Arab statesmen to resolve the conflict, and isolated Israel from it. In particular, the United States did not contest the right of Egypt to seize the canal company provided that it paid adequate compensation as required by international law. When the war erupted, Eisenhower and Dulles moved quickly to end it and to force the belligerents to withdraw from the territory they occupied. Such action seemed essential to keep Egypt from embracing an extremist disposition that would redound to the benefit of the Soviet Union. In short, U.S. officials found it impossible to achieve a peaceful solution of the canal issue that both satisfied the European allies and mollified Egyptian nationalism.[19]

The Eisenhower Doctrine

As a consequence of the Suez War, President Eisenhower declared a major new security policy in the Middle East. The Anglo-French-Israeli military assault on Egypt had demolished British and French prestige in the region, vaulted Nasser's stature to stratospheric levels, and seemingly left the remaining pro-Western leaders vulnerable to Nasserist uprisings. U.S. leaders feared the specter of Soviet intrusion into the region. "We have no intention of standing idly by," the president declared in December 1956, "to see the southern flank of NATO completely collapse through Communist penetration and success in the Mid East."[20]

Determined to act, the president proposed the Eisenhower Doctrine in January 1957. The doctrine pledged that the United States would distribute economic and military aid and, if necessary, use military force to contain communism in the Middle East. Congress approved the doctrine in March, despite misgivings about the administration's perspective on the Middle East, the preservation of Israeli interests under the doctrine, and the surrender of congressional prerogatives to the executive branch. Special envoy James P. Richards toured the region, dispensing tens of millions of dollars in economic and military aid to Turkey, Iran, Pakistan, Iraq, Saudi Arabia, Lebanon, and Libya.[21]

Although never formally invoked, the Eisenhower Doctrine guided U.S. policy in three controversies. In spring 1957, Jordanian army officers and Palestinians who were sympathetic to Nasser challenged the authority of Jordan's King Hussein. Eisenhower feared that the collapse of the monarchy would cause the spread of either Egyptian or Israeli power into Jordan, perhaps triggering a war in which the Soviets would gain. Thus he provided $10 million in economic aid to Amman and dispatched the U.S. Sixth Fleet to the Eastern Mediterranean to bolster the king.[22]

The Eisenhower Doctrine also shaped U.S. policy during a crisis involving Syria that erupted several months later. U.S. observers detected rising communist influence in Damascus as the government there denounced the Eisenhower Doctrine, accepted additional Soviet weapons, suppressed conservative opposition, and apparently fomented revolt in

Jordan. In August, the Syrian regime foiled what appears to have been a U.S. covert operation to unseat it. Worried that the Soviet Union might annex Syria or subvert neighboring pro-Western regimes, Eisenhower concentrated U.S. naval and air forces in the region; sent weapons to Iraq, Lebanon, and Jordan; and nudged Turkey to overthrow the regime in Damascus. As Turkey massed 50,000 soldiers along its border with Syria, Egyptian pilots and soldiers trickled into Syria, and Cairo and Damascus formed a joint command to defend against Turkey. The threat of war persisted for several weeks, abating only when Egypt and Syria merged into the United Arab Republic (UAR) on February 1, 1958.[23]

The most intensive application of the Eisenhower Doctrine occurred in 1958 in response to revolutionary unrest in three Arab states. In Jordan, nationalists continued to pose a threat to the throne of King Hussein. In Lebanon, discontent with the government of President Camille Chamoun, a Christian, fed a popular uprising among the country's Muslims, who were apparently enamored of Nasser. Chamoun demanded U.S. military intervention to deny the country to the radicals, but Eisenhower initially refrained from such action on the calculation that it would produce undesirable consequences. In Iraq, radical revolutionaries suddenly and violently overthrew the pro-Western government in July.[24]

Alarmed by the revolt in Baghdad, Eisenhower ordered military intervention in the region. Concluding that Lebanon and Jordan seemed vulnerable to the threat of sudden revolution by pro-Nasser nationalists or communists, the president dispatched U.S. Marines to occupy Beirut and suppress the popular uprising there. Then he directed diplomats to supervise a transfer of power, from Chamoun to General Fuad Chehab, that restored stability to the country. Eisenhower also endorsed and logistically supported a parallel move by British forces into Jordan that shored up King Hussein. U.S. forces remained in Lebanon for three months.[25]

Dealing with Nasser

Nasser remained a difficult challenge for U.S. leaders after the Suez War. Profoundly mistrustful toward the West, the Egyptian premier delayed the postwar clearance and the reopening of the Suez Canal, rejected Western solutions to the question of canal ownership, attacked the prestige of pro-Western leaders in Lebanon and Iraq, criticized the Eisenhower Doctrine, and accepted Soviet military and economic aid. U.S. officials identified Nasser as a chief threat to their objectives in the Middle East because his neutralist foreign policy opened the region to Soviet influence.

U.S. Navy intelligence officers estimated that he was "literally engaged in a cold war against the West."[26]

The rapid formation of the UAR in early 1958 surprised and concerned U.S. officials but, ironically, contained the seeds of an improvement in U.S. relations with Nasser. Overcoming his initial alarm at the expansion of Nasser's influence to Damascus, Eisenhower soon reasoned that the merger of Egypt and Syria would arrest the spread of communism in Damascus, absorb Nasser's political ambitions, and perhaps stoke tension between Cairo and Moscow. The State Department formally recognized the UAR on February 25.[27]

To draw Nasser away from Moscow, moreover, Dulles proposed a series of deals, beginning with U.S. military equipment sales and economic aid, to build better relations. Eisenhower told Mostafa Kamel, who became UAR ambassador to Washington in August 1958, that their two governments must "work together cooperatively and intelligently to find an equitable solution" to the problems between them. Nasser welcomed the "new page" in Egyptian-U.S. relations.[28]

In 1958–59, U.S. and UAR officials laid a foundation for a rapprochement. Nasser revealed that he was troubled by Soviet influence in Iraq and ready to make amends with the West. The United States agreed to provide food aid worth some $110 million, in exchange for which the UAR pledged to promote anticommunist political initiatives in Iraq and to tone down its anti-Western propaganda. Nasser saw "no real problem in US–UAR relations," he told U.S. Ambassador G. Frederick Reinhardt, "other than the problem of Israel." When Eisenhower and Nasser met face to face in September 1960 in New York for a full and frank discussion, the issue of Israel added a frosty tone to their encounter.[29]

Building on Eisenhower's lead, President Kennedy nurtured a rapprochement with Nasser on the calculation that he would better serve U.S. interests by accommodating rather than confronting the Egyptian leader. The rapprochement rested on several foundations. Kennedy and Nasser traded a series of long, personal correspondences that established a sense of trust and mutual respect. They agreed to put the Arab-Israeli dispute "in the icebox" and move on to other matters. As a courtesy, Kennedy took care to explain U.S. arms sales to Israel—which he knew Nasser would not like—before finalizing the deals, and Nasser reciprocated by refraining from public criticism of the sales. Kennedy convinced Congress to approve major new food aid to Egypt, and Nasser responded positively to Kennedy's regional arms control proposals.[30]

Despite its promising start, the rapprochement soon stumbled over the situation in Yemen, a tiny country in southwest Arabia. In late 1962, rebels sympathetic to Nasser deposed their theocratic monarchy and declared the Yemen Arab Republic. Nasser sent tanks and warplanes to bolster the new regime against counterrevolutionary royalist forces that were armed and encouraged by Saudi Arabia. As violence wracked Yemen, the Saudis complained bitterly to the United States about Nasser's involvement, and in November 1963, Congress moved to curtail U.S. aid to Egypt. Just before his death, Kennedy indicated that Nasser had dispirited and frustrated him.[31]

Once Lyndon B. Johnson occupied the White House in November 1963, U.S.-Egyptian relations declined sharply. A long-time sympathizer of Israel and critic of Nasser, Johnson signaled his distaste for Kennedy's efforts to coddle the Egyptian leader. After a mob burned down a U.S. Information Agency library in Cairo, Johnson eliminated economic aid to Egypt, provoking Nasser to declare that Johnson could "go and drink . . . from the sea!" The U.S. president further groused that Nasser stirred unrest in Congo, encouraged the newly formed Palestine Liberation Organization to attack Israel, expressed sympathy for the Viet Cong, and criticized the pro-U.S. monarchies in Iran and Saudi Arabia. When Egyptian bellicosity toward Israel stimulated the tensions that erupted in the Six Day War of 1967, Johnson dismissed Nasser as a dictator at odds with the United States. President Richard M. Nixon, who took office in January 1969, remained suspicious of Nasser at the time of the Egyptian leader's death in 1970.[32]

Conclusion

Mohammed Mossadegh and Gamal Abdel Nasser exemplified the nationalist movements that swept the Third World in the mid-twentieth century. These leaders sought to lead their peoples from the shadow of European imperialism into the aura of national sovereignty and independence. They contested the economic, military, and political influence that Western powers had claimed in their homelands. They questioned the wisdom and the necessity of aligning their countries with the West in the Cold War.

U.S. officials viewed the wave of revolutionary movements in the Middle East with some concern. Although American idealism championed the right of peoples to practice self-determination and endorsed anticolonialism, U.S. leaders viewed revolutionary nationalist movements as dangerous because they threatened to destabilize the Middle East and open it to Soviet influence. Although most officials in Washington seemed to realize that Mossadegh, Nasser, and other such leaders were not communists, those American officials could not shake the fear that the nationalists would somehow advance the Soviet cause by breaking with the West.

Therefore, U.S. officials practiced a counterrevolutionary policy in the Middle East. They engineered a coup against Mossedegh in 1953, and they sought to contain the influence of Nasser—by firmness and occasional accommodation—through the 1950s and 1960s. Under the Eisenhower Doctrine, the United States declared its intent to stabilize the Middle East by whatever means were necessary, and it subsequently intervened in Jordan, Syria, and Lebanon to defend friendly regimes and contest adversarial ones. In the 1950s and 1960s, the United States enacted a conservative, counterrevolutionary policy that it would practice for decades.

CHAPTER 4

UNENDING CONTROVERSY

The Arab-Israeli Conflict, 1961–1982

LEFT UNSOLVED BY THE TRUMAN AND Eisenhower administrations, the Arab-Israeli conflict festered from the 1960s into the 1980s. Perpetual tension and border violence were punctuated by short but intense wars in 1967, 1973, and 1982 that altered borders, inflamed passions, and gravely destabilized the Middle East. Distracted by overseas issues such as the Cold War and Vietnam as well as domestic affairs such as Watergate, U.S. officials sought in principle to prevent Arab-Israeli hostilities and to promote final peace settlements in the region. While they would claim certain successes, the Arab-Israeli conflict persisted.

The United States and the Arab-Israeli Conflict, 1961–1967

U.S. leaders pursued three broad objectives in the Middle East in the early 1960s. First, they underscored the importance of practicing anti-Soviet containment in the region. National security advisers cautioned that the Soviet Union sought to gain influence in the Middle East by supporting revolutionary, anti-Western regimes and political movements. The Soviets, Harold H. Saunders of the National Security Council (NSC) staff cautioned in June 1966, "are gaining ground" turning the United Arab Republic (UAR), Syria, and Iraq against the West. In view of the region's oil resources, military facilities, lines of communication, and human resources, U.S. officials resolved to stop such Soviet expansionism.[1]

Second, U.S. officials sought political stability in the Middle East. They aimed to preserve the territorial integrity of all states in the region against external attack, especially by the Soviet Union. They sought to ensure the survival of Israel against Arab opposition. To safeguard Western oil interests, they worked to preserve the conservative monarchy in Saudi Arabia. To provide a buffer against the spread of anti-Western Arab influence or the renewal of conflict between Israel and radical Arab states, they bolstered Jordan with financial aid. The United States also sought to reduce Arab-Israeli tensions over territory, fresh water, arms supply, and the status of Palestinian refugees, and to prevent the recurrence of Arab-Israeli war or the eruption of hostilities between Arab powers.[2]

Third, U.S. officials aimed to maintain a delicate balance between antagonistic factions in the region. To facilitate their quest for regional peace, they sought friendly relations with both Israel and its Arab neighbors. The administration also sought to negotiate a resolution of a UAR-Saudi clash in Yemen. "Carrying water on both shoulders

In the crisis of 1967, precipitated by the expulsion of United Nations (UN) peacekeepers from the Sinai by Egyptian president Gamal Abdel Nasser, President Lyndon B. Johnson sought a peaceful resolution to the conflict by encouraging both sides to work with the UN. He both condemned Egypt's unlawful actions and urged Israel to exercise restraint. This photo from May 26, 1967, shows Johnson (seated on couch) in a meeting with his foreign policy advisers and representatives of Israel to discuss the current tensions. The delicate balancing act did not work, however, and on June 5, Israel launched military strikes against Egypt and then Syria and Jordan. Yoichi R. Okamoto, photographer, Lyndon Baines Johnson Library sometimes seems immoral and is always difficult," Saunders explained, in reference to the U.S. practice of maintaining friendly relations with all powers. However, the only alternative was "being driven to choose half our interests, sacrifice half and let the USSR pick up our losses."[3]

U.S. officials achieved only partial success in their endeavor to nurture friendship with all powers in the Middle East. U.S.-Israeli political relations appeared to rest on solid foundations of friendship and cooperation. In 1961, Vice President Lyndon B. Johnson told Israeli Prime Minister David Ben-Gurion that "I am sure you know that you have many friends here." Three years later, as president, Johnson assured Prime Minister Levi Eshkol that he was "foursquare behind Israel on all matters that affected their vital security interests." Robert Komer of the NSC staff and Israeli Foreign Minister Golda Meir affirmed in 1965 that "US/Israeli relations were on a solid footing."[4]

Yet U.S.-Israeli relations were not without problems. Johnson vigorously promoted nuclear nonproliferation in the Middle East, for instance, and he deeply regretted Israel's refusal to renounce nuclear weapons. The U.S. government also criticized Israel's policy of conducting major reprisals against neighboring states for terrorist attacks that apparently originated on their soil. Certain U.S. officials, moreover, regretted the domestic political pressure to back Israel unconditionally. Komer encouraged Johnson to insist that Israel "not . . . keep trying to force us to an all-out pro-Israeli policy" in light of "our Arab interests and our common aim of keeping the Soviets out of the Middle East."[5]

The Johnson administration also sought, with partial success, to nurture close relations with Arab states. Admitting that he was attracted to Jordan by "my deep interest in the Bible," Johnson assured King Hussein that he sought "close and cordial relations." Likewise, the president assured Saudi Crown Prince Faisal that "we are resolved as ever to stand solidly and steadfastly beside our valued friends in the area, including Saudi Arabia." U.S. relations with the UAR, by contrast, remained problematic. Johnson applauded Egyptian Premier Gamal Abdel Nasser's willingness to accept U.S. initiatives on nuclear nonproliferation, but as chapter 3 explained, U.S.-UAR tensions mounted when Nasser issued anti-U.S. propaganda, intervened in the civil war in Yemen, and accepted Soviet arms supply.[6]

The issue of arms supply revealed the complexity and difficulty of the U.S. quest to promote containment, stability, and balance in the Middle East. Citing Soviet arms supplies to the UAR, Israel requested permission to purchase U.S. tanks in 1964. Although he sensed that such a sale during an election year would earn domestic political rewards, Johnson initially declined the request on the reasoning that it would undermine relations with Arab powers. Then, in 1965, U.S. officials deemed it essential to provide tanks to Jordan, both to enhance the stature of King Hussein and to deter him from accepting such weapons from the Soviet Union. To the modest disappointment of Israeli leaders, Johnson decided to offer tanks to both Israel and Jordan. Similarly, in 1966, Johnson sold advanced military aircraft to both countries to counter Soviet sales of such weapons to the UAR. These arms deals, Saunders noted, were contrived to achieve "a deterrent balance" in the region.[7]

The Johnson administration's policy in the Middle East faced obstacles. Violence flared along the Israeli-Syrian border, first as Israel used force to stop Syrian efforts to avert the headwaters of rivers flowing into Israel in 1964, and then, in 1965 and after, as Palestinian guerrillas based in Syria launched attacks into Israel and Israel retaliated with reprisal raids. Less intense violence also erupted along the Jordan border. The Palestine Liberation Organization (PLO), established in 1964 with the expressed purpose of destroying the Jewish state, added to the tension. To complicate this situation, Soviet political overtures to the UAR, Syria, and Iraq limited the ability of the United States to remain friendly to those countries, indirectly threatened the integrity of Saudi Arabia and Jordan, and portended a resurgence of Arab-Israeli conflict. U.S. arming of Israel and Soviet arming of Arab states raised tensions and increased destructive capabilities across the region.[8]

In late 1966 and early 1967, Middle East political conditions deteriorated rapidly. Arab infiltrators committed deadly acts of violence along Israel's borders with the UAR and Syria, and Israel responded with forceful reprisals. UN authorities proved unable to settle tensions, and hostile rhetoric and passions escalated on all sides. Israeli fighters engaged and downed Syrian jets on April 7, 1967, and in May, a wave of violence in northern Israel prompted an Israeli threat to occupy Damascus. Amidst reports of an Israeli mobilization and of UAR-Syrian military consultations, the Johnson administration counseled caution on all parties.[9]

The Six Day War of June 1967

To the consternation of American officials, a Middle East crisis erupted on May 16, 1967, when Nasser expelled the UN troops that had policed the Sinai since the end of the Suez-Sinai War in 1957. Stung by criticism from other Arab leaders of his recent passivity toward Israel, Nasser ordered his forces to occupy evacuated UN bases on Israel's border. Rumors circulated that Israel would launch a preemptive strike against this provocation. Johnson asked Israel, Syria, and the UAR to show restraint and to cooperate with UN Secretary General U Thant, who visited Cairo in search of a peaceful resolution to the crisis. Johnson also advised Syria to curtail exfiltration of terrorists to Israel, the UAR to readmit UN soldiers to the Sinai, and Israel to refrain from a preemptive attack. Yet the crisis deepened on May 22, when Nasser closed the Straits of Tiran to Israeli shipping and Israeli leaders threatened to fight to reopen the waterway.[10]

As tensions mounted, U.S. officials took four steps to head off war. First, Johnson promptly and publicly declared the UAR blockade "illegal" and "potentially disastrous to the cause of peace," and he sent a special envoy to Cairo to urge Nasser to reverse it. Second, resolving to "play every card in the UN," Johnson encouraged the UAR and Israel to cooperate with Secretary General Thant to end the crisis. Neither of these initiatives bore fruit. Nasser refused to yield on the blockade and Israeli Ambassador Abba Eban told Secretary of State Dean Rusk that Israeli officials "have absolutely no faith in the possibility of anything useful coming out of the UN."[11]

Third, U.S. officials discouraged Israel from launching a military attack on the UAR to reopen the Straits of Tiran. Johnson and his advisers realized that offering Israel either no support or unconditional support might trigger Israeli military action. Thus they aimed to perform a delicate balancing act both by firmly warning Israel against the use of force and by offering alternative means to guarantee freedom of the seas. Johnson assured Eban on May 26 that "we will pursue vigorously any and all possible measures to keep the Strait open." The record of the conversation reveals that "with emphasis and solemnity, the President repeated twice, Israel will not be alone unless it decides to go alone." Johnson also refused to guarantee Israeli security on the grounds that he lacked congressional support and constitutional authority, without which a security pledge "wouldn't be worth ten cents."[12]

Fourth, U.S. officials organized concerted action by Western powers to break Nasser's blockade of the Straits of Tiran. The State and Defense Departments conceived of a plan in which naval forces of various Western maritime powers would position ships in the Red Sea and pledge to protect merchant ships that plied the straits bound for Israel. Other Western naval vessels would concentrate in the eastern Mediterranean to deter Nasser from resisting the operation in the straits and to provide reinforcement if shooting erupted. U.S. officials estimated that they would need three weeks to prepare an international agreement and put the plan in motion.[13]

Unfortunately for the United States, such efforts to head off war encountered serious problems. For instance, Israeli insecurity mounted amidst reports that UAR units in the Sinai were armed with chemical weapons. After Jordan and the UAR signed a mutual defense treaty on May 30, Eshkol wrote to Johnson that in the absence of an ironclad U.S. security guarantee, U.S. appeals for restraint "will lack any moral or logical basis." Johnson sensed, moreover, that Congress would not endorse any U.S. operation in the Middle East that risked hostilities. "The problem of 'Tonkin Gulfitis,'" Rusk and Secretary of Defense Robert McNamara advised, in reference to the mounting backlash against the war in Vietnam, "remains serious."[14]

U.S. officials also realized that the maritime plan faced political, economic, and military obstacles. State Department experts predicted that the UAR would oppose the operation, even to the point of armed resistance to Western ships. If such a confrontation developed, Arab oil-producing states might embargo oil exports to Western powers, triggering economic dislocation across the industrialized world. Pentagon tacticians who surveyed the deployment of military forces admitted that the United States lacked the assets in the Middle East to ensure a triumph in any conflict with the UAR over the straits, and they added that even a military victory would not guarantee the reopening of the waterway.[15]

By early June, U.S. officials realized that they were boxed in by an impossible situation. Johnson and his top advisers remained convinced that Israel would escalate to war unless the UAR rescinded its blockade of the Straits of Tiran. Yet State Department and CIA officials warned that the maritime plan to reopen the straits appeared to Arab leaders as a U.S. capitulation to Israel, forced the pro-Western Arab states to endorse Nasser's position, eroded U.S. influence in the Arab world, and opened the door to Soviet influence. Such officials urged Johnson to adopt a "hands off" approach to the crisis.[16]

Scholars have debated the substance of diplomatic signals that Johnson sent to Israel in the critical days of early June 1967. Archival evidence indicates that some U.S. officials realized the futility of trying to stop an Israeli strike on Egypt and the advantages that would accrue from such a blow to Nasser's stature. Circumstantial evidence suggests that Johnson conveyed to Israeli leaders that he would not oppose, while not specifically endorsing, an Israeli strike. On the other hand, however, documents reveal that Johnson anticipated limited Israeli military action against the Egyptian blockade in the straits rather than a wider war. "We are sorry this [war] has taken place," Johnson told the NSC on June 7, two days after Israel attacked the UAR in a major offensive. "By the time we get through with all the festering problems we are going to wish the war had not happened." Johnson recalled in his memoirs that the news of war deeply disturbed him because he had worked hard to avert such hostilities, which seemed "potentially far more dangerous than the war in Southeast Asia."[17]

The Middle East crisis indeed turned into war on June 5 when Israeli forces suddenly demolished the Egyptian air force in aerial attacks and then rapidly occupied the Gaza Strip and the Sinai. When Jordan and Syria entered the fray on the UAR's side, Israel delivered similar blows to their forces and occupied the West Bank and the Golan Heights. By the time the final ceasefire took effect on June 10, Israel had soundly defeated its three adversaries and occupied enormous portions of their territory.[18]

A dramatic victory for Israel, the Six Day War damaged U.S.-Arab relations. Within hours of the outbreak of fighting, National Security Advisor Walt Rostow declared to Arab diplomats in Washington that Johnson had tried to prevent hostilities and sought to restore peace. As their military fortunes collapsed, however, various Arab leaders charged that U.S. warplanes actually participated in the Israeli aerial attacks against them. U.S. officials rejected these charges as specious, evidence of scapegoating by leaders facing embarrassing military setbacks. In any case, anti-U.S. passions soared in Arab countries, mobs threatened the safety of U.S. nationals, and Arab governments severed diplomatic relations with the United States.[19]

U.S.-Israeli relations also suffered setbacks during the Six Day War. On June 8, Israeli warplanes attacked the *Liberty*, a U.S. Navy intelligence-gathering ship sailing off the coast of the UAR, killing thirty-four U.S. sailors. For reasons that remain mysterious, Johnson called off a counterstrike by nearby naval units. Israel later explained the incident as a result of errors in reconnaissance and communications and apologized for it, and Johnson accepted the apology and refrained from publicly investigating the episode.[20] "There is no excuse for repeated attacks on a plainly marked U.S. naval vessel," an NSC official wrote. Israeli apologies "do not change the fact that this most unfortunate attack occurred."[21]

The United States adopted a three-track policy toward the Six

Day War. First, it sought to end the war as soon as possible. On June 6, U.S. officials pushed a ceasefire resolution through the UN Security Council, resisting a Soviet amendment ordering Israel to evacuate the territory it occupied. U.S. diplomats helped broker mutual Israeli-Jordanian acceptance of the ceasefire on June 7, and Israeli-Egyptian acceptance the next day. They elicited Syrian acceptance of the ceasefire on June 9, but the fighting continued at Israeli initiative. Ordered by Johnson to "put pressure on Israel," the State Department secured Israeli compliance on June 10 by warning that the Soviets were "busy saber rattling."[22]

Second, Johnson sought to prevent Soviet political or military involvement in the war, which would seriously imperil Western interests in the Middle East and perhaps lead to a global conflict. In a series of "hot line" messages, Johnson appealed to Soviet Premier Alexei Kosygin to collaborate on UN ceasefire resolutions. Kosygin supported such resolutions in principle, although he proposed a proviso to demand Israeli withdrawal from occupied territory, a proviso that Johnson refused. Superpower tensions peaked on June 10, when Kosygin severed relations with Israel and warned Johnson that "necessary actions will be taken, including military," unless Israel accepted the ceasefire with Syria. Prudently, Johnson ordered the Sixth Fleet to move toward the Eastern Mediterranean and pressed Israel to stand down. The mood around the White House became somber until news arrived that Israel had complied. Only then did U.S. officials celebrate that the war spelled a major defeat for the Soviet Union because its client states had performed miserably. "The Russians," Johnson noted on June 14, "had lost their shirts in the Middle East war."[23]

Third, the United States sought to build a permanent peace settlement over the ashes of the Six Day War. The Johnson administration realized that this task would prove difficult. The war had left Arab leaders angry and bitter, and at a summit meeting in Khartoum in August–September 1967 they adopted resolutions declaring the famous "three noes": no recognition of Israel, no peace with Israel, no negotiations with Israel. Flushed with their dramatic victory over three Arab states, for their part, Israeli leaders gradually resolved to use the occupied territories as bargaining chips to secure their own terms in any peace settlement. Meanwhile, Johnson's aides reminded him that domestic public opinion strongly favored peace terms consistent with Israeli demands. "Our powers to make peace," Rostow advised, "are extremely limited."[24]

In such a context, U.S. peacemaking diplomacy achieved little. The Johnson administration proposed a UN resolution to base a peace settlement on the principles of Israeli withdrawal from the territories occupied in June 1967 and Arab recognition of Israel's right to exist as a state. But Israel's position seemed to harden, the NSC noted in September, even as the Arab positions moderated. On November 22, the UN Security Council passed Resolution 242 (UN 242) as a basis for peace-making. That resolution, however, included two crucial ambiguities: it provided that Israel would withdraw from "territories" rather than "the territories," a loophole that gave Israel legal footing to claim permanent retention of some of the land it had occupied in June; the resolution also failed to specify whether Israeli withdrawal should precede or follow Arab recognition. "The outlook for the moment," Rusk reported to the Cabinet, "is for deadlock."[25]

The War of Attrition

Despite the end of hostilities and the passage of UN 242, the Middle East remained ripe for conflict in the shadow of the Six Day War. Eager to recover from the humiliation of 1967, Egypt accepted massive Soviet arms supplies and surpassed its prewar military capability by late 1968. Johnson and President Richard M. Nixon provided Israel with advanced military jets (Skyhawks and Phantoms) to assure military balance, to gain a potential lever on Israeli diplomacy, and to enhance their domestic political interests. Nasser offered to make peace through a UN-brokered settlement if Israel withdrew from all occupied territory, but Israel, indicating a newfound determination to base its security on land rather than agreements, refused to go along. Johnson, distracted by Vietnam, and Nixon, wary of Soviet inroads in Arab states, refrained from compelling Israel to make concessions.[26]

In this context, sporadic violence along the Egyptian-Israeli border escalated into the so-called War of Attrition. Calculating that he could challenge the Israeli occupation of the Sinai and provoke the great powers' political intervention in the situation, Nasser ordered artillery and air strikes on Israeli units east of the Suez Canal in March 1969. Responding with similar measures, Israel quickly achieved air superiority and the ability to strike Egyptian targets virtually at will. By January 1970, Israeli war jets bombed targets deep in Egyptian territory, including Cairo, with the purposes of signaling Israel's firmness, securing the frontier, and triggering Nasser's downfall. But Nasser reacted by traveling to Moscow to secure Soviet assistance, including modern antiaircraft guns, surface-to-air missiles, radar systems, MiG fighters, and 15,000 Soviet soldiers as advisers (including 200 pilots). By June 1970, Soviet pilots battled Israeli airmen in dogfights near the Suez Canal, and casualties mounted on both sides of the waterway. Despite the long American quest to avoid it, the Arab-Israeli dispute became entangled in the Cold War.[27]

Internal divisions limited the ability of the Nixon administration to deal with the War of Attrition. Secretary of State William Rogers, confined to Middle East affairs by Nixon and National Security Adviser Henry Kissinger, eagerly sought to broker a settlement in concert with European powers and the Soviet Union. Kissinger, who disliked Rogers and mistrusted the Soviets, however, quietly discouraged Israel from working with the secretary of state. On December 9, 1969, Rogers proposed a plan for peace based on UN 242 plus a settlement of the refugee issue. Israeli leaders rejected the scheme as damaging to their interests and instead escalated the War of Attrition with strategic bombing.[28]

Persisting in peacemaking, Rogers achieved some success in 1970. In June, he floated a second plan calling for a ceasefire, affirmation of UN 242 by Israel, Jordan, and Egypt, and peace negotiations led by UN mediator Gunnar Jarring. Egypt and Jordan immediately accepted this so-called Rogers Plan B. Israel followed suit, but only after Nixon assured Golda Meir, who had become Israel's prime minister in early 1969, that Israel would be forced neither to absorb Palestinian refugees nor relinquish territory in the absence of a final peace treaty. On these terms, the War of Attrition ended on August 7. Despite suffering heavy casualties, Nasser reached his goals of restoring his political image, gaining Soviet weapons, proving the limits of Israeli superiority, and triggering U.S. involvement in peacemaking. Yet the situation remained fraught with peril.[29]

Soon after the ceasefire, U.S. officials faced a crisis in Jordan. For some time, King Hussein had allowed PLO militants to use his territory to stage raids into Israel. By 1970, however, the king decided that the price of his complicity had become too severe, in terms of both Israeli reprisals on his kingdom and the open defiance that Palestinians showed for his authority. In September 1970, following an incident in which the PLO landed four highjacked commercial airliners only miles from his palace, the king ordered his army to crush the PLO. Crisis loomed when Syria sent tanks into northern Jordan to help the Palestinians. After Hussein's army routed PLO units, however, his air force struck the Syrian tanks, forcing them to retreat. Meanwhile, Nasser died at age fifty-two of a heart attack apparently provoked by exhaustion from conducting diplomacy during the crisis.[30]

U.S. officials were satisfied by the outcome of the episode. The Soviet Union seemingly retreated from a potential involvement in the crisis in the face of U.S. resolve, manifest in the deployment of the Sixth Fleet to the Eastern Mediterranean. U.S. diplomats encouraged King Hussein to secure a pledge from Israel to back him if necessary in a fight against Syria, which relieved Nixon from the burden of having to consider sending U.S. forces to rescue the king. In the end, U.S. officials were heartened by Jordan's defeat of the radical PLO and the resulting indirect blow to Soviet prestige.[31]

The War of 1973

During the early 1970s, the stage was set for another major Arab-Israeli war. As directed by Rogers Plan B, UN Mediator Gunnar Jarring promoted a peace deal in 1971 based on UN 242. Egyptian President Anwar Sadat, who consolidated power in Cairo after Nasser's death in 1970, conditionally accepted the plan. But Israel rejected it, as well as a more modest Egyptian proposal that Israeli forces withdraw from the Suez Canal area as a gesture to start a peace process. Prime Minister Meir decided that continued deadlock in peacemaking negotiations would enable Israel to exploit its military superiority in order to achieve maximalist territorial ambitions. In so doing, Avi Shlaim argues, she missed a chance to avoid the 1973 war.[32]

The Nixon administration's policy toward this conflict evolved in favor of Israel. At Rogers's behest, Nixon initially endorsed Egypt's peace plan and advised Israel to compromise. Gradually, however, Nixon adopted Kissinger's view of Israel as a regional client state that, consonant with the Nixon Doctrine (discussed in chapter 5), would serve American interests by containing both Soviet communism and Arab radicalism. While the State Department believed that withholding arms from Israel would induce it to compromise and that diplomatic stalemate advanced Soviet interests, Kissinger asserted that an insecure Israel would never compromise and that the deadlock undermined Soviet credibility among Arab leaders. The president also realized the domestic political advantages of backing Israel as he approached the election of 1972. In December 1971, Meir met Nixon and convinced him to declare the Rogers Plan dead in exchange for which Israel would consider only a partial withdrawal from the Suez Canal area.[33]

Alignment with Israel blinded the Nixon administration to the harbingers of the 1973 war. Sadat declared his intention to recover the Sinai, asked for American diplomatic support, and expelled Soviet advisers from his country in July 1972 as a means of achieving independence of action. Kissinger, however, interpreted this action as a sign of Egyptian weakness rather than activism. In the autumn of 1973, shortly after Nixon named him secretary of state as well as national security adviser, Kissinger engaged in talks with Israeli, Jordanian, and Egyptian officials, but the negotiations failed to break his complacency, to change Israel's determination to stay the course of deadlock, or to provide Sadat hope of reaching his goals via diplomacy. The war in Vietnam, the pursuit of détente in Beijing and Moscow, and the unfolding Watergate crisis at home also distracted Nixon and Kissinger from the Middle East in 1972–73.[34]

War erupted on October 6, 1973, when Egyptian and Syrian armies launched a coordinated, surprise offensive against Israeli forces in the occupied Sinai and Golan. Launched at the height of the Jewish Yom Kippur holiday, the attack caught the Israelis off guard. The Arab armies, benefiting from a Soviet airlift of supplies that began on October 10, made impressive advances for several days. Armed by the United States at the height of the war, however, Israel repelled the Arab offensives, reoccupied the Golan, coming within twenty miles of Damascus, and crossed to the west side of the Suez Canal, thereby isolating the entire Egyptian Third Army in the Sinai. Although Israel thus expanded its territorial reach before the ceasefire took effect on October 22, the early Arab advances and the relatively high Israeli casualty rates convinced the Arab world that the war was a draw, that Israel was not invincible, and that Arab states had recovered their prestige and honor so badly mauled in 1967.[35]

Surprised by the outbreak of war, Kissinger immediately took action to end the fighting and to build a foundation for a lasting peace. Initially hoping that the war would end indecisively so that he could negotiate a lasting territorial settlement, he refused to arm either side, and he tried to persuade both sides to accept a ceasefire on October 12. Headstrong with success, Egypt refused. Thus Kissinger convinced Nixon to authorize the massive airlift of military supplies to Israel. Such a step offered to secure the United States a diplomatic role in the conflict, to ensure an indecisive outcome to the fighting, to match the Soviet arms supply to Arab armies, and to please domestic public opinion, which remained very sympathetic to Israel. Perhaps Kissinger also feared that Israel might use its nuclear arsenal if necessary to stave off defeat, an option that Israeli officials at least implicitly acknowledged. "Without being told in so many words," William Quandt, an aide to Kissinger, later wrote, "we knew that a desperate Israel might activate its nuclear option." Beginning on October 13, the American airlift delivered thousands of tons of war materiel that enabled Israel to launch its successful counterattacks. On October 18, Congress formally allocated $2.2 billion to fund the airlift.[36]

Even as he arranged to arm the Israelis, Kissinger deftly moved to end the war on terms favorable to the United States. He flew to Moscow to negotiate with the Soviets the terms of UN Security Council Resolution 338, passed on October 22, which called on the belligerents to honor a ceasefire and to negotiate a "just and durable peace" on the basis of UN 242. Then he flew to Israel and convinced Meir to honor the ceasefire.[37]

Ironically, the war moved through its most dangerous phase after the ceasefire resolution took effect. With Kissinger's apparent sanction, the Israeli Defence Forces (IDF) moved to encircle the Egyptian Third Army and sever Egyptian supply lines, in violation of the ceasefire resolution, to gain tactical advantages in the event of future hostilities. Sadat complained bitterly, and Soviet Premier Leonid Brezhnev warned

President Nixon meets with Israeli Prime Minister Golda Meir and Secretary of State Henry Kissinger, March 1, 1973. Nixon's and Kissinger's support for Israel hindered efforts to conclude an Egyptian-Israeli peace. The region erupted in war again in October 1973 when Egyptian and Syrian forces attacked Israel. At this point, Nixon and Kissinger reevaluated their policy and focused on stanching the fighting and building a foundation for a lasting peace.
National Archives and Records Administration

starkly on October 24 that he would send Soviet troops to defend Egypt if necessary. "I will say it straight that if you find it impossible to act jointly with us in this matter," he warned Nixon, "we should be faced with the necessity urgently to consider the question of taking appropriate steps unilaterally." To avert a crisis, Kissinger worked through diplomatic channels to reign in the Israelis and to mollify the Soviets. With Nixon's backing, however, he also placed U.S. worldwide forces on alert and leaked reports of this move to the news media, in part to demonstrate U.S. firmness to the Soviets, in part to establish U.S. prestige in the eyes of Middle East leaders, and in part to deflect attention from the Watergate scandal. The Israeli troop movements ground to a halt on October 25.[38]

The 1973 war proved costly to the United States. Angry at U.S. rearmament of Israel, Arab oil-producing states imposed an artificial price hike and production limits on the sale of oil to the United States and other Western powers, seriously damaging their economies. The war also eroded the appeal of Nixon's détente strategy by revealing that U.S.-Soviet rivalry remained intense on peripheral issues, like the Arab-Israeli conflict, despite the apparent relaxation of tensions on strategic questions. The war also inflamed Arab-Israeli passions and limited the U.S. image of impartiality by encouraging the pro-Israel tendency in American public opinion. In 1975, seventy-six U.S. Senators signed a public letter to President Gerald R. Ford laden with phrases such as "the special relationship between our country and Israel" and "the United States . . . stands firmly with Israel."[39]

Undaunted by the challenge, Kissinger worked to transform the ceasefire into a full-fledged peace process. In an exhaustive initiative known as "shuttle diplomacy," he repeatedly visited Arab states and Israel from October 1973 to summer 1974 and hosted a five-power (United States, Soviet Union, Israel, Jordan, and Egypt) conference at Geneva in December 1973. Kissinger aimed for disengagement of Arab and Israeli troops in the war zones and insertion of UN peacekeepers along both fronts, and he achieved this in an Egyptian-Israeli accord signed on January 18, 1974, and a Syrian-Israeli deal signed on May 31. Along the way, Kissinger also reestablished U.S. diplomatic relations with Egypt, which had been severed since 1967, and he convinced Arab states to resume shipments of oil to Western states in March 1974. Kissinger impressed many observers with his tireless personal effort and his ability to abate a crisis with the skill of a master chess player. *Time* magazine called him "the miracle worker."[40]

Building on the foundation of the disengagement agreements, Kissinger secured the so-called Sinai II agreement between Egypt and Israel in September 1975. The deal broadened the UN buffer zone to include the strategically sensitive Mitla and Gidi passes, from which Israel withdrew. Both Israel and Egypt established monitoring/early warning stations in the passes, Egypt's built by the United States and staffed by American civilians. Israel withdrew from the oil fields at Abu Rodeis. Egypt and Israel accepted limits on the numbers of tanks, artillery, and personnel stationed near the UN zone, and both powers agreed to work toward a final settlement through peaceful means rather than war. To overcome Israeli reluctance to sign anything short of a full peace treaty, the Ford administration used a combination of sticks (such as a warning that Ford would reassess his policy toward Israel if it remained stubborn) and carrots (such as massive economic aid and a secret pledge by Kissinger not to negotiate with or recognize the PLO or launch any diplomatic initiatives in the region without first consulting Israel). Ford secured Egyptian cooperation by pledging to seek a follow-up accord between Israel and Syria and to seek a settlement of the Palestinian refugee problem.[41]

Jimmy Carter and the Peace Process

Motivated in part by his Christian faith, President Jimmy Carter took office in January 1977 intent on achieving a comprehensive Arab-Israeli peace agreement. Carter considered Middle East peace "an urgent priority," National Security Adviser Zbigniew Brzezinski recorded. "Occasionally Carter would also say that he was willing to lose the Presidency for the sake of genuine peace in the Middle East, and I think he was sincere." Carter envisioned a settlement involving an Israeli withdrawal to its pre-1967 borders, on the reasoning that Israeli security should be based on compromise rather than territorial retention. Carter also expressed a willingness to work with the PLO, if it accepted UN 242, and to establish a Palestinian state. Shedding Kissinger's reluctance to work with the Soviets, the president suggested an international conference at Geneva to discuss the prospects for Middle East peace.[42]

Carter's quest for peace faced several major obstacles. Tensions along Israel's northern borders had escalated since the eruption of civil war in Lebanon in 1975, when a decades-old rivalry between Maronite Christians and Muslims exploded in violence. The situation was aggravated by the presence of Palestinians, who had arrived in droves after the Six Day War of 1967 and the clash in Jordan in 1970 and who rallied behind the PLO. Israel supported the Maronites in hope that they would sign a peace treaty and form an antiradical alliance. Syria looked to Lebanese Muslims and PLO fighters as allies in its attempt to counterbalance both Israel and Egypt. Syria occupied central Lebanon in 1976 to exert influence, and by early 1977, the PLO became prominent in south Lebanon, from where it waged attacks on northern Israel. Following a major terrorist assault in March 1978, Israel sent 20,000 soldiers to occupy south Lebanon for three months, remove unfriendly local leaders and bolster the Maronites, and trigger the flight of 100,000 civilians.[43]

In addition, Middle East leaders were skeptical of Carter's call for a major international conference. The PLO turned cold to the idea after Carter replaced his call for a Palestinian state with a pledge only to consult the Palestinians at Geneva. Menachem Begin, elected prime minister of Israel on May 17, 1977, ideologically opposed evacuating Golan or the West Bank, the latter of which he called by its Biblical names of Judea and Samaria, and he feared that U.S.-Soviet cooperation at Geneva might damage his interests or advance a Palestinian state. Sadat feared that Egypt might lose at Geneva if the United States backed Israel and the Soviet Union promoted Syria and the PLO.[44]

Sharing reluctance toward Carter's Geneva initiative, Egypt and Israel started a bilateral peace process. In November 1977, Sadat mentioned to journalists that he would visit Jerusalem, if invited, to discuss peace terms, and Begin surprised the world community by issuing the suggested invitation. Within weeks, Sadat visited Jerusalem, addressed the Knesset, and affirmed with Begin the principle of "no more war." Although Syria, Libya, South Yemen, and Algeria adopted a "rejectionist" pose of berating both Israel for refusing to make a comprehensive peace and Egypt for selling out the united Arab front, the Egyptian-Israeli dialogue continued.[45]

Upstaged by Sadat's dramatic initiative, Carter devoted himself to nurturing the Egyptian-Israeli peace process to fruition. When the bilateral talks deadlocked, Carter invited Sadat and Begin to conduct face-to-face negotiations at Camp David in September 1978. There the president carefully brokered terms for peace. "He showed himself to be a skillful debater, a master psychologist, and a very effective mediator," Brzezinski noted. "Without him, there would have been no agreement." On September 17, Carter presided over the signing of the Camp David Accords. The first agreement, "A Framework for Peace in the Middle East," sketched a three-year plan for a transition of the West Bank and Gaza from occupied territories to self-governing districts under Palestinian autonomy with Israeli security interests guaranteed. The second accord, "A Framework for the Conclusion of a Peace Treaty between Egypt and Israel," provided for Israeli withdrawal from the Sinai, demilitarization of the Sinai under UN oversight, and opening of diplomatic relations between the two powers. "The world prayed for the success of our efforts," Carter intoned, "and I am glad to announce to you that these prayers have been answered."[46]

Carter also intervened decisively when Egyptian-Israeli talks bogged down in early 1979 on several issues, including minor matters such as implementation logistics and major questions such as linkage between the two Camp David agreements. The president visited Cairo and Jerusalem in March 1979 and brokered compromises on all the issues. The linkage issue was finessed by a letter of understanding that Israel and Egypt would negotiate the issue. In an historic treaty signed at the White House on March 26, 1979, Egypt and Israel made peace and exchanged diplomatic relations. "All of official Washington was present"

For President Jimmy Carter, peace in the Middle East was "an urgent priority." Despite the misgivings of Egyptian President Anwar Sadat and Israeli Prime Minister Menachem Begin, both leaders took the political risk of initiating a bilateral peace dialogue. With the help of skillful negotiation by President Carter, that process culminated in the signing of the Camp David Accords on September 17, 1978, pictured above. Full diplomatic relations were established two years later. Jimmy Carter Library at the ceremony, Secretary of State Cyrus Vance noted, "and everyone was euphoric." To his credit, Carter facilitated an important peace treaty between Israel and its largest, most populous, and most prestigious Arab adversary. Granted, Egyptian and Israeli willingness to make peace was a crucial factor, but Carter exercised substantial influence in clinching the settlement.[47]

Carter's achievement had clear limits. It did not secure a more general, regional peace. In fact, Begin soon indicated that he had no intention of withdrawing from the West Bank or Golan, of granting Palestinians any meaningful form of sovereignty, or of curtailing Israeli construction of settlements in the occupied territories. Various Arab states complained that the peace treaty affirmed Israel's unilateral control of Jerusalem and gave it a legal basis to contest the withdrawal provisions of UN 242. The Arab League expelled Egypt, most Arab states broke diplomatic relations with Cairo, and the PLO vowed to fight on. Distracted by the revolution in Iran, the Soviet invasion of Afghanistan, and an energy crisis at home, Carter lost the initiative for action. Besieged in his own reelection campaign, he became reluctant to pressure Israel to make concessions.[48]

Developments of 1981 further diminished hope for a comprehensive peace settlement. On June 7, Israeli war jets preemptively attacked and destroyed an Iraqi nuclear reactor at Osirak, near Baghdad, on the supposition that it was destined to produce nuclear weapons that would be used against Israel. While the event inflamed Arab anger, it seemed to resuscitate the flagging political fortunes of Begin, who narrowly won the Israeli election of June 30 and thereafter formed an even more conservative government. October witnessed the deaths of two of the architects of the 1979 peace treaty—Anwar Sadat, who was assassinated in Cairo by an army officer, and Israeli Foreign Minister Moshe Dayan, who succumbed to cancer. In December, Begin pushed through the Knesset a bill providing annexation of the Golan Heights, a move that violated UN 242, the Israeli-Syrian disengagement accord of 1974, and the Camp David Accords.[49]

The War in Lebanon

The tensions that mounted after the Egyptian-Israeli peace treaty triggered an Israeli invasion of Lebanon in 1982. Cross-border attacks like those that had provoked Israel's 1978 incursion continued sporadically through the Camp David peace process. After an artillery duel rocked the border areas in both Lebanon and Israel, U.S. special envoy Philip

Habib brokered a ceasefire agreement between Israel and the PLO in July 1981. According to Charles Smith, however, Begin grew to regret the ceasefire because it implied Israeli recognition of the PLO, provided cover for the PLO to rearm, and implied equal U.S. treatment of the PLO and Israel. Considering the PLO more dangerous as a political entity under a truce than as a military threat, Begin itched to destroy it. He authorized Minister of Defense General Ariel Sharon to plot a major invasion of Lebanon that would eradicate the PLO, neutralize Syrian forces, and ensconce in power Maronite leader Bashir Gemayel in the hope that he would sign a peace treaty with Israel.[50]

Secretary of State Alexander Haig indirectly if unintentionally encouraged Israeli belligerence. In early 1982, Sharon openly discussed with Haig the prospects of taking the war on the PLO into Lebanon and warned that the IDF would retaliate forcefully against the next provocation. Haig's response was ambiguous and, in retrospect, controversial. On the surface, he urged Sharon to show restraint, advising that any reprisal must be proportionate and launched only in reaction to an "internationally recognized provocation." Yet by not specifically warning Sharon to hold back or threatening any punishments for offensive action, Avi Shlaim posits, Haig implicitly encouraged Sharon's offensive propensity. Israeli officials apparently interpreted Haig's remarks as a green light for offensive action.[51]

Thus the stage was set for war. On June 3, a faction of the PLO shot and wounded an Israeli diplomat in London. Israel retaliated by bombing PLO targets in and near Beirut, and PLO assets in south Lebanon responded by shelling Galilee. On June 6, the IDF invaded Lebanon in force. Although the Cabinet authorized an attack against PLO targets within some forty kilometers of the border, Sharon, as commanding officer, broadened the scope of the conflict by engaging Syrian forces and occupying territory as far north as Beirut. Even after a U.S.-brokered ceasefire took effect on June 11, IDF units continued secretly moving northward until the IDF linked up with Christian Lebanese militias and besieged PLO units in Beirut. Reluctant to absorb the casualties that would result from a frontal attack on the city, the IDF bombarded PLO strongholds, occupied the airport, and probed around the city's borders in an effort to intimidate the PLO into surrender.[52]

The Roanld Reagan administration quickly became involved in the war. Deeply angered by Israel's offensive action, President Reagan pressured Begin to relent. He also accepted Haig's resignation on June 25, perhaps in part to repudiate the secretary's endorsement of Israeli action. The new secretary of state, George Shultz, sent veteran envoy Philip Habib to broker a settlement. Under a deal signed on August 12, U.S., French, and Italian troops arrived in Beirut to supervise the relocation of some 11,000 PLO fighters to various Arab states distant from Israel. Among those deported was Yasser Arafat, who had formed the Palestine National Liberation Movement (Fatah) in 1958 and assumed leadership of the PLO in 1969. The evacuation was completed by September 1, and the Western soldiers departed Lebanon.[53]

Israeli leaders also used their occupation to influence political developments in Lebanon. They meddled in the Lebanese elections of August 23, ensuring the election of Bashir Gemayel as president. But Israel's hope that Gemayel would sign a peace treaty evaporated when he was assassinated on September 14. Sharon reacted to the murder by ordering the IDF to reoccupy parts of Beirut and enabling Phalangist militias to massacre hundreds of Muslim civilians in the Sabra and Shatila refugee camps. (While Israelis did not participate in the killing, an Israeli judicial investigation later determined that the IDF was complicit in the massacre, and the Israeli Cabinet fired Sharon as minister of defense.) Worse for Israeli leaders, Bashir Gemayel's brother and successor Amin Gemayel indicated no desire to cooperate with Israel.[54]

The war in Lebanon impelled President Reagan to promote peacemaking. Quoting Scripture, he told the American people on September 1 that peacemaking was "a moral imperative." He asserted that Israel must honor UN 242 and thus rejected Israeli claims to sovereignty over Golan and the West Bank. Hoping to isolate the PLO, however, he also denied Palestinian statehood, indicating support for Palestinian autonomy in confederation with Jordan and in peace with Israel. Reagan apparently tried to provide Arab leaders a choice between liberation of the West Bank under moderate control or prolonged Israeli occupation. In any case, the Reagan plan fell flat. Israel rejected it on territorial grounds, and Arab leaders, meeting at a summit in Fez, Morocco, in early September, reaffirmed that the PLO, as the sole representative of the Palestinian people, must be included in any deal.[55]

The Reagan peace plan rejected, Secretary of State Shultz worked to repair the damage of the Israeli invasion. He brokered a deal, signed on May 17, 1983, that formally terminated the war between Israel and Lebanon, provided for a retreat of IDF units to a security zone of some 40 kilometers width in southern Lebanon, and introduced UN troops as peacekeepers to the north of Israeli forces. The IDF consolidated a presence in south Lebanon destined to last nearly twenty years. In the wake of its departure from central Lebanon, internecine fighting erupted on several fronts, vastly complicating the Lebanese civil war.[56]

Conclusion

The Arab-Israeli conflict moved through several crisis points between 1961 and 1982. The tensions emanating from the disputes of earlier decades mounted in the early and middle 1960s, sparking the Six Day War of June 1967 in which Israel militarily defeated Egypt, Syria, and Jordan and occupied large swaths of their territory. The War of Attrition of 1969–70, an Egyptian-Israeli struggle along the battlefront established by the 1967 war, generated casualties and bolstered resolve on both sides. In the October 1973 war, Arab armies recovered some of their prestige by launching a surprise assault on Israeli forces that enjoyed tactical success before Israel turned the tide and achieved a draw. The Israeli invasion of Lebanon in 1982 completed the cycle of intense military conflict between Israel and neighboring Arab states.

On behalf of their interests in the Cold War, U.S. officials favored resolution of this conflict. The hostilities generated political instability that seemed to advance Soviet interests by radicalizing Arab states and threatened the oil resources on which Western security and economic health depended. Thus U.S. officials sought some means to bring peace to the region.

American peacemaking efforts achieved only partial success in 1961–82. While U.S. officials contributed to the ceasefires that ended each round of hostilities in this period, they could not prevent the next round from starting. While the United States successfully brokered a major peace treaty between Egypt and Israel, it was unable to achieve a more sweeping settlement that might have averted the 1982 Israeli invasion of Lebanon. International peace and stability in the Arab-Israeli relationships would await a future decade.

CHAPTER 5

REVOLUTION, WAR, AND TERRORISM

The Middle East at Center Stage, 1970s–1980s

IN ADDITION TO THE ARAB-ISRAELI conflict, U.S. foreign policy makers faced several other challenges in the Middle East in the 1970s and 1980s. A revolution with deep anti-American undertones swept Iran, setting the stage for a crisis involving the seizure of American hostages in Tehran. The Soviet Union invaded Afghanistan, raising fears in Washington that Moscow sought to extend its influence through the region. Lebanon remained unstable in the aftermath of Israel's 1982 invasion, and acts of anti-Western terrorism occurred across the entire region. The Iran-Iraq War of 1980–88 produced massive casualties, threatened oil supplies, antagonized political relations throughout the region, and eventually embroiled the United States in military operations.

The United States faced these challenges through the lens of the Cold War. While the turmoil in the Middle East resulted from myriad factors related to the political, cultural, and historical dynamics of the region, U.S. officials shaped policies on the grounds of their anti-Soviet containment objectives. As its involvement in the Middle East deepened, the United States found itself at the center of complex and dangerous predicaments.

Trouble in Iran

In the eyes of U.S. officials, Iran remained politically stable for more than two decades after the Anglo-American covert operation of 1953 restored Shah Mohammed Reza Pahlavi to the throne in Tehran (discussed in chapter 3). Indeed, in the 1950s, Iran emerged as an important U.S. ally. In 1955, it joined CENTO and garnered extensive U.S. economic and

military aid (some $1 billion by 1960). Hundreds of U.S. military person-
nel trained Iran's national police and army. In 1964, the Shah granted
these U.S. soldiers the legal right of extraterritoriality (essentially, diplomatic immunity from Iranian law), thereby eroding Iranian sovereignty.[1]

The U.S.–Iranian partnership blossomed during the Nixon presidency. As part of his global strategy for containing Soviet communism
through new and efficient means, the president declared under the so-
called Nixon Doctrine that the United States would equip and rely on
various client states to resist revolution and otherwise stabilize each region of the world. Nixon viewed Iran as his Middle East client, especially
after Britain announced that it would relinquish its commitments to security interests east of Suez in 1971. He also hoped to repair the stark trade
imbalance caused by American consumption of Iranian oil, especially
after the sharp price hike of 1973 earned Iran windfall revenues. For

*The U.S.-Iranian partnership thrived during Richard Nixon's presidency. With pro-Western
Shah Mohammed Reza Pahlavi at the helm, the U.S. treated Iran as a client state that
would promote U.S. security and economic goals in the region. The Shah's close ties to the
West—this photo from 1973 shows him meeting with President Nixon in the Oval Office—
earned him political problems at home that culminated in his overthrow during the Iranian
revolution of 1978–79.* Robert L. Knudsen, photographer, National Archives

these security and economic reasons, Nixon nurtured a close relationship with the Shah and offered to sell him any nonnuclear weapon systems the Shah desired. In 1972–77, Iran increased its defense budget by nearly 700 percent and purchased U.S. weapons valued at $16.2 billion. The CIA formed a close partnership with SAVAK, the Shah's secret police force. By 1978, there were 50,000 Americans in Iran, many of them holding executive positions in government and the oil industry.[2]

The more the Shah cozied up to the United States, however, the more he seemed troubled by domestic problems. Those Iranians who had admired Mohammed Mossadegh in the early 1950s viewed the Shah as a discredited lackey of Western imperialism. Such sentiments deepened as the Shah welcomed American advisers, granted them extraterritoriality, and paid them salaries deemed outlandish by local standards. Others regretted the urban blight, housing shortages, and economic dislocations that accompanied the Shah's efforts to modernize Iran. Yet others resented the Shah's creeping absolutism, manifest in his banning of political parties; his ostentatious display of regal splendor; and his unleashing of SAVAK to repress dissent with censorship and torture.[3]

Gradually, the Ayatollah Ruhollah Khomeini organized an opposition movement among Iran's conservative Shi'a Muslim clerics. After leading anti-Shah protests at Qom in 1963, Khomeini was jailed and sentenced to death, but in 1964, the Shah commuted his sentence to exile to Iraq. The Shah's act came back to haunt him as the exiled ayatollah soon emerged as leader-in-exile of a widespread opposition movement. Khomeini's 1971 book *Islamic Government* called for the destruction of the old order and the establishment of an Islamist government in Iran. Khomeini's vision caught the imagination of the Iranian people who chafed under the Shah's rule and resented the American prominence in their country. Through a network of supportive clerics, Khomeini spread his influence throughout the country.[4]

The situation in Iran collapsed during Jimmy Carter's presidency. In November 1977, a cycle of unrest prompted Carter to bolster the Shah by inviting him to Washington. Ominously, the welcoming ceremony on the White House lawn was disrupted by the angry shouts of thousands of anti-Shah demonstrators milling just outside the grounds. Worse, after local police dispersed the crowd with tear gas, the wind carried the gas over the White House lawn, moistening the eyes of Carter, the Shah, and their wives and forcing an abrupt end of the ceremony. The next month, Carter compounded his woes during a visit to Tehran, where he publicly toasted the Shah for making Iran "an island of stability" and for "the admiration and love which your people give you."[5]

The November–December episodes portended, and perhaps triggered, the Iranian revolution that unfolded in 1978. In January, a violent clash between anti-Shah marchers and state police left six people dead and touched off a cycle of mounting violence in which anti-Shah rebels grew more bold and confrontational and SAVAK grew more brutal and oppressive. Suspicious that Khomeini directed the insurgency from Iraq, the Shah pressured Iraq to deport the ayatollah in June. That step proved to be a blunder, as Khomeini relocated to Paris, where he gained access to the Western media and direct telephone lines to Tehran. Vaulted to international fame and leadership of the revolution, Khomeini demanded the abdication of the Shah. In November, the Shah declared martial law, but he refrained from using his army to restore order on the hunch that common soldiers would defect before killing civilians.[6]

The Carter administration proved ineffectual at curbing the revolution in Iran. National Security Adviser Zbigniew Brzezinski, known for his hawkish disposition toward communism and disorder, advised Carter to issue the public toast to the Shah, to forbid the CIA or military intelligence from contacting the insurgents, and to urge the Shah to use his army to retain power. Secretary of State Cyrus Vance, known for his more progressive instincts, urged Carter to dissuade the Shah from using force and to work secretly with the opposition to help moderates take power in Tehran. Torn by such conflicting advice, Carter equivocated for many months, taking no action. Finally, the president sided with Brzezinski in late 1978 and advised the Shah to use force to crush the rebellion, but this step was too little, too late. In January 1979, the Shah appointed a moderate prime minister and fled the country, never to return. Within weeks, Khomeini returned from exile, deposed the Shah's prime minister, and established a fundamentalist, absolute, and theocratic regime in Tehran.[7]

Carter found the new government quite challenging. As Khomeini consolidated power in Tehran, he attacked the United States in propaganda. Mobs routinely filed past the U.S. embassy chanting anti-American slogans, and in February 1979, a throng entered the embassy compound before Tehran police ousted it. U.S. businessmen departed the country. The U.S. Embassy remained open, albeit with a skeleton staff of sixty (reduced from some fourteen hundred before the revolution), led by Ambassador William H. Sullivan, who advised his superiors in Washington to seek accommodation with the new regime. By September, the demonstrations outside the embassy had diminished in intensity, and top officials in the Carter administration began exploring the possibility of achieving more stable relations.[8]

Trouble developed, however, after the exiled Shah petitioned Carter for entry into the United States to gain access to advanced treatment for the cancer that had afflicted him since 1974. Sensitive to Iranian passions, Carter resisted such a move for months. The embassy in Tehran warned in September that admitting the Shah "would almost certainly result in an immediate and violent reaction" that Khomeini would prove unable or unwilling to contain. Yet Brzezinski, other conservative voices, and various members of Congress urged Carter to admit the Shah on

On November 4, 1979, Iranian militants stormed the U.S. Embassy in Tehran and took hostages, demanding that the U.S. turn over the Shah to be tried. In this photo taken four days later, anti-American protesters are shown chanting outside the embassy, holding a poster with a caricature of President Carter that reads: "U.S. can not do anything." AP/Wide World Photos

humanitarian grounds. Carter was persuaded, and in late October 1979, he extended permission for the Shah to enter the United States.[9]

Khomeini responded to Carter's move by provoking the infamous Iran hostage crisis. Perhaps the ayatollah feared that the United States might try to restore the Shah or his son to power in Tehran; perhaps he sought vengeance against his hated nemesis. For whatever motive, he urged his followers to take to the streets of Tehran to protest Carter's decision; on November 1, a throng of three million persons gathered in Tehran to march past the U.S. Embassy and condemn the United States as the "Great Satan." Three days later, hundreds of militants stormed the embassy and seized the Foreign Service officers and Marines on duty there. As the captives were blindfolded, interrogated, paraded before cameras, and threatened with execution by firing squads, Khomeini applauded the mob action against the "nest of spies." The ayatollah soon clarified his terms: he would release the captives in exchange for "the deposed and criminal Shah." The ayatollah's move triggered copycat expressions of anti-Americanism across the Muslim world: extremists briefly took control of the Great Mosque in Mecca, Saudi Arabia, the holiest site in Islam, and mobs attacked the U.S. embassies in Islamabad, Pakistan, and Tripoli, Libya.[10]

The Carter administration's reaction to the crisis showed its trademark uncertainty and vacillation. Brzezinski advised the president to order military action to rescue the hostages and punish Khomeini. A timid response would encourage other thugs and extremists to attack U.S. interests around the world, he argued, while a forceful response would signal American resolve and provide a means to end the Khomeini regime. Vance, by contrast, urged Carter to employ diplomacy, cautioning that military action would imperil the hostages, whose lives were not in immediate danger. It would also stimulate a wave of protests across the entire Third World, spark other acts of hostage-taking, and drive Khomeini into the arms of the Soviets. Initially siding with Vance, Carter implemented a series of diplomatic options: he froze Iranian assets (worth about $10 billion) in U.S. banks; expelled Iranian diplomats and students from the United States; isolated Iran diplomatically and organized international financial sanctions; secured a censure of Iran's actions by the International Court of Justice; sought to secure the release of the hostages through back-channel negotiations; and in April 1980, broke off diplomatic relations with Tehran.[11]

Because the crisis remained deadlocked after months of diplomacy, however, Carter shifted gears in April 1980, when he ordered the military rescue mission that Brzezinski had urged all along. According to the plan, eight Air Force helicopters would fly from an aircraft carrier, below radar and under cover of darkness, to a remote site code-named Desert One, near Tabriz. There they would rendezvous with troop transport airplanes, refuel, take on commandos, and fly to a staging area near Tehran, from which point the commandos would rescue the hostages on the following night. Soon after the plan was put into action on April 24, however, problems developed. Two of the eight helicopters malfunctioned en route to Desert One, and a third broke down upon arrival. The remaining five helicopters lacked the capacity to transport the rescue team and the freed hostages. Personally monitoring the operation in the White House, Carter ordered an abort. Then, in haste to depart Desert One, a helicopter and an airplane collided and exploded, killing eight soldiers.[12]

The botched rescue mission was a severe setback for the United States. Khomeini was quick to publicize the operation as a U.S. invasion, and Iranian notables went to Desert One to poke at the charred remains of the U.S. soldiers before television cameras. The hostages were then dispersed to many sites to render other rescue attempts impossible. Vance resigned his office in protest against the mission. Carter later called the day of the mission "one of the worst of my life," and his popularity at home and abroad sank perceptibly. "The disastrous failure at Desert One," NSC staff member Gary Sick later recorded, "was a terrible blow to the United States at a moment when it badly needed a victory."[13]

Worse from Carter's personal perspective, the hostage ordeal significantly influenced the presidential election of 1980. From the outset of the crisis, concern for the hostages became a national phenomenon, as citizens held candlelight vigils and displayed yellow ribbons and as the mass media provided intensive daily news coverage of the event. Carter nurtured such activity, for example by dimming the lights on the national Christmas tree in December 1979, and he adopted the so-called Rose Garden strategy, pledging to confine himself to the White House and work nonstop to solve the hostage crisis rather than campaign for office. He apparently calculated that he could exploit a successful resolution of the crisis to win reelection, and for several months polls revealed a groundswell of public support. As the crisis persisted, however, Carter's popularity fell. Perhaps electoral considerations encouraged the president to order the doomed rescue mission in April 1980. Certainly, the tragedy at Desert One damaged his image among voters even as Republican challenger Ronald Reagan lambasted the president for poor leadership on a variety of issues. Confronted by gloomy political forecasts, Carter abandoned the Rose Garden strategy in summer 1980.[14]

Carter also intensified his efforts to resolve the hostage crisis on the hope that a so-called October surprise—a release of the hostages on the eve of the election—might save his embattled presidency. The death of the Shah in July 1980 raised hopes that a settlement was possible. Through back-channel negotiations arbitrated by Algeria, U.S. and Iranian officials discussed the possibility of a deal in which the hostages would be released in exchange for the unfreezing of Iranian financial assets, needed for the war against Iraq that had erupted in September. Negotiations stalled, however, and as the hostages languished so did Carter's political fortunes: Reagan was elected president on November 4. As a lame duck, Carter continued negotiations, and in early January 1981, he struck a deal to trade the hostages for the release of Iran's financial assets. As a final snub to Carter, Khomeini freed the hostages on January 20, 1981 (the U.S. Inauguration Day), loading them on an airplane at Tehran Airport but then delaying the aircraft's departure until minutes after Reagan took the oath of office in Washington.[15]

Since the election of 1980, several political insiders have alleged that Republican Party leaders unlawfully and immorally interfered in the hostage crisis to secure Reagan's victory. Carter administration negotiators claimed that steady progress toward a settlement with Iran stalled abruptly in October 1980 when Iran inexplicably turned stubborn. Some of them came to suspect that top officials of the GOP—perhaps including vice presidential nominee George H. W. Bush—had ventured to Paris that month to meet a Khomeini envoy and pledge to send Khomeini arms if he held the hostages through Election Day. (Indeed, within a few years, Reagan would covertly send such weapons to Tehran.) Such shenanigans, Gary Sick aptly notes, would have been "not only strictly illegal but border[ing] on treason" and would have constituted "nothing less than a political coup." While such charges are plausible, they have been denied vehemently by Republican leaders. No conclusive proof has ever been presented to sustain the charges.[16]

Trouble in Afghanistan

Simultaneously with the Iran hostage crisis, Carter also faced a confrontation with the Soviet Union over Afghanistan. Carter had taken office intent on developing a more stable and amicable relationship with Moscow, but tensions mounted steadily in 1977–79 over several issues. Soviet leaders had been concerned for some time by instability in Afghanistan, where nationalists challenged a pro-Soviet ruling elite. After the Iranian revolution of 1979, they feared the prospect that anticommunist Islamic fundamentalism might seep from Iran to Afghanistan and even to the Muslim peoples of the southern Soviet Union. On December 25–27, 1979, some 80,000 Soviet soldiers invaded Afghanistan, officially under an invitation from Premier Hafizullah Amin to restore order. However, Amin was soon killed by Soviet forces, who proceeded to occupy much of the country.[17]

The Soviet invasion, involving the largest Soviet military movement outside Eastern Europe since World War II, profoundly disturbed President Carter. He called the attack perhaps "the most serious threat to the peace" since 1945 and, falling completely under Brzezinski's influence, implemented a series of firm countermeasures. The president suspended official diplomatic contacts with the Soviets; imposed embargoes on the export of wheat, technology, and various other goods to Russia; increased the Pentagon's budget and pushed the readiness of combat forces; earmarked foreign aid for Pakistan and other local states resisting Soviet expansion; covertly funneled arms and aid to Afghans resisting Soviet occupation; resumed selective service registration of young men to bolster military readiness; and imposed a boycott of the 1980 summer Olympic Games in Moscow. Suspecting that the Soviets had territorial aspirations on the oil-rich region south of Afghanistan, the president also issued the so-called Carter Doctrine in January 1980. "An attempt by an outside force to gain control of the Persian Gulf region," he intoned, "will be regarded as an assault on the vital interests of the United States of America, and such an assault will be repelled by any means necessary, including military force."[18]

President Ronald Reagan moved quickly to contest the Soviet presence in Afghanistan. He acted under the so-called Reagan Doctrine, a commitment to support anti-Soviet forces and promote freedom and democracy around the world. "We must not break faith with those who are risking their lives—on every continent, from Afghanistan to Nicaragua," Reagan explained in 1985, in his most concise articulation of the doctrine, "to defy Soviet-supported aggression and secure rights which have been ours from birth." To implement this vision, Reagan relied on covert operations and selective applications of Pentagon muscle, masterminded by William Casey, a veteran of the wartime Office of Strategic Services who served as Director of Central Intelligence from 1981 to 1987. "I wanted to remind [Soviet Premier] Leonid Brezhnev that we knew what the Soviets were up to," Reagan later wrote, "and that we weren't going to stand by and do nothing while they sought world domination."[19]

Acting under the Reagan Doctrine, the United States seriously challenged the Soviet occupation of Afghanistan. The Reagan administration covertly organized and armed Afghan partisans via secret supply lines through Pakistan; in 1979–89, U.S. aid topped $3 billion. Some sixty U.S. soldiers were secretly inserted into Afghanistan, where they trained partisans in resistance tactics. Mercenaries from around the Muslim world—including a Saudi national named Osama bin Laden—were recruited to resist Soviet imperialism in Afghanistan. "Their sustained countrywide struggle against tyranny and oppression," Secretary of State George P. Shultz said of the Afghan fighters, "is worthy of our esteem." By the mid-1980s, the U.S.-orchestrated resistance inflicted a significant toll on Soviet forces, and Reagan's decision to arm the rebels with portable Stinger antiaircraft missiles in 1986 seemed to seal the Soviets' fate. Despite sending more than 100,000 soldiers to Afghanistan and sustaining some 40,000 casualties, the Soviets could not secure control of the country. In the context of major reforms in Soviet foreign policy, Soviet Premier Mikhail Gorbachev announced in April 1988 that he would withdraw Soviet forces from Afghanistan.[20]

Reagan's Strategic Consensus

The situations in Afghanistan and Iran were only two of several challenges facing Reagan in the Middle East. "No region of the world," the president later remarked, "presents America with more difficult, more frustrating, or more convoluted problems than the Middle East." To practice anti-Soviet containment in such a volatile region, Alexander Haig, who served as secretary of state in 1981–82, envisioned a "consensus of strategic concerns" among such friendly regional powers as Egypt, Israel, Saudi Arabia, Turkey, and Pakistan. By arming and aiding these countries, the administration would aim to build a pro-American, anti-Soviet bastion in the Middle East.[21]

But the strategic consensus came under immediate tests that revealed its central flaw—a disregard for intra-regional tensions. In 1981, Israel bitterly (and futilely) contested Reagan's decision to sell five advanced Airborne Warning and Command Systems (AWACS) aircraft to Saudi Arabia on the grounds that such weapons, purportedly earmarked for use against the Soviet Union, imperiled Israel. Israel's June 1981 attack on the Iraqi reactor at Osirak (discussed in chapter 4), moreover, violated Saudi airspace and thus angered the government in Riyadh.[22]

The strategic consensus suffered severely in the wake of Israel's 1982 invasion of Lebanon. As discussed in chapter 4, the Israelis occupied much of Lebanon, and once the PLO leadership evacuated the country under the supervision of U.S., French, and Italian forces, the Israeli army retreated to a security zone in the southern part of the country. After the massacres at the Sabra and Shatila refugee camps in September, Reagan ordered the redeployment of some twelve hundred Marines to Beirut as a stabilizing force. But those Marines enjoyed no influence over the PLO remnants in northern Lebanon, Syrian forces in eastern Lebanon, or Israeli units in southern Lebanon. Rather, the U.S. soldiers gradually came to be identified with the country's Maronite elite, and thus increasingly came under fire from Muslim rebels.[23]

Before long, the Marines found themselves caught in the middle of the Lebanese civil war. After months of small-scale exchanges of gunfire, a truck bomb attack on the U.S. Embassy in Beirut in April 1983 killed sixty-three persons. In September, Reagan ordered the U.S. Navy to shell the positions of Druze militias that occupied territory in the Shouf Mountains east of Beirut, which Israeli forces had evacuated over American

Lebanon, which Israel had invaded in 1982, became increasingly explosive in 1983, as Israeli presence in the south, Syrian presence in the east, Palestinian Liberation Organization (PLO) presence in the north, and twelve hundred American Marines in Beirut created a volatile atmosphere. While President Ronald Reagan intended the Marine presence to stabilize the area, stability proved elusive, and on April 18, 1983, a truck-bomb attack on the U.S. Embassy killed sixty-three people. This photo, taken the next day, shows the extent of the destruction. Several months later, 241 Marines were killed when their barracks was bombed. AP/Wide World Photos objections. Anti-Maronite insurgents responded the next month by launching another suicidal truck bomb attack that demolished a Marine Corps barracks and killed 241 Marines. Reagan retaliated by ordering shelling and bombing raids on Syrian and other adversaries' positions in Lebanon and vowing to remain in the country indefinitely. As he contemplated his reelection campaign in early 1984, however, the president redeployed the Marines from Beirut to Navy ships patrolling offshore, and soon thereafter withdrew the Marines from the region. "The War in Lebanon grew even more violent," Reagan later observed, "and the Middle East continued to be a source of problems for me and our country."[24]

Critics emphasize that Reagan's policy in Lebanon was utterly disastrous. Although U.S. personnel suffered hundreds of fatalities, Lebanon remained torn by sectarian and international strife and Arab states and peoples grew deeply anti-American. The United States seemingly rewarded Israel's aggressive tendencies with massive military and economic aid and did nothing to address the root causes of Palestinian resistance. In the process, Reagan lost the political integrity and motivation needed to broker a broader Arab-Israeli peace settlement. Reagan's policy, moreover, was so contradictory and inconsistent that it raised serious questions about his administration's goals and competence. It was no wonder that Reagan pulled out, with guns blazing to cover his retreat, on the eve of his reelection bid.[25]

Reagan's hope of knitting a strategic consensus also failed to take into account the emergence of Islamic fundamentalist ideology. Secular Arab nationalism had lost its luster after the military defeats of Egypt, Syria, and Jordan in 1967 and Jordan's suppression of the PLO in 1970. Sunni Muslim fundamentalists were encouraged by Mawlana Mawdudi, a prolific Pakistani thinker and visionary, to pursue a cultural and political revival of Islam, and they were inspired by Sayyid Qutb, an Islamist ideologue hanged by the government of Egypt in 1966, to seek such objectives by militant means. Such fundamentalists sought to overthrow secular regimes from Cairo to Islamabad, and the triumph of Khomeini's Shi'a revolution in Iran encouraged them to action. Islamic fundamentalism fed the anti-Western dynamics of the Lebanon civil war. Egypt's Islamic Jihad assassinated Egyptian President Anwar Sadat in 1981 because he was seen as a secular puppet of the West who sacrificed Islamic purity and interests by making peace with Israel. The Reagan administration's preoccupation with anti-Soviet containment blinded it to this new dynamic in the politics of Muslim states.[26]

Reagan's strategic consensus was also challenged by the growing threat of terrorism in the Middle East. Terrorism had intensified into a new global challenge during the 1970s for several reasons. The accumulated frustrations of dispossessed peoples of the Third World—for example, the Palestinians, who endured dispersion, poverty, statelessness, and fruitless diplomacy—led them to favor violence over the traditional modes of international law and diplomacy. The proliferation of weapons gave non-state actors the means to inflict violence. The development of global media networks both projected images of American materialism and licentiousness that repulsed conservative communities around the world, and instantly broadcast news of terrorists' attacks, which served the terrorists' psychological warfare objectives. The rise of religious fundamentalism provided some perpetrators justification for extreme action, including suicidal aggression. Western governments mobilized to confront the Soviet adversary were unprepared to meet the threats posed by shadowy, non-state actors who defied diplomatic and legal conventions. Terrorists proved effective at finding vulnerabilities in Western embassies, business assets, and civilian airliners and at striking on terms of their own choosing, thereby neutralizing the military superiority of more powerful states.[27]

Although many groups worldwide embraced terrorism by the early 1980s, Reagan decided to strike back against Libya's erratic dictator Moammar Qaddafi, who since taking power in a coup in 1969 had brazenly endorsed the methods of anti-Western extremists (as well as leaned his country toward the Soviet strategic orbit). In 1981, intent on flexing American muscle, Reagan expelled Libyan officials from the United States, embargoed the importation of Libyan oil, and sent the U.S. Sixth Fleet into the disputed Gulf of Sidra off Libya's coast. In August, U.S. Navy jets downed two Libyan fighters that fired upon them. Qaddafi seemingly redoubled his covert support of anti-American terrorists, and 1984 and 1985 witnessed a series of incidents including attacks on Western airports, the shooting of an anti-Qaddafi exile in London, and several highjackings of airliners and cruise ships. The U.S. Navy returned to the Gulf of Sidra in March 1986 and, when challenged, destroyed several Libyan patrol boats and radar sites. Within weeks, a bomb devastated a West Berlin discotheque popular among U.S. soldiers, killing two people and wounding dozens. When intercepts of cables linked Qaddafi to the deed, Reagan wrote later, "I knew we had to do something about the crackpot in Tripoli." The president ordered U.S. warplanes to bomb Tripoli and other military sites in Libya. The air strikes killed Qaddafi's daughter and narrowly missed the dictator himself.[28]

Reagan's attack on Libya produced mixed results. Most Americans endorsed the raid and concluded, in the short term, that it seemed to humble and pacify Qaddafi. "After the attack," Reagan boasted, "we didn't hear much more from Qaddafi's terrorists." Yet critics charged that Reagan had misrepresented evidence linking Syria to the West Berlin disco bombing and gunned for Libya because it posed a softer target, and that the attack merely strengthened Qaddafi at home by forcing potentially rebellious military officers to rally around the flag. World opinion criticized Reagan's display of power, especially since U.S. bombs strayed from military targets and killed civilians. Worse, Libya retaliated in December 1988, when agents of Qaddafi's intelligence service placed a bomb aboard Pan Am Flight 103, which exploded over Lockerbie, Scotland, killing 270 people, including 189 Americans. (Some thirteen years later, a Scottish court convicted and imprisoned for life a Libyan intelligence officer, whom Qaddafi had extradited to escape the pinch of sanctions, for the crime.)[29]

Iran-Iraq War

The Iran-Iraq War of 1980–88 also confronted Reagan with a difficult challenge. After Khomeini seized power in Tehran in 1979, he declared his intentions to export Islamic fundamentalism to Iraq and beyond. Saddam Hussein, a secularist as well as a ruthless and ambitious member of the Iraqi regime, addressed this threat (and aimed to extend Iraq's territorial domain and oil assets) by taking power in Baghdad and attacking Iran. In September 1980, Iraqi forces invaded Iran along a broad battlefront and occupied 10,000 square miles of the country. By 1982, however, Iran launched a counteroffensive, liberated its own territory, and moved into Iraq. Hussein suggested a truce and restoration of the status quo antebellum, but Khomeini insisted that Iraq must depose Hussein and pay reparations as conditions for peace. In 1984, Hussein widened the war by attacking Iranian oil tankers, in hopes of cutting off Iran's oil revenues, while Iran retaliated by attacking tankers registered in Kuwait and Saudi Arabia, Iraq's material supporters. This "war of the tankers" was followed in 1985 by a "war of the cities," in which both sides bombed or fired missiles against civilian population centers. In addition, a series of major offensives by ground troops proved generally ineffective at breaking the stalemate. By 1988, the two powers had suffered more than one million casualties.[30]

While officially neutral, the Reagan administration essentially sided with Iraq in this war. Although Saddam Hussein was a ruthless dictator, officials in Washington came to fear an Iranian military triumph after

Khomeini's armies gained momentum in 1982. Indeed, the ayatollah called for the spread of Islamic fundamentalism worldwide, and officials in Washington nervously monitored a series of episodes in which Iranian agents attempted revolutionary activity in Saudi Arabia, Kuwait, Bahrain, and North Yemen in 1981–82. U.S. intelligence also detected Iranian support of the radical groups behind the attacks on U.S. forces in Lebanon and the kidnappings of U.S. nationals in that country. In this context, Reagan bolstered Baghdad by providing economic aid and military supplies and by restoring diplomatic relations in November 1984. The State Department also organized an international embargo on arms supply to Iran. In reference to Tehran's covert agents across the Middle East, Reagan declared that "the United States gives terrorists no rewards and no guarantees. We make no concessions. We make no deals."[31]

Despite Reagan's words and tilt toward Iraq, his administration surreptitiously provided weapons to Iran. In a series of deals executed in 1985–86, White House staff members secretly supplied Khomeini's regime with hundreds of antitank and antiaircraft missiles. Reagan later claimed that these arms shipments were intended to improve the badly strained U.S. relationship with Iran, an oil-rich state of critical importance to the West, as well as win the release of several Americans held hostage by radical Islamic groups in Lebanon. When disclosed by the media, however, public criticism mounted against the president. Even Secretary of State Shultz commented that the deals "grossly violated" Reagan's stated refusal to deal with terrorists and his official embargo against arms sales to Iran. While the arms supply seemed to win the release of several captives in Lebanon, moreover, it also seemed to stimulate the taking of additional hostages. The coincidental news that Reagan aides had illegally diverted proceeds of the Iran arms sales to the Contra rebels in Nicaragua tarnished the administration's reputation.[32]

In 1987, finally, Reagan applied a mixture of diplomacy and firmness to promote an end to the Iran-Iraq War. In July, the United States secured a unanimous resolution of the UN Security Council calling for a ceasefire under the terms of the UN Charter and imposing sanctions against noncompliers. Khomeini refused to accept such terms, and instead escalated the war by firing missiles on Iraqi cities and ordering so-called final offensives of epic proportions. To pressure Iran, Reagan arranged the reflagging of Kuwaiti oil tankers as U.S.–flag ships and then ordered the Navy to escort them through the Persian Gulf. Iran contested the U.S.–flag tankers with speedboat assaults and marine mines. Before long, the U.S. Navy was at war with the navy of Iran. Major clashes ensued in July–October 1987 and April–July 1988, as U.S. forces struck at Iranian minelayers, speedboats, oil platforms, and frigates. Tragedy capped the violence: on July 3, 1988, following a clash with Iranian naval vessels, the USS *Vincennes* accidentally downed an Iranian civilian airliner flying overhead, killing 290 passengers and crew.[33]

In the end, Reagan's two-track policy of diplomacy and force seemed to work, as Iran, on July 18, 1988, accepted the 1987 UN ceasefire resolution. The financial and human costs of the war—the latter accentuated by the airbus disaster—had exceeded Khomeini's tolerance, and Iranian public morale had waned as Iraq regained the military initiative, fired missiles at Iranian cities, and used poison gas on Iranian soldiers.

This 1986 political cartoon by Herb Block satirizes Reagan's covert dealings with Iran in order to receive help securing the release of American hostages held in Lebanon by Iranian terrorists. In exchange for Iranian help, the Reagan administration supplied Iran with antitank and antiaircraft missiles, which violated the U.S. arms embargo against Iran and Reagan's own policy of not dealing with terrorists. In the cartoon, Reagan appears on TV to announce the release of the hostages at the same time that he hands Ayatollah Khomeini an "arms payoff for hostage release." The Herb Block Foundation

The decision to make peace was "in the best interests of the revolution," Khomeini declared to his people, although it "is more lethal to me than poison." A ceasefire took effect on August 20, ending the Iran-Iraq War.[34]

Conclusion

The United States faced several crises in the Middle East in the 1970s and 1980s. A fundamentalist revolution in Iran carried that country beyond the American orbit and resulted in a hostage crisis that beleaguered the United States on the global stage and paralyzed the presidency of Jimmy Carter. The Soviet invasion of Afghanistan stoked fears of militant communism capturing vital oil assets in the Persian Gulf region. The U.S. government faced a wave of terrorism with Middle East roots that victimized Americans in the region and elsewhere. The Iran-Iraq War imperiled the oil of the Persian Gulf and eventually drew American soldiers into harm's way.

The Carter and Reagan administrations found it difficult to deal with these challenges. Carter was baffled by the Iranian revolution, consumed by the hostage crisis, and embarrassed by the debacle at Desert One, all of which undermined his bid for reelection in 1980. Alarmed by the Soviet invasion of Afghanistan, Carter in effect drew a line in the sand, vowing to wage world war if the Soviets crossed that line in a military move into the Persian Gulf states.

Reagan was perhaps only modestly more successful at sorting out the problems in the Middle East. The serendipitous end of the Iran hostage crisis in January 1981 bolstered American confidence and relaxed overseas tensions at the dawn of Reagan's presidency. Reagan's covert aid to Afghan partisans proved important in checking Soviet expansionism in Afghanistan. And the president's belated intervention in the Iran-Iraq War helped guide those two war-weary nations toward a truce.

However, Reagan seemed unable to achieve a cogent strategy for stabilizing the Middle East. His strategic consensus never materialized in any meaningful sense, as his costly failure to achieve stability in Lebanon demonstrated. He proved unable to stop terrorist attacks on the United States despite using military power to strike at apparent perpetrators. Even his successes in Afghanistan and the Persian Gulf would prove to have ripple effects that would bounce back to haunt the United States in the 1990s and after.

CHAPTER 6

PEACE PROCESS

The U.S. Approach to the Arab-Israeli Conflict, 1982–2005

HE UNITED STATES REMAINED CONCERNED WITH the Arab-Israeli dispute in the late 1900s and early 2000s. The conflict threatened to undermine vital American interests in the waning years of the Cold War, and it thereafter remained an impediment to the American goal of stability in the Middle East. Thus officials in Washington consistently sought ways to abate the tensions between the two sides and to achieve a final and formal peace agreement. Although American peacemaking proved muted and accomplished little in the 1980s, several major breakthroughs were achieved in the 1990s, when the peace process enjoyed its most sustained period of success. But the early 2000s witnessed a shift in focus from the interstate conflict of previous decades to a brutal civil war between Israelis and the Palestinians who resided in the territories occupied by Israel since 1967. The United States found the latter type of conflict as destabilizing and as difficult to solve as the former kind.

Peacemaking in the Doldrums, 1982–1990

President Ronald Reagan belatedly and passively became involved in Arab-Israeli peacemaking. In the wake of the Israeli invasion of Lebanon, the president proposed a peace plan in September 1982, calling for self-government of Palestinians in association with Jordan (discussed in chapter 4). The Reagan plan refused to recognize the Palestine Liberation Organization (PLO) and opposed formal Israeli territorial expansion although it did not oppose Israeli settlements. Israel rejected the plan, and Arab leaders at Fez declared that the PLO, as the sole representative of the

Palestinian people, must be part of any deal, that a Palestinian state must be established, and that Israel must evacuate all land gained in the 1967 war, including East Jerusalem. Distracted by numerous other diplomatic challenges, Reagan did not follow up. Under his strategic consensus policy, he was reluctant to accentuate Arab-Israeli differences or to put at risk a potential strategic partnership with Israel needed to contain Soviet influence in Syria and Iraq.[1]

Reagan, moreover, showed little interest in peace plans developed by others. In February 1985, PLO chief Yasser Arafat and King Hussein of Jordan signed a memorandum embracing aspects of the Reagan plan of 1982. They offered to form a confederation once Israel departed from the occupied territories and to negotiate jointly with Israel at an international conference. The government in Washington, however, was cool to the idea of a conference that would grant the Soviets a place at the table or become a means of pressuring Israel to make unilateral concessions. Reagan insisted that the PLO first accept UN 242, thus recognizing Israel, before any negotiations would begin. By early 1986, Hussein and Arafat had a falling out and their initiative died.[2]

Reagan's lack of enthusiasm helped undermine another round of peacemaking in 1987. In April, King Hussein brokered a deal with leaders of Israel's Labor Party—then in the inferior position in the complicated power-sharing arrangement between the Labor and Likud parties—to hold an international conference. The Reagan administration refused to endorse the idea, however, on the grounds that it could not interfere in Israeli domestic politics. Yitzhak Shamir, the Likud prime minister, firmly rejected the plan. In September, Shamir and Reagan agreed to the idea of Reagan and Soviet Premier Mikhail Gorbachev inviting Shamir and King Hussein to meet with them during a U.S.-Soviet summit, as a symbolic gesture to jumpstart peace talks, but the king rejected the idea as too risky in the context of inter-Arab politics. Thereafter, Reagan grew reluctant to engage in Middle East diplomacy because he wished to protect his party's interests in the presidential election of 1988.[3]

In this context, the territories occupied by Israel since 1967 exploded in a violent uprising, known as the *intifada* (Arabic for "shaking off"), in late 1987. In retrospect, the origins of the rebellion were clear. Having languished for forty years without a state and for twenty years under Israeli occupation, the Palestinians had become dispirited by their poverty, disillusioned with the PLO and the Arab states, humiliated by Israeli curfews and restrictions, and frustrated by the bravado of Israeli settlers. These conditions provided the kindling for a brushfire war, and a spark was lit on December 9, 1987, when a motor vehicle accident in Gaza left four Palestinians dead; local crowds blamed an Israeli truck driver for the incident. Street protests erupted and grew quickly into a widespread resistance movement throughout the occupied territories. Thousands of Palestinians—most younger than age twenty-five—took to the streets to demonstrate, throw rocks and incendiaries, and burn tires. Reputedly ordered by Minister of Defense Yitzhak Rabin to "break their bones," Israeli security forces responded with curfews, closures of universities, mass arrests, crowd control measures ranging from water cannons to live ammunition, and economic sanctions. By mid-1990, Israeli authorities had killed more than 800 Palestinians (including 200 children younger than age sixteen) and imprisoned some 17,000. Another 250 were murdered by fellow Palestinians on suspicion of collaboration. Palestinians killed about 50 Israelis. The uprising, Avi Shlaim notes, "may be seen as the Palestinian war of independence."[4]

The intifada dramatically changed Palestinian political dynamics. Although the uprising started spontaneously, Arafat's PLO gradually and skillfully took leadership of it and coordinated resistance activities, thereby gaining prestige among the masses. Yet the intifada also spawned the rise of the Islamic Resistance Movement (also known by its Arabic acronym Hamas, which means "zeal" in Arabic), a more radical group, based in Gaza, that advocated extreme measures against Israel and vied with the secular PLO for support from Palestinians. On July 31, 1988, King Hussein renounced Jordan's annexation of the West Bank and declared that he would no longer represent Palestinians. Seeing danger in Hamas and opportunity in King Hussein's move, Arafat took action. On November 14–15, the Palestine National Council (PNC) voted to approve UN Resolutions 242 and 338, to accept the UN partition plan of 1947 and thereby implicitly affirm the legitimacy of Israel, and to declare "the establishment of the State of Palestine on our Palestinian territory and with its capital Jerusalem." Within days, twenty-seven Arab and Muslim nations recognized Palestine.[5]

The intifada also created a difficult situation for Israel. Televised images of Israeli suppression of the uprising resulted in worldwide reproach of the Jewish state, and the UN General Assembly censured Israel for its harsh methods. Yet Prime Minister Shamir refused to ease the suppression of the uprising. He declared that the PLO declarations of November 1988 were too vague to rest Israeli security on them. He accused Arafat of engineering "a deceptive propaganda exercise, intended to create an impression of moderation" while the violence continued.

His Likud party stated forthrightly that Israel was entitled to the West Bank and Gaza.[6]

The prospect of the intifada fomenting extremism prompted Secretary of State George P. Shultz to take action. In March 1988, he proposed essentially an acceleration of the Camp David peace process and a reaffirmation of the land-for-peace formula of UN Resolutions 242 and 338. The Shultz initiative called for negotiations between Israel and a joint Jordan-PLO delegation, arbitrated by the United States and aiming to reach a final agreement on the occupied territories within one year and to complete a transitional settlement within three years. A UN-backed conference would jumpstart the process. Despite active efforts by Shultz to sell the plan during several visits to region, Shamir seemed cold to the idea and King Hussein dragged his feet. The plan collapsed when King Hussein relinquished all claims to the West Bank on July 31.[7]

In the sunset of the Reagan presidency, Shultz achieved a modest diplomatic breakthrough. Arafat applied for a U.S. visa to visit New York City for the purpose of addressing the UN General Assembly, but Shultz denied the request, citing ties between Arafat and terrorist groups. Unhappy with Shultz's action, the General Assembly reconvened in Geneva and welcomed Arafat there. Yet Arafat also seemed to relent to U.S. pressure. He signed a statement that the PLO accepted UN Resolutions 242 and 338, "undertakes to live in peace with Israel," and "condemns individual, group, and State terrorism in all its forms." In his address to the General Assembly on December 13, 1988, Arafat called for a UN-sponsored conference among the Palestinians, Israel, and neighboring states and the replacement of Israeli occupation forces with UN troops. The next day, Arafat firmly renounced terrorism during a press conference, and Shultz promptly declared that the United States would speak to the PLO.[8]

The administration of George H. W. Bush, who succeeded Reagan as president in 1989, tried to build on Shultz's breakthrough. To head off a U.S.-PLO dialogue, Israeli leaders offered to negotiate with non-PLO Palestinians. In an address to an AIPAC convention in Washington in May 1989, Secretary of State James Baker approved this approach as "an important and positive start" toward peace negotiations but then criticized Israel's construction of settlements on the West Bank and the Likud Party ideology that underlay it. "For Israel," he intoned, "now is the time to lay aside, once and for all, the unrealistic vision of a greater Israel. Israeli interests in the West Bank and Gaza—security and otherwise—can be accommodated in a settlement based on Resolution 242. Forswear annexation. Stop settlement activity. Allow schools to reopen. Reach out to the Palestinians as neighbors who deserve political rights." When Baker tried in September 1989 to arrange a meeting of Israelis and Palestinians in Cairo, however, Shamir condemned it. Israeli-American tensions also grew over Shamir's determination to increase settlement construction and Baker's announcement that U.S. economic aid would depend on a settlement freeze. Baker concluded that Shamir "was trying to strangle the U.S. initiative in its cradle."[9]

Baker's peacemaking diplomacy ended in the spring of 1990. On May 20, the murder of seven Palestinians by an Israeli army veteran sparked a new wave of armed resistance and Israeli repression. On May 30, the Israeli military thwarted a terrorist attack involving Palestinian commandos landing on a beach near Tel Aviv. Responsibility for the attack was claimed by the Palestinian Liberation Front, a radical faction based in Baghdad. When Arafat refused to condemn the planned raid, however, Baker felt compelled to suspend the dialogue with the PLO on June 20. In remarks aimed at Shamir and Arafat, a frustrated Baker publicized the White House telephone number and stated, "When you're serious about peace, call us." Within weeks, the Persian Gulf War of 1990–91 (discussed in chapter 7) brought peacemaking to a standstill.[10]

The Peace Process in the Golden Era of the 1990s

The Persian Gulf War and the end of the Cold War in 1990–91 changed the political landscape in the Middle East and thus raised U.S. hope of resuming the peace process. The U.S.-led victory over the expansionist Iraqi army in the Gulf War earned the United States the goodwill of moderate Arab states such as Saudi Arabia and Egypt and even the begrudging appreciation of Syria, and it gained President Bush worldwide respect as a leader with a mandate for action. It also embarrassed King Hussein and Arafat, who had expressed sympathy for Iraqi Premier Saddam Hussein, and made them seem anxious to make amends. Indeed, the absence of Soviet opposition to U.S. wartime policy and the end of the Cold War put at risk the traditional Soviet sustenance for radical Arab leaders and raised the possibility of American-Russian cooperation in peacemaking. Iraqi missile attacks during the war awakened Israeli leaders to the dangers from afar, even as the end of the Cold War raised their fear that the United States, its containment objectives reached, might retreat from the region. "There will never be a better time to move than now," Baker told Shamir in March 1991, "when the radicals are weak and discredited, when our Arab friends feel strong and confident, when American credibility is at its height."[11]

To capitalize on this opportunity, Baker engaged in a vigorous shuttle diplomacy to organize a peace conference involving Israel, Jordan, the Palestinians, Syria, Egypt, and Lebanon. In countless hours of wearying negotiations, the secretary of state used a combination of inducements and firmness to convince the Middle East powers to attend. "It was maddeningly simple," Baker later recorded. "You can't make peace if you won't talk." His labor paid off on October 30, 1991, when Bush and Gorbachev presided over the Madrid conference, a face-to-face meeting of the principals to the conflict. Although the conferees achieved nothing concrete beyond the reaffirmation of UN Resolutions 242 and 338, Baker considered the conference "a resounding triumph. . . . After forty-three years of bloody conflict, the ancient taboo against Arabs talking with Israelis had . . . been dramatically consigned to the back benches of history."[12]

Despite Baker's euphoria, the peace process inched along in the wake of the Madrid conference. Israeli-Arab and Israeli-Palestinian negotiations, prescribed at Madrid, tended to bog down in endless discussions on procedural issues, reflective of a lingering unwillingness on all sides to make concessions on the essential issues of territory, Jerusalem, and the rights of Palestinian refugees. Shamir antagonized the Palestinians—and the Bush administration—by continuing to build Jewish settlements on occupied territory in the West Bank, and Bush pressed back by denying Shamir U.S. financial aid needed to build housing for the tidal wave of Russian immigrants flowing into Israel. Hope gleamed after the June 1992 election of Israeli Prime Minister Yitzhak Rabin, who released Palestinian prisoners, slowed settlement construction, and made other goodwill gestures. When Hamas intensified its violence against Israelis, however, Rabin deported 416 suspected militants to Lebanon in December 1992 and sealed the borders of the territories in March 1993.[13]

Yet in this depressing environment a major breakthrough was reached through secret negotiations in Oslo. Norwegian officials sponsored a series of stealth meetings between Israeli and Palestinian officials in January–August 1993 that resulted in the initialing of a Declaration of Principles on Interim Self-Government Arrangements (later known as the Oslo I Accord) on August 20. Under the deal, the PLO would renounce terrorism and recognize Israel; Israel would withdraw from Jericho and the Gaza Strip; and the two parties would thereafter negotiate all points of contention including Jerusalem, borders, refugees, and settlements. The two sides would "strive to live in peaceful coexistence and mutual dignity and security and achieve a just, lasting, and comprehensive peace settlement and historic reconciliation."[14]

President Bill Clinton, inaugurated in January 1993, monitored the secret talks at Oslo and immediately endorsed the Declaration of Principles. He invited Rabin and Arafat to sign the Oslo Accord formally on the lawn of the White House on September 13, during an elegant ceremony witnessed by three thousand guests—including two former presidents, eight former secretaries of state, and the entire Washington diplomatic corps—as well as a worldwide television audience. "This bold new venture today," Clinton asserted, "this brave gamble that the future can be better than the past, must endure." The tenor of the day was even more poignantly expressed by Rabin, who declared that "we who've fought against you, the Palestinians, we say to you in a loud and clear voice, enough of blood and tears. Enough!" In dramatic fashion, Clinton then nudged Rabin to shake Arafat's extended hand in an historic gesture of peace.[15]

In the heady days following the White House ceremony, U.S. officials nurtured the peace process on all fronts. After Israel and Jordan opened peace talks in October 1993, Secretary of State Warren Christopher encouraged the negotiations by arranging $900 million in economic and military aid to Jordan. In July 1994, Rabin and King Hussein visited Washington jointly to declare the termination of hostilities between their two states. A formal peace treaty was signed on October 27, with Clinton cosigning as witness, and diplomatic relations were opened the next month. "Neighbors who had known only hostility," Christopher later wrote, "were about to embark on a new relationship, and the United States had helped to make it happen." Following Jordan's lead, other Arab states began to interact with Israel. Morocco and Tunisia opened negotiations, while the Gulf Cooperation Council, led by Saudi Arabia, eased off its economic boycott against Israel.[16]

Progress was also reached on the Israeli-Palestinian front. In May 1994, the IDF departed Gaza and Jericho. In July, Arafat returned to Gaza to loud celebrations and established the Palestine Authority (PA), which soon fielded a police force, printed postage stamps, issued travel documents, and otherwise acted like a state. In October 1995, Israel and the PA signed the Israeli-Palestinian Interim Agreement on the West Bank and Gaza, alternatively known as the Taba Accord or Oslo II, which provided for the withdrawal of the IDF from nine major Palestinian towns. Meanwhile, the State Department hosted a conference in Washington at which forty-six countries pledged some $2.5 billion in economic aid for the Palestinians. On January 20, 1996, Palestinian voters elected Arafat as president and elected an eighty-eight-member legislature. On April 24, the PNC overwhelmingly voted to amend its charter to excise those passages that called for the violent destruction of Israel. A day later, Israel's Labor Party declared that it no longer opposed Palestinian statehood.[17]

Yet the Oslo peace process was continually threatened by violence perpetrated by extremists in both camps who wished to derail it. In February 1994, during the Muslim holy month of Ramadan, an American-born Jewish settler killed twenty-nine worshippers at the Mosque of Abraham in Hebron, in what U.S. special envoy Dennis Ross called "an act of murder designed also to kill the Oslo process." Suicide bombers of Hamas and Islamic Jihad blasted four Israeli buses between October 1994 and August 1995, killing dozens of Israelis. Perhaps the biggest blow to the peace process came on November 4, 1995, when an Israeli extremist, claiming to be acting on God's orders to preserve Israeli control of holy lands, assassinated Rabin. Within weeks of Arafat's election as president in early 1996, moreover, fifty-nine Israelis died in four major terrorist attacks in Jerusalem and Tel Aviv.[18]

In addition, energetic U.S. efforts to encourage Israeli-Syrian peace came to naught. Secretary of State Christopher shuttled repeatedly between Jerusalem and Damascus in 1993–96 trying to broker a settlement in which Israel would withdraw from the Golan Heights in exchange for a peace treaty. His efforts were marred, however, by violence on the ground, such as the June 1993 Israeli air strikes on Syrian artillery in the Bekaa Valley of Lebanon, in retaliation for rocket attacks on northern Israel by the Syrian-supported Hizballah. Christopher was heartened when Rabin, in August 1993, proposed that Israel would evacuate the Golan over a five-year period if Syria would make peace and normalize relations. But American hopes soured when Hafiz al-Asad, who had ruled Syria since 1970, refused to make peace or even to open negotiations with Israel unless Israel promptly and unconditionally withdrew from the Golan. Not even a personal visit from President Clinton, who stopped in Damascus in October 1994 on his way home from witnessing the Israel-Jordan treaty, softened Asad's stance. The State Department sponsored Israeli-Syrian negotiations at the Wye River Conference Center in Maryland in December 1995–January 1996, but those talks broke down when Asad refused to condemn a recent wave of suicide bombings in Israel. Additional Hizballah rocket attacks into northern Israel provoked Israeli countermeasures and froze Israeli-Syrian relations.[19]

In the aftermath of Rabin's assassination, moreover, the political climate in Israel shifted away from peacemaking. In May 1996, Israeli voters elected Prime Minister Benjamin Netanyahu, whose campaign theme of firmness on all security matters found credence in an electorate terrorized by the recent wave of suicide bombings. Netanyahu officially continued the peace process—even shaking Arafat's hand on September 4—but he clearly lacked the passion or commitment displayed by Rabin. Indeed, within weeks of meeting Arafat, Netanyahu permitted the opening of the ancient, recently excavated Hasmonean Tunnel in Jerusalem. After Palestinians charged that the tunnel threatened the structural integrity of the Dome of the Rock, rioting erupted, claiming the lives of fourteen Israelis and fifty-eight Palestinians. Clinton called Arafat and Netanyahu to Washington for an emergency meeting to end the violence, and within weeks, Israel and the PA agreed on a partial Israeli withdrawal from Hebron. But Netanyahu thereafter allowed the resumption of settlement construction in East Jerusalem, and rioting and a new wave of suicide bombings followed. "The peace process, on a respirator since Rabin's death," Secretary of State Madeleine Albright observed, "seemed about to be unplugged."[20]

Clinton took the initiative to try to resuscitate the peace process in 1997–98. He dispatched Albright and Ross to the region to encourage implementation of the Oslo Accords, and they persuaded Arafat and Netanyahu to attend a summit meeting in October 1998 at the Wye River center. There, with Clinton serving as energetic arbitrator, the two adversaries agreed to sign a memorandum that would jumpstart the stalled peace process. Netanyahu agreed to transfer an additional 13 percent of the West Bank to Palestinian control, to assure safe passage of Palestinians between Gaza and the West Bank, and to release certain Palestinian prisoners from Israeli jails. Arafat pledged to renounce terrorism, to imprison certain perpetrators of violence against Israel, and to undertake various measures to prevent attacks by Palestinian extremists. Both powers agreed to cooperate in certain civil and economic enterprises and to resume the final status talks by May 4, 1999. The peace process, Clinton concluded, "was still alive."[21]

Indeed, the Wye River Memorandum restarted the peace process. Clinton visited Gaza in December 1998 to witness firsthand the PNC's vote to remove from its charter those passages calling for the destruction of Israel. It was, he later wrote, "a moment that made the whole trip worthwhile." Clinton also welcomed Arafat to the White House in March 1999 and issued a letter supporting "the aspirations of the Palestinian people to determine their own future on their own land" and censuring Jewish settlement building. Arafat, having threatened to declare statehood on May 4, 1999, when the five-year interim deal expired, backed off at the last minute on the calculation that such a move would boost conservatives in the imminent Israeli election. Indeed, the moderate Ehud Barak was elected Israeli prime minister in that polling. Albright then visited the Middle East to encourage final status talks, brokering the Sharm al-Sheikh agreement of September that committed both parties to seek a Declaration of Principles by February 2000 and a final settlement by September 2000. As U.S. officials arbitrated talks in several venues, Israel conceded additional portions of the West Bank and Arafat jailed fugitives. But a final settlement remained elusive.[22]

Clinton tried to break the logjam by inviting Barak and Arafat to Camp David in July 2000, for their first face-to-face meeting. Both leaders declared a desire for a final settlement, and Clinton desperately tried to grasp a crowning jewel for his beleaguered presidency. But after two weeks of intense negotiations arbitrated by the president, no agreement resulted. On the issue of land, Barak offered to withdraw from some 90 percent of the West Bank and to offer territorial compensation for those portions that Israel retained. He also offered to recognize Palestinian sovereignty over most of East Jerusalem as well as the Muslim and Christian Quarters of the Old City, a Palestinian capital in the city, and Palestinian custodianship over Haram al-Sharif. He further pledged to show flexibility on the refugees and security issues. Clinton pressured Arafat hard to accept these terms, but Arafat refused to accept anything less than Israeli withdrawal to the 1967 borders, complete Palestinian sovereignty over East Jerusalem, and Israeli recognition of the right of return among the some four million Palestinian refugees. By Clinton's private estimation, such stubbornness made Arafat "the skunk at the party." Blaming Arafat for scuttling a deal, Clinton later recorded, "I shut down the talks. It was frustrating and profoundly sad."[23]

Clinton made a final push for peace during his last months in office, after the start of the second intifada (discussed later in this chapter). In addition to promoting a ceasefire, in December 2000 the president also proposed comprehensive peace terms even more generous to the Palestinians than the Camp David plan. Under the scheme, Palestine would become a state with its capital in East Jerusalem and sovereignty over Haram al-Sharif, with 95 percent of the West Bank and with additional lands from Israel to compensate for the missing portions. The Israeli army would withdraw from the West Bank in stages. The refugee issue would be compromised. "It was a hard deal," Clinton noted, but "fair to both sides." Barak approved the terms on December 25, but Arafat refused the deal on the grounds that Israel must withdraw immediately and that he would not concede on the refugee issue. Clinton considered Arafat's decision "a colossal mistake . . . , an error of historic proportions." Arafat "definitively demonstrated that he could not end the conflict," Ross concluded. He "succeeded as a symbol and failed as a leader."[24]

Clinton also failed to get a Syrian-Israeli peace deal. The president convinced Asad and Barak to resume direct talks, after a five-year suspension. Clinton and Albright brokered meetings between Barak and Syrian Foreign Minister Farouk Shara in Shepherdstown, West Virginia, in January 2000. Having agreed in principle on Israeli withdrawal from the Golan, Israel and Syria disagreed on such particular issues as the timetable of the withdrawal and of the subsequent opening of diplomatic relations, the composition of personnel in teams that would monitor the frontier, and the prospect of Israel retaining terrain on the eastern shore of Lake Tiberias. At Shepherdstown, Clinton found the Syrians "positive and flexible" and was "disappointed" by Barak's rigidity that seemed to stalemate the conference. When the president met with Asad in Geneva two months later, by contrast, Asad firmly rejected a pitch

The 1990s saw slow but significant progress towards an Israeli-Palestinian peace. While neither terrorism nor settlements stopped definitively, together Israeli and Palestinian delegates attended the Madrid Conference, the Oslo meetings, the Wye River summit, and the summit held at Camp David. Above, President Bill Clinton (left) meets with PLO chair Yasser Arafat (right) and Ambassador Dennis Ross (center) at Camp David during the two-week long summit in July 2000. No peace yet exists, but these meetings laid groundwork for future peacemaking. William J. Clinton Presidential Library from Clinton that included new concessions by Israel. "The problem is not one of kilometers," Shara explained. "It is one of dignity and honor." The Geneva meeting ended in what Ross called "a high visibility failure," and Asad died of a heart attack in June, his dream of recovering the Golan unrealized.[25]

Worse, an Israeli withdrawal from south Lebanon that had the potential to dissipate Israeli-Syrian tensions actually encouraged extremism among many Palestinians. The Israeli occupation of south Lebanon had become increasingly controversial among Israelis in 1995–99, when intensifying attacks by Hizballah had left more than one hundred IDF soldiers dead. As a candidate for office, Barak pledged that he would withdraw from Lebanon within a year, on the calculation that Israel lacked vital interests in that country and that an Israeli concession on Lebanon might facilitate a peace treaty with Syria. As prime minister, Barak fulfilled his campaign pledge by ordering the IDF to depart Lebanon in spring 2000. But Asad remained stubborn on the Golan, and Arafat lost face as many Palestinians concluded that Hizballah's armed resistance rather than Arafat's diplomacy had compelled the Israeli retreat. "Suddenly, there was a new model for dealing with Israel: the Hizballah model," Ross noted. "Don't make concessions. Don't negotiate. Use violence. And the Israelis will grow weary and withdraw."[26]

The Second Intifada

The failure in the Clinton-brokered Israeli-Palestinian peace process in late 2000 set the stage for a renewal of Israeli-Palestinian violence on a grand scale. Palestinians became deeply frustrated with the peace process launched at Oslo, especially when it appeared that the Israeli withdrawal from south Lebanon was compelled by Hizballah armed resistance. For their part, Israeli conservatives rallied around the idea of keeping the Golan and perpetuating the occupation of the West Bank. In this context, Likud leader Ariel Sharon, in a political gimmick designed to affirm his hard-line credentials, marched across the Temple Mount on September 28 under a heavy police guard and vowed in a speech that Israel would never surrender the land that held the Al-Aqsa Mosque. Within twenty-four hours, Palestinians rioted across the West Bank in protest. Albright likened Sharon's move to "throwing a lighted match into a gasoline can with all the children in the neighborhood standing by." But she also faulted Arafat for not containing the violence. "Instead of using the incident to demonstrate Palestinian maturity in the face of Sharon's provocative act," she commented, "he reminded the world why even the most open-minded Israelis have misgivings about a Palestinian state."[27]

The rioting of late September quickly spread into a second intifada that proved to be more intense and deadly than the first. The second uprising featured Palestinian terrorist attacks during religious holiday celebrations, the grisly murder of two Israeli soldiers after they sought refuge in a Palestinian police station, the fatal shootings of Palestinian children by Israeli soldiers, and countless Israeli air strikes and tank barrages. More than ninety suicide bombers attacked Israeli targets between September 2000 and June 2003, including seven who struck in seven days during the Israeli Passover holiday of 2002. By January 2005, the violence claimed the lives of some 3,500 Palestinians and 1,000 Israelis. More than a dozen proposed ceasefires failed to stop the carnage. The uprising threatened to become an international conflict in October 2003, when Israel, following a suicide terrorist attack, bombed what it claimed was an Islamic Jihad training base fourteen miles northwest of Damascus, the first Israeli attack on Syria in ten years.[28]

The violence completely soured Israeli-Palestinian political relations. His reputation for hawkishness confirmed by his visit to the Temple Mount, Ariel Sharon defeated Prime Minister Barak in the Israeli elections of February 2001 by a commanding 63–35 percent margin and easily won reelection in January 2003. Sharon adamantly refused to consider making any concessions on territory, Jerusalem, or refugees, downgrading Israel's aim from a formal peace agreement to suppression of terrorism. The prime minister did not disguise his disgust with Arafat, whom he accused of aiding and abetting terrorism. After two suicide bombers killed six Israelis and a Scottish student in September 2002, Israeli tanks besieged Arafat's headquarters in Ramallah. For more than two years, Arafat remained in virtual house arrest, either unable to leave the compound or unwilling to try, for fear of being exiled permanently by Israel. The attention of the world was perhaps the only factor that kept Sharon from deporting Arafat or taking his life. The era of historic handshakes was surely over.[29]

U.S. officials tried, with no success, to stem the bloodletting. Clinton encouraged Barak and Arafat to meet a few times to discuss ceasefire terms, but the fighting continued. The George W. Bush administration also worked diligently, and futilely, to end the violence and resume the peace process. A commission, appointed by Clinton and chaired by Senator George Mitchell, composed a three-step peace plan in May 2001. The Mitchell Commission urged that the Palestinians and Israel, first, reaffirm commitments to past agreements, curb violence, and re-

sume security cooperation; second, make gestures (what diplomats called "confidence-building measures") such as cessation of settlement construction and renunciation of terrorism; and third, resume peace negotiations. "It is clear—now more than ever," Secretary of State Colin Powell declared, "there can be no military solution . . . to this conflict, and that negotiation provides the only path to a just, lasting and comprehensive peace in the Middle East." Although Sharon and Arafat endorsed the Mitchell plan, however, the violence continued unabated. Thus Bush dispatched to the region CIA Director George Tenet, who composed a "security work plan" of steps to implement the Mitchell Plan. Then the president sent retired Marine Corps General Anthony Zinni on several missions to convince both parties to accept the Tenet plan. But Tenet and Zinni achieved little.[30]

President Bush became personally involved in the Israeli-Palestinian issue only belatedly. In contrast to Clinton's activism, Bush adopted a passive pose during his first year in office. "I don't see much we can do over there" in light of Clinton's inability to reach a settlement, Bush told the National Security Council in January 2001. "I think it's time to pull out of that situation." In the aftermath of the September 11, 2001, attacks (discussed in chapter 7), however, Bush showed new interest in the Arab-Israeli situation. "For the sake of all humanity, things must change in the Middle East," he intoned in a major address on June 24, 2002. "My vision is two states, living side by side in peace and security." Because Arafat's government was "compromised by terror" and "official corruption," however, the president called on the Palestinian people to elect new leaders and adopt a constitutional democracy that would renounce terror and live in peace. He further challenged Israel "to take concrete steps to support the emergence of a viable, credible Palestinian state," including withdrawal of forces occupying the West Bank, cessation of settlement construction, economic development among the Palestinians, and an end of the post-1967 occupation on the basis of UN Resolutions 242 and 338.[31]

Bush promoted this new initiative by cosponsoring the Roadmap, a new, three-stage peace plan. The so-called Quartet (the United States, Russia, the European Union, and the United Nations) composed "a performance-based and goal-driven roadmap, with clear phases, timelines, target dates, and benchmarks aiming at progress through reciprocal steps by the two parties in the political, security, economic, humanitarian, and institution-building fields." In phase 1 (through May 2003), the Roadmap envisioned an end to terror and violence, the building of Palestinian in-

stitutions, the relaxation of Israeli civil restrictions, and a freeze on Israeli settlement construction. Phase 2 (May–December 2003) would entail a Quartet-sponsored conference to establish a State of Palestine with provisional borders, adoption of a Palestinian constitution establishing a democratic government, and discussions on refugees, water, and development issues. During Phase 3 (2004–5), the Quartet would host a second conference to start final status negotiations between Israel and Palestine on such issues as borders, Jerusalem, refugees, and settlements, and it would negotiate Israeli-Lebanese and Israeli-Syrian peace treaties.[32]

In June 2003, Bush ventured to the Middle East to sell the Roadmap. At a meeting in Sharm el-Sheikh on June 4, he elicited endorsements from the leaders of Egypt, Saudi Arabia, Jordan, and Bahrain after pledging to seek a "permanent reconciliation . . . no matter how difficult it is." The next day, the president met Sharon and Palestinian Prime Minister Mahmoud Abbas (also known as Abu Mazen) in Aqaba. "The journey we're taking is difficult, but there is no other choice," Bush declared. "No leader of conscience can accept more months and years of humiliation, killing, and mourning." Abbas affirmed Israel's right to exist and pledged to suppress terrorist attacks on all Israelis, including settlers and soldiers. Sharon agreed to accept in principle a Palestinian state with contiguous borders and to remove "unauthorized" settlements in the West Bank. Jordan's King Abdullah, who succeeded King Hussein in February 1999, endorsed the Roadmap by asserting that "blowing up buses will not induce the Israelis to move forward. And neither will the killing of Palestinians or the demolition of their homes and their future. All this needs to stop." To promote the Roadmap, Bush appointed the U.S. Coordination Monitoring Mission in Jerusalem, a ten-person team headed by Assistant Secretary of State for Nonproliferation John S. Wolf and under the personal direction of National Security Adviser Condoleezza Rice, to monitor the situation in the Middle East.[33]

Despite the declarations of support, the Roadmap faced rather imposing obstacles. For starters, both Israelis and Palestinians hinted that they remained unwilling to make the necessary concessions on central issues such as the control of Jerusalem and the rights of Palestinian refugees. In addition, Israeli conservatives rallied behind a vigorous defense of the West Bank settlements. By 2003, 225,000 Israelis resided in 145 such settlements, and in 1998–2003, those settlers had established an additional 117 "outposts" (new land claims on which settlements could be built in the future). The settlers, many of whom were émigrés from America, tended to adhere to a religious ideology that portrayed the West

Bank as the biblical lands of Judea and Samaria, promised by God to the Jewish people, and that considered settlement of that land the highest form of Zionism. In May 2003, Sharon, who had vigorously promoted settlement construction since the 1970s, approved permits to add 11,000 new homes in four existing settlements in the West Bank. "There is no restriction here," the prime minister told settlers, "and you can build for your children and grandchildren, and I hope for your great-grandchildren as well." When Sharon pledged to Bush that he would dismantle certain outposts that defied Israeli law, settlers organized massive protest demonstrations in Jerusalem.[34]

Contradictions also existed between the Roadmap and Israel's construction of a massive wall as a safeguard against infiltration of terrorists into Israel. In the wake of a series of suicide bombings, the Sharon government began constructing a thirty-foot-high concrete barrier roughly paralleling the pre-1967 border of the West Bank (although well within the West Bank). Projected to run hundreds of miles, the wall promised Israelis, settlers included, physical security via separation from the Palestinians. Backed by much of world opinion, however, the Palestinians bitterly protested that the wall consumed Palestinian territory, amounted to a massive land grab, encircled key West Bank towns, and disrupted the livelihoods of thousands of Palestinians. If completed, the wall would contain some 58 percent of the West Bank. In 2004, the International Court of Justice and the Israeli Supreme Court ruled that the wall must not violate the rights of Palestinians. Sharon conceded only that he would dismantle or reroute the wall if peace were achieved.[35]

For his part, Arafat resisted the Roadmap. Initially, he seemed to relent to U.S. pressure to establish new leadership by agreeing in April 2003 to appoint Abbas as prime minister of the PA. A long-time PLO official, Abbas had earned a reputation as a dove for promoting peaceful dialogue with Israel. But Arafat packed Abbas's cabinet with his own loyalists, refused to relinquish control of Palestinian militias, remained chair of an executive committee that retained the authority to review peace negotiations, and flexed his muscle by delaying a meeting between Abbas and Sharon in May 2003. After a series of such power struggles, Abbas resigned as prime minister in September 2003. His successor, Ahmed Qorai, faced similar battles in 2003–4 with Arafat, who refused to relinquish control over the PA's security forces or finances.[36]

Violence also threatened the Roadmap. Within weeks of the president's June 2003 visit to the region, Hamas militants killed four Israeli soldiers and sent a suicide bomber to demolish a Jerusalem bus, killing seventeen Israelis. Israel responded by firing missiles into Gaza, killing nineteen Palestinians. On June 29, the Islamic Jihad, Hamas, and Fatah declared ceasefires on the condition that Israel reciprocated, but Israeli spokesmen widely scorned the ceasefires as a ploy to rearm. In March 2004, Israel assassinated Hamas founder Sheikh Ahmad Yassin by firing rockets on his car in Gaza, and in August, Hamas retaliated by sending two suicide bombers into Hebron, where they blew up two buses, killing sixteen people and wounding ninety-four.[37]

In late 2004, American officials became guardedly hopeful that the Israeli-Palestinian situation might soon improve. Israeli Prime Minister Sharon implemented a plan to abandon the Gaza Strip and forcibly evacuate the 8,000 Israeli settlers there. Even more promising, the Palestinian people elected the moderate Mahmoud Abbas as president of the PA to succeed Yasser Arafat, who died in November 2004. Having netted 62 percent of the vote in the January 2005 polling, Abbas quickly moved to halt terrorist attacks against Israel and to convince such groups as Hamas to reform into peaceful political parties. His election seemed to answer Bush's call for new leadership to guide the Palestinian people into an era of peace and constitutional democracy.[38]

Yet reasons for caution remained. There was no certainty that Abbas would prevail over dissident Palestinian factions intent on inflicting violence on Israel. Thus the prospects of both Palestinian democracy and moderation toward Israel remained imperiled. For his part, Sharon also faced a difficult domestic political environment. To provide political cover of his Gaza withdrawal plan, he felt compelled to order a series of armed forays into the territory that left dozens of Palestinians dead, and he resolved permanently to retain vast swaths of the West Bank. Still, ultra-conservative Israeli settlers—many of whom lionized Rabin's assassin—threatened to use violence to derail the Gaza withdrawal plan and hinted that Sharon might pay for his peacemaking with his life.[39]

Conclusion

In 1982–2005, American peacemaking in the Arab-Israeli context experienced mixed success. During the last decade of the Cold War, U.S. officials tempered their traditional determination to make peace with a reluctance to take steps that might imperil their anti-Soviet objectives in the Middle East. As a result, the peace process nurtured by Henry Kissinger and Jimmy Carter in the 1970s remained in the doldrums caused by Israel's 1982 invasion of Lebanon. Although certain U.S. officials occasionally floated plans for reconciliation, they neither exerted the energy nor conceived the terms necessary to build on the foundation of the Egyptian-Israeli peace treaty of 1979. In addition, the local states and peoples showed little enthusiasm for settlement, and the Palestinians of the Israeli-occupied territories launched an uprising against Israel in 1987.

In 1989–91, by contrast, the end of the Cold War and the outcome of the Persian Gulf War reinvigorated the peace process. Those two watershed events sufficiently changed the political dynamics of the Middle East to make international peace an alluring prospect in the minds of the region's leaders. Sensing opportunities, officials in the first Bush and the Clinton administrations engaged in intensive diplomacy designed to facilitate formal treaties. Such efforts resulted in several notable accomplishments, including a formal peace agreement between Israel and Jordan, increased interaction between Israel and other Arab states, and vigorous Israeli-Syrian negotiations.

Unfortunately for the advocates of harmony, the peace process of the 1990s fell short of complete success. Despite their enormous effort, U.S. officials proved unable to broker a peace treaty between Israel and Syria. Nor could they convince Yasser Arafat to accept a compromise settlement—which included several notable concessions by Israel—on which a State of Palestine could be erected. Worse, the early 2000s witnessed a new uprising among the Palestinian people that triggered ghastly violence, political turmoil, and growing extremism among the Palestinians and the Israelis. While they could celebrate the fact that the international peace arrangements of earlier decades held, U.S. officials faced the difficult and perhaps insurmountable task of curtailing the violence, drawing Israel and the Palestinians back to the table of diplomacy, and leading them into the dawn of a new day.

CHAPTER 7

MESSY LITTLE WARS

U.S. Operations in the Middle East Since 1990

W HILE TRYING TO SOLVE THE ARAB-Israeli conflict, the United States also faced a series of new challenges in the Persian Gulf region. Most of the trouble centered on oil-rich Iraq, ruled by Saddam Hussein. The 1990s opened with a war in which the United States led a multinational coalition that reversed the Iraqi conquest of Kuwait. The decision to leave Hussein in power resulted in a long, postwar struggle to disarm and contain him, which the government in Washington pursued for a decade through a variety of diplomatic and military means. Meanwhile, the United States also faced a mounting threat by a shadowy coalition of terrorists, who struck most devastatingly on September 11, 2001. President George W. Bush conflated the Iraq problem with the scourge of terrorism and launched a preemptive invasion of Iraq in 2003.

The Persian Gulf War, 1990–1991

During the Iran-Iraq War of 1980–88, the United States followed a policy of bolstering Iraq as a counterweight against expansionism by the fundamentalist government in Tehran (discussed in chapter 5). President George H. W. Bush, who took office in January 1989 in the wake of the Iran-Iraq ceasefire, initially sought to build a better relationship with Iraq. Bush worried about Saddam Hussein's record of brutality and aggressiveness, his use of chemical weapons against domestic and foreign foes, and his maintenance of a disproportionately large army. But the president calculated that an improvement in U.S.-Iraqi relations might pay such dividends as discouraging Iraq from developing its chemical, biological, or

105

nuclear weapons capabilities (what experts called weapons of mass destruction [WMD]), winning Iraqi cooperation in brokering Arab-Israeli peace settlements, and gaining economic opportunities in Iraq's oil industry. In October 1989, Bush signed National Security Directive–26 (NSD-26), indicating that his administration would seek "normal relations" with Iraq and offer "economic and political incentives" for Hussein to moderate his policy. Secretary of State James A. Baker asked Foreign Minister Tariq Aziz for Iraq's help in starting Arab-Israeli negotiations and, as an incentive, proposed an aid package of some $1.2 billion. In a harbinger of trouble, however, Aziz responded by accusing the CIA of plotting to overthrow Hussein.[1]

Indeed, U.S. leaders reconsidered their effort to normalize relations with Iraq within months. In early 1990, the Hussein regime intensified its anti-American rhetoric and executed an Iranian-born British journalist for espionage. U.S. and British authorities seized steel tubes—of a type needed to build nuclear weapons—on the verge of shipment to Iraq. Probably recalling Israel's 1981 air raid against the Iraqi nuclear reactor at Osirak (discussed in chapter 4), Hussein declared on April 2 that if Iraq were again attacked, "by God, we will make fire eat up half of Israel." The White House called Hussein's words "deplorable and irresponsible." To signal his displeasure with these developments while not closing the door to normal relations, Bush suspended financial aid programs to Iraq but refrained from imposing complete economic sanctions.[2]

The U.S. perspective on Iraq was no doubt influenced by the end of the Cold War. As the Soviet Union disintegrated in 1989–91, the Pentagon conducted a sweeping review of threats facing American security. In the so-called New Strategy or Regional Defense Strategy of spring 1990, officers posited that newly emerging regional powers—dubbed "rogue states" or "outlaw states"—would pose threats to U.S. security interests after the demise of Soviet power. Rogue states were identified by dominant regional status, possession of large militaries and WMD, and expansionist goals. Under the Rogue Doctrine, the Pentagon asserted that it must maintain the ability to fight any two such states simultaneously. Saddam Hussein's trouble-making in early 1990 confirmed in U.S. minds both the validity of the Rogue Doctrine and the need to confront Iraq.[3]

Indeed, in summer 1990, Hussein picked a fight with his Arab neighbors. Although Kuwait had backed Iraq during the 1980s war, Iraq had nursed a grudge about the wealth Kuwait had accumulated while Iraq had spent its own treasure on the battlefields. In 1990, Hussein accused the gulf monarchies of conspiring with the United States to deflate oil prices, which made it impossible for Iraq to retire its war debts, and he charged that Kuwait had stolen Iraqi oil worth some $2.5 billion from well fields near the border. On July 17, Hussein threatened to do "something effective" to redress his grievances, and two days later, he advanced two divisions of Republican Guards to Kuwait's border. Even as Arab statesmen negotiated with him, Hussein moved 100,000 Iraqi troops to his southern border by July 31.[4]

Uncertain of Hussein's intentions, the United States aimed to deter military action by Iraq. Bush ordered the Navy to deploy additional ships into the Persian Gulf and to conduct drills with the navy of the United Arab Emirates. Baker directed Ambassador to Baghdad April Glaspie repeatedly to warn Hussein that the United States would oppose the use of force to settle intra-Arab disputes. Yet Bush also showed some reservation about vigorous action. Saudi officials encouraged him to allow the Arab states to resolve the situation. Glaspie cautioned that excessive U.S. criticism might spur Hussein to take drastic action even if it proved self-destructive. Such a measured approach, however, did not discourage Hussein. After one meeting with Glaspie, he claimed that the United States was indifferent to his dispute with Kuwait and that the American people lacked the political will to intervene if there were a risk of major casualties. U.S. officials could only hope that Hussein was using the threat of force to extort favorable concessions from his neighbors.[5]

U.S. hopes to the contrary, the Iraqi army invaded Kuwait on August 2 and easily overpowered its tiny army. Hussein justified the attack as a settlement of the oil dispute and, alluding to British action to establish Kuwait in 1922, as a correction of an anomaly of Western imperialism set up by "the colonialists, to ensure their petroleum interests." U.S. leaders feared that Iraq's huge army might also seize the oil fields of northern Saudi Arabia or perhaps occupy that entire kingdom and dismantle its monarchy, especially after three reported incidents in which Iraqi troops breached the Saudi border on August 3–6. Had Hussein entertained such grand goals, Bush later commented, "he would have had a free run" against the badly outnumbered Saudi military, and he could thereby have gained control of enormous oil resources as well as the military bases eventually used by the United States against him. But Hussein paused. As Michael Palmer has observed, he showed a degree of caution similar to that displayed in his invasion of Iran in 1980, when he halted an initial, successful thrust and sought to consolidate his gains through diplomacy.[6]

In the face of the immediate threat, Bush took action to ensure the security of Saudi Arabia. Within days of the attack on Kuwait, he ordered warships at Diego Garcia to head to the Persian Gulf and rushed two squadrons of F-15 fighters and the Eighty-Second Airborne Division to Saudi Arabia. Under the so-called Desert Shield plan, some 100,000 U.S. forces reached the kingdom by the end of August. The immediate threat to the Saudi state subsided when Hussein relocated several elite units from the frontier to reserve positions in southern Iraq, although both Iraq and the United States continued to build up forces in the area.[7]

Having secured Saudi Arabia, Bush also took a variety of steps to contest Iraq's conquest of Kuwait. He demanded "the immediate, unconditional, and complete withdrawal of all Iraqi forces from Kuwait," imposed economic sanctions on Iraq, and encouraged other states to follow suit. At the UN Security Council, U.S. diplomats pushed through Resolution 660, which condemned the Iraqi aggression, demanded Iraqi withdrawal, and encouraged settlement of intra-Arab disputes through negotiations. Bush telephoned other leaders around the world to promote the idea of collective action to reverse the aggression. He declared publicly on August 5 that "this will not stand, this aggression against Kuwait." But Hussein defied such admonitions, asserting that Kuwait no longer existed and telling his own people to prepare for the "mother of all battles." The conflict over Kuwait soon became an armed standoff.[8]

In October, Bush began to take steps that would lead to the use of military force to liberate Kuwait. With diplomacy stalled, he worried that the coalition showed signs of fracturing as Arab leaders chafed at Israeli-Palestinian violence and Soviet leaders, having watched their European empire tumble, showed an inclination to protect their traditional client in Baghdad. Just after the U.S. midterm elections on November 8, Bush announced that he would relocate 200,000 U.S. soldiers from Germany to Saudi Arabia, which implicitly signaled a resolve to take offensive action. On November 29, the United States also pushed through the UN Security Council Resolution 678, which ordered Iraq to withdraw from Kuwait by January 15, 1991, and authorized member states, if Iraq remained defiant, "to use all necessary means . . . to restore international peace and security in the area." Bush convinced leaders of twenty-eight other countries to contribute troops to such an operation, and yet other powers to bankroll it. On January 9, Baker met Aziz in Geneva, but neither statesman would budge on his government's policy on Kuwait. "There was now no question in my mind," Baker later wrote, "we were going to war." On January 12, the House and Senate voted by margins of 250–183 and 52–47, respectively, to authorize the president to use force to liberate Kuwait.[9]

Having secured international and domestic legal sanction to wage war to liberate Kuwait, Bush ordered the start of offensive military action on January 17, 1991. Under Operation Desert Storm, U.S. and allied aircraft launched a massive aerial blitz, first, against command, control, and communications facilities in Iraq and Iraqi-occupied Kuwait, and, eventually, against Iraqi ground troops in Kuwait. On the first day alone, the Allies flew some 2,400 combat missions, gaining complete control of the skies, inflicting massive damage, and suffering relatively few losses. Hussein resisted by launching Scud missiles against Allied positions in Saudi Arabia, Bahrain, and Qatar, as well as against Israel; although most missed their targets, one Scud hit a U.S. base in Saudi Arabia, killing twenty-seven GIs. Hussein also tried to stymie the assault by occupying the Saudi border town of Khafji in late January, but U.S. Marines rather easily repulsed that move.[10]

The Iraqi Scud missile attacks on Israel, which was not officially a member of the military coalition arrayed against Baghdad, threatened to change the course of war dramatically. Hussein fired the missiles in order to provoke an Israeli response that would splinter the American partnership with other Arab states. The attacks, which began on January 18 and continued for several days, enraged Israeli leaders. Citing Israel's security doctrine of launching reprisals for assaults on its people, Prime Minister Yitzhak Shamir indicated his intent to retaliate against Scud launching sites in western Iraq. Secretary of Defense Richard Cheney advised Bush to unleash Israel, but Chairman of the Joint Chiefs of Staff General Colin Powell reasoned that "if we were going to preserve the Arab end of the coalition, we had to keep the Israelis out of this fight." National Security Adviser Brent Scowcroft prevailed on the president to restrain Israel by "deconfliction," meaning withholding identification codes that Israeli pilots would need to traverse the war zone safely. To ease the pressure, Bush also dispatched Patriot missile crews to Israel to defend against Scuds, diverted U.S. soldiers to western Iraq to root out Scud sites, dispatched Deputy Secretary of State Lawrence Eagleburger to Jerusalem "to hold the Israeli hand," and signaled Iraq that any use of WMD would invite a massive retaliation in kind. "There is a limit to Israeli restraint," Eagleburger cabled at one tense moment, "and we are close to it." But the leash held, and Hussein's ploy to fracture the alliance failed.[11]

Soviet Premier Mikhail Gorbachev also posed a wartime diplomatic challenge to Bush by adopting the role of peace broker. Apparently upset by U.S. air attacks on Baghdad, and perhaps seeking to burnish his faltering reputation as world leader, Gorbachev proposed in late January a deal including a ceasefire, an Iraqi withdrawal from Kuwait, and negotiations on the issue of Palestine. Bothered by the prospect of Hussein keeping his army intact, Bush immediately rejected these terms as inconsistent with the UN resolutions demanding unconditional withdrawal. Then Gorbachev, on February 15, convinced Hussein to accept UN Resolution 660, but the Iraqi leader added certain conditions pertaining to a ceasefire, an American withdrawal, revocation of other UN resolutions, and Israeli policy. Bush promptly rejected these terms as well, calling Hussein's offer "a cruel hoax" that raised but then spoiled the hopes of his own people for peace. The steady erosion of Soviet power and decline of Cold War tensions in 1990–91, moreover, gave Bush the confidence to disregard Soviet wishes.[12]

As the air war and the Soviet-inspired diplomacy unfolded, Bush gradually came to the conclusion that he must launch a ground war to finish the task at hand. Many of Bush's top advisers, including Pentagon officers, had identified several perils in a ground war, including substantial casualties, the prospect of facing Iraqi chemical weapons, and the political fallout of attacking an Arab state. But Bush reasoned that if he allowed Hussein to save his army, then Iraq would remain a menace to its neighbors far into the future, longer than the United States could afford to contain it. "We had to act now," Scowcroft later wrote, "while we were mobilized and in place." Hussein's brazen aggression and diplomatic audacity, together with reports of Iraqi atrocities against Kuwaitis and environmental depredation, further convinced Bush that Hussein deserved little mercy. On February 21, Hussein offered to withdraw from Kuwait if the United States ceased its aerial attacks. But Bush responded the next day by issuing an ultimatum that Iraq must leave Kuwait within twenty-four hours.[13]

The February 22 ultimatum triggered the final phase of the war. Hussein failed to comply with U.S. demands, so Bush ordered a major ground assault against Iraqi troops in Kuwait on February 23. The Iraqi army collapsed quickly in death, retreat, and surrender; the Allied powers destroyed the bulk of Iraqi armor and artillery; and Kuwait was liberated in a combat phase that lasted exactly one hundred hours. As American airpower decimated Iraqi units heading north from Kuwait City—on the so-called highway of death—Bush called off the attack to avoid criticism in the media that he had abetted a slaughter. The United States achieved the liberation of Kuwait at a cost of 148 combat fatalities.[14]

The rapid success in Kuwait naturally raised the prospect of pressing on with the war, occupying Baghdad, and deposing Hussein. Some observers suggested that danger loomed as long as Hussein remained in power, given his aggressiveness, chemical weapons, nuclear research, missiles, and army. But Bush decided not to advance, later explaining:

> I firmly believed that we should not march into Baghdad. Our stated mission, as codified in UN resolutions, was a simple one—end the aggression, knock Iraq's forces out of Kuwait, and restore Kuwait's leaders. To occupy Iraq would instantly shatter our coalition, turning the whole Arab world against us, and make a broken tyrant into a latter-day Arab hero. It would have taken us way beyond the imprimatur of international law bestowed by the resolutions of the Security Council, assigning young soldiers to a fruitless hunt for a securely entrenched dictator and condemning them to fight in what would be an unwinnable urban guerrilla war. It could only plunge that part of the world into even greater instability and destroy the credibility we were working so hard to reestablish.

The president's "absolutely correct judgment," Baker added, was "enthusiastically endorsed by the military, our coalition partners, the Congress, and American public opinion."[15]

Yet the outcome of the war and subsequent events caused many to reconsider the wisdom of Bush's restraint. Hussein was able to preserve the prowess of his elite Republican Guard units to a greater extent than U.S. officials had realized. Worse, shortly after Bush called on Iraqi army officers to overthrow Hussein, rebellions erupted among the Kurds of northern Iraq and the Shiites of the south, and Hussein was able to crush those rebellions mercilessly, in the process reinvigorating his stature among Iraq's dominant Sunni community. Although moved by the tragedy of these events, Bush reasoned that intervention would entail "incalculable human and political costs." Empowering the Kurds would anger Turkey, assisting the Shiites would embolden Iran, dividing Iraq into three states would upset the delicate balance of power in the Gulf region, and taking any action would cost American lives. "It is naïve . . . to think," Colin Powell later explained, "that if Hussein had fallen, he would necessarily have been replaced by a Jeffersonian in some sort of desert democracy where people read *The Federalist Papers* along with the Koran. Quite possibly, we would have wound up with a Saddam by another name." Bush calculated that the best long-term plan was to stay out of Iraq, preserve the anti-Hussein coalition, promote Arab-Israeli peace, and contain Iraq through UN diplomacy.[16]

The Containment of Iraq, 1991–2002

Bill Clinton, who won the White House in the 1992 presidential election, inherited and applied George H. W. Bush's strategy of containing Saddam Hussein. Indeed, when Bush ordered an air strike on Iraq during his last week in office in January 1993 because Iraq violated UN resolutions, the president-elect publicly endorsed the move. Clinton embraced the major features of Bush's postwar apparatus for containing Iraq, including restrictions on its military mobility, international financial sanctions enforced by a multinational naval presence in the Persian Gulf, and a rigorous system of inspections to ensure Iraq's compliance with the disarmament provisions of UN resolutions. Clinton calculated, his UN Ambassador and eventual Secretary of State Madeleine Albright later recorded, that "the combination of sanctions, inspections, military pressure, and possible air strikes had placed him [Hussein] in a box." While Bush had declared that sanctions would remain in force until Hussein fell from power, Clinton raised the prospect of ending sanctions if Hussein adhered to all resolutions.[17]

Clinton also extended the Bush administration's enforcement of so-called no-fly restrictions in two zones of Iraq. In the northern zone, comprising about one-tenth of the country, U.S. and Allied warplanes based in Turkey protected Iraq's Kurdish population from Iraqi air assaults. In the southern half of the country, U.S. fighters based in Saudi Arabia and aboard carriers ensured that Iraqi airpower neither threatened the territorial security of Kuwait nor harmed Iraqi Shiite communities. The so-called Operations Northern Watch and Southern Watch grew more extensive as the 1990s passed; in 2000, more than 10,000 U.S. sorties were flown. On many occasions, Iraqi units either fired upon Allied aircraft or locked on their radars. Routinely, Allied aircraft bombed and strafed Iraqi artillery and radar stations.[18]

Clinton also ordered occasional military strikes on Iraq. In early 1993, Kuwaiti intelligence broke up an Iraqi conspiracy to assassinate former president Bush as he toured the liberated kingdom. Charging that the plot on Bush was "an attack against our country and all Americans,"

Clinton ordered a strike with twenty-three cruise missiles on Iraqi intelligence facilities in Baghdad. In October 1994, when Hussein threatened another move on Kuwait by sending 10,000 Republican Guards toward the border, Clinton deployed 36,000 U.S. troops to Kuwait, backed by an aircraft carrier battle group. "Saddam got the message," Secretary of State Warren Christopher declared, "stopped dead in his tracks, and pulled back." In September 1996, Clinton ordered the bombings of Iraqi army units that approached the Kurdish town of Irbil, forcing them to retreat.[19]

The Clinton administration also attempted to enforce a UN-backed system of inspections to ensure Iraqi disarmament. UN Security Council Resolution 687 of April 1991 demanded that Iraq submit to inspections by the International Atomic Energy Agency (IAEA) and the newly created UN Special Commission (UNSCOM) to verify destruction of Iraq's WMD capabilities and its ballistic missiles with ranges of more than 150 kilometers. For several years, the inspections seemed to work effectively. Inspectors clarified the extent of Hussein's WMD arsenals and verified the destruction of large stockpiles of them. The inspection

United Nations Special Commission (UNSCOM) members inspect mustard agent artillery projectiles in Iraq, circa 1991. UNSCOM was created following the first Gulf War to verify that Iraq destroyed its weapons of mass destruction capabilities and ballistic missiles in accordance with UN resolutions. The inspections seemed to work effectively until 1997, when Iraqi president Saddam Hussein began interfering with the inspectors' work and later forced them out of the country. UN/DPI Photo.

process enjoyed a windfall in 1995, when two of Hussein's sons-in-law defected to Jordan and divulged details of Iraq's WMD capabilities and thus led inspectors to major discoveries. By the mid-1990s, Albright claimed, UN inspectors had eliminated more Iraqi WMD capability than Iraq had lost in the Gulf War.[20]

Yet gradually, the inspection process broke down. Accusing the inspectors of serving U.S. intelligence agencies, Hussein began to interfere with inspections in 1997 and to insist on the removal of American nationals from UNSCOM. Meanwhile, the international consensus on financial sanctions also began to crumble, as Hussein convinced various communities around the world that the sanctions impoverished his people and as France and Russia, which had substantial business interests in Baghdad, proposed a change in policy. Unable to identify a viable military solution to the standoff, the Clinton administration used diplomacy to strengthen the international resolve for sanctions. Finally, Russian Foreign Minister Yevgeny Primakov persuaded Hussein to allow the resumption of inspections.[21]

Hussein challenged the inspection process for a second time in early 1998, when he demanded that UNSCOM suspend surprise inspections and consider presidential sites off limits. After canvassing the globe, Albright claimed to find more than a dozen states, including Britain and France, grimly ready to consider military action against Baghdad. But when Clinton tried to rally public opinion to that option, ironically, he found a groundswell of opposition. Eventually, UN Secretary General Kofi Annan brokered a deal in which Hussein allowed inspections to resume on the condition that UN-appointed diplomats would accompany inspectors to presidential sites. The UN Security Council also reaffirmed that future Iraqi noncompliance might result in severe consequences.[22]

Despite the warning, Hussein unilaterally halted all UNSCOM inspections in December 1998, triggering a Western military reaction. Although he realized that force would not reopen the door to inspectors, Clinton ordered a massive strike against Iraqi military facilities. U.S. and British forces sent some 650 aircraft and 400 missiles to hit Iraqi military facilities over four days. Hussein's breaking of his promise to allow inspections justified the raids, Clinton explained. "Iraq has abused its final chance." Privately, the president figured that even if the raids did not demolish Iraq's WMD facilities, they at least weakened his overall warmaking capabilities.[23]

Thereafter, Clinton adopted a firm policy toward Iraq known as "containment plus." With inspections clearly over, the United States bolstered its military presence in the region, toughened its enforcement in the no-fly zones, and increased its strikes on Iraqi radar facilities. The president also signed into law a bill authorizing the expenditure of $97 million to fund Iraqi opposition forces committed to ousting Hussein. The Iraqi leader threatened "the security of the world," Clinton declared. The "best way to end that threat once and for all is with a new Iraqi government."[24]

Yet Clinton's containment-plus approach provided no more security against Iraqi WMD capability than the previous inspections approach. In December 1999, the Security Council affirmed the precedent of inspections to ensure Iraq's riddance of WMD, and it replaced the obsolete UNSCOM with the United Nations Monitoring, Verification, and Inspection Commission (UNMOVIC), with responsibility for conducting "a reinforced system of ongoing monitoring and investigation." But UNSCOM, in a final report issued in 1999, indicated that Iraq might still possess up to 6,000 chemical bombs, nine surface-to-surface missiles, 26,000 liters of anthrax, and 1.5 tons of VX gas. UNMOVIC would be hard pressed to monitor such armaments in the foreseeable future.[25]

Terrorism

While the number of terrorist incidents worldwide declined from the 1980s to the 1990s, the latter decade witnessed a steady series of anti-American terrorist attacks among disaffected Muslims who acted on religious motivations. Several factors indigenous to the Muslim states of the Middle East encouraged this trend. High birthrates and economic underdevelopment created youthful populations with few opportunities to improve their standard of living, and authoritarian regimes left little room for peaceful, democratic reform. The modern media imported images of Western wealth and moral laxity, which bred both resentment and abhorrence. In such conditions, violence became an attractive option for political expression. In addition, the ease of travel in the post–Cold War era of globalization and the widespread availability of electronic communications made it easier for terrorists to operate without detection around the globe.[26]

Moreover, a fundamentalist ideology that emerged in the 1980s gave religious sanction to political violence. Encouraged by such developments as the Iranian revolution, the assassination of Anwar Sadat, and the Soviet defeat in Afghanistan (discussed in chapter 5), Islamists preached a utopian vision of a God-centered political order that would restore righteous living and replace the repressive, secular regimes of the region. Their ideology embraced a historical view of Western repression of

Muslim peoples, manifest in the Crusades and, more recently, in the West's defeat of the Ottoman Empire in World War I, capture of Ottoman territory as mandates, creation of Israel, and support of the secular regimes. Propagandists readily blamed the United States and the international Jewish community for the suffering of Muslims everywhere.[27]

Embracing such an ideology, Islamists surged in political influence in the late 1980s and early 1990s. Heady with success, the so-called Afghan Arabs—Arabs who had fought in Afghanistan— fanned across the Middle East, South Asia, North Africa, and the Muslim areas of the former Soviet empire looking for opportunities to replicate their success. An Islamist, Hassan al-Turabi, seized power in Sudan. Hamas contested the power of the Palestine Liberation Organization (PLO), by dispatching suicide bombers against Israeli targets, and Iran backed Hizballah fighters in Lebanon. To destabilize the secular government of Hosni Mubarak in Egypt, Islamic Jihad and Gamaa Islamiya launched a campaign of terrorism that claimed one thousand victims in 1992–97. Islamists also plotted to overthrow the secular government in Pakistan and the pro-Western monarchy in Saudi Arabia. In Algeria, the Islamist party Front Islamique du Salut (FIS) won popular elections in December 1991, only to see the Algerian Army nullify the elections and seize power in January 1992.[28]

Despite this surge, Islamism met its limits by the late 1990s. The Algerian Army maintained power by crushing a civil insurrection by the Islamists who had won the 1991 balloting. The PLO prevailed over Hamas for influence among the Palestinian people. Surviving an assassination attempt in 1995, Mubarak maintained power through a combination of repression of Islamists and economic reform that preserved popular loyalty to the state. Muslims in Bosnia repudiated Islamism when they accepted the Dayton peace accord of 1995. By the late 1990s, moderates solidified control or came to power in Saudi Arabia, Pakistan, Indonesia, Turkey, Algeria, and Sudan. The Iranian people elected the moderate Mohammad Khatami as prime minister in May 1997 (although the radical anti-American Supreme Leader Ayatollah Ali Khamenei retained control of the country's security apparatus, which apparently continued to abet terrorist activities through the Middle East).[29]

During the late 1990s, Afghanistan emerged as the strongest Islamist bastion. Energized by the Soviet withdrawal, the mujaheddin seized control of Kabul in 1992 and nurtured transnational networks of experienced fighters. The Taliban, a political sect advocating strict adherence to Islamic law, seized control of Afghanistan in 1996. Initially, Western governments welcomed the regime because it stabilized the country and raised the prospect of building an oil pipeline across the land. But the mood soon soured, as the Taliban suppressed civil rights and practiced ultra-conservative Islamic law.[30]

Worse, from the Western view, the Taliban gave sanctuary to Osama bin Laden. A wealthy and educated Saudi, bin Laden had gained prominence and demonstrated organizational brilliance in the 1980s, while resisting the Soviet occupation of Afghanistan in partnership with the United States. In the process, he embraced an extreme version of Islamism, networked with compatriots who flocked to Afghanistan from around the Muslim world, and compiled a database of holy warriors (jihadists) known as al-Qaeda ("The Base" in Arabic). When Iraq overran Kuwait in 1990, bin Laden offered to organize an army of jihadists to defend Saudi Arabia against Iraq, but King Fahd decided to rely on American military power. The presence of American soldiers in Arabia—the site of Mecca and Medina, Islam's holiest cities—enraged bin Laden because it violated Islamic strictures against granting infidels access to holy lands. In 1991, he relocated to Sudan, revived contacts with al-Qaeda members, and plotted both to oust American troops from Saudi territory and to overthrow the Saudi regime that had welcomed them. Expelled from Sudan in 1996, bin Laden found his way to Afghanistan, where, under Taliban protection, he trained legions of Islamists for jihad around the world.[31]

In the late 1990s, bin Laden essentially declared war on Saudi Arabia and the United States. He accused Saudi leaders of "polytheism" because they followed "laws fabricated by men . . . , permitting that which God has forbidden." In August 1996, bin Laden issued a "Declaration of Jihad against the Americans Occupying the Land of the Two Holy Places," asserting that "God willing, I will expel the Jews and the Christians from Arabia." In February 1998, bin Laden and Ayman al-Zawahiri, the leader of Al-Jihad in Egypt, cosigned the charter of the International Islamic Front against Jews and Crusaders. The charter called on Muslims "to kill Americans and their allies, whether civilians or military personnel, in every country where this is possible." To bin Laden, the United States of the 1990s resembled the Soviet Union of the 1980s—an apostate, occupying power deserving of resistance. He also apparently calculated that attacks on the United States would rejuvenate public support for Islamism and reverse its decline across the region.[32]

Once freed from their preoccupation with Soviet expansionism, U.S. officials grappled to understand and contain Islamism in the 1990s. The George H. W. Bush administration, for instance, quietly supported the Algerian Army's nullification of the FIS electoral victory of 1991. "We are suspect of those who would use the democratic process to come to power, only to destroy the very process in order to retain power and political dominance," Assistant Secretary of State Edward Djerejian declared in June 1992. "While we believe in the principle of one person, one vote, we do not support one person, one vote, one time." Officials of the Bush and Clinton governments advocated democratic reform in the Middle East, recognized the peaceful inclinations of Islam, and denied the inevitability of conflict between Muslim and non-Muslim civilizations.[33]

Yet despite the larger decline of Islamism across the 1990s, the Clinton administration faced a mounting threat of Islamist terrorism. In February 1993, Islamic terrorists exploded a bomb in a parking garage at the World Trade Center in New York City, killing six and injuring more than one thousand persons (although failing to destroy the buildings as intended). Although law enforcement officials arrested, tried, and convicted the perpetrators, the bombing highlighted the vulnerability of American institutions and citizens to major acts of terrorism by anti-American foreigners. Popular fears about terrorism at home were stoked by the Oklahoma City bombing of April 1995—the work of a domestic political extremist—which claimed 168 lives. News of the March 1995 nerve gas attack on a Tokyo subway by a religious cult, moreover, raised concerns that terrorists might use WMD in the United States. Widespread reports that former Soviet nuclear and biological weapons were unaccounted for added to the worry.[34]

In reaction to these developments, Clinton pursued various counterterrorism policies. At home, he pushed through Congress a bill broadening the powers of law enforcement officials to prevent terrorist attacks and to prosecute those perpetrating such acts, and he initiated planning for the government's response to any WMD attack inside the country. Overseas, the president promoted multilateral cooperation in law enforcement and nuclear nonproliferation, and he tried to organize international sanctions against Iran on the grounds that it provided some $100 million per year to Hamas and Hizballah. In March 1996, Clinton joined leaders of twenty-five other nations, including fourteen Arab states, at the "Summit of Peacemakers" in Sharm el-Sheikh, for the purpose of morally condemning terrorism in Israel and elsewhere. While Clinton claimed to have foiled terrorist plots to blow up tunnels in New York City and to highjack airliners in the Philippines, he also realized that counterterrorism must become a long-term, sustained effort. He told a group of students in the spring of 1996 that terrorism was "the threat of their generation just as nuclear war had been the threat for those of us who had grown up during the Cold War."[35]

Despite Clinton's efforts to avert terrorism, he soon became involved in an escalating confrontation with Islamic extremists in the Middle East and elsewhere. In June 1996, unidentified terrorists parked a truck laden with explosives in an unguarded lot next to Building 131 of the Khobar Towers complex in Dhahran, Saudi Arabia, the barracks of U.S. Air Force personnel. The ensuing blast killed nineteen and wounded hundreds of U.S. airmen, as well as injuring hundreds of nearby civilians. In addition to relocating the troops in Saudi Arabia to more secure facilities, the U.S. government also probed connections between Iran and the Khobar bombers and focused its intelligence lenses on bin Laden, then residing in Sudan. The CIA established an office devoted exclusively to tracking bin Laden and al-Qaeda. The United States pressured Sudan to deport bin Laden, who relocated to Afghanistan as the Taliban consolidated power. In spring 1998, Clinton authorized the CIA to conduct a "snatch operation" to capture bin Laden in Afghanistan.[36]

From his sanctuary in Afghanistan, bin Laden escalated his war on the United States. In August 1998, he orchestrated simultaneous bombings of the U.S. Embassies in Kenya and Tanzania that killed 257 people—including 12 Americans and 40 local employees of the embassies—and wounded more than 5,000. In response, Clinton beefed up the physical security of embassies, partnered with other nations to break up terrorist plots, invested in counterterrorism planning and technology development, and prepared to deal with future attacks on the home front. Law enforcement efforts achieved some gains: officials in Jordan and Egypt foiled al-Qaeda strikes in those countries, and American authorities stopped a December 1999 attack on Los Angeles International Airport. In May 2001, four al-Qaeda operatives were convicted in New York of involvement in the 1998 embassy bombings and sentenced to life imprisonment.[37]

Clinton also escalated his war against al-Qaeda. Two weeks after the African embassy bombings, he ordered a retaliatory strike with seventy-nine cruise missiles against terrorist targets in two countries. The missiles wrecked an al-Qaeda camp and killed some twenty operatives in Afghanistan and demolished a factory in Sudan where, the CIA believed, al-Qaeda had manufactured VX gas. The Clinton administration also pressured the Taliban to surrender bin Laden to U.S. authorities, warned that the United States would hold the Taliban accountable for future violence perpetrated by al-Qaeda, and organized international financial sanctions on Afghanistan. "After the African slaughter," Clinton later wrote, "I became intently focused on capturing or killing him [bin Laden] and with destroying al Qaeda." The president signed orders authorizing the use of lethal force against bin Laden and his top aides, pressed the CIA to pinpoint his whereabouts, alerted air and missile units near Afghanistan to remain ready to strike, and directed the Pentagon to plan commando operations into Afghanistan. But Clinton held back from an outright invasion of Afghanistan because he doubted that U.S. or world opinion would support such a drastic move.[38]

The conflict continued to the end of the Clinton presidency. In early 2000, Clinton ordered the positioning of two submarines in the Arabian Sea, ready to fire missiles at any site where bin Laden was found. In October, al-Qaeda terrorists aboard a small boat detonated a bomb adjacent to the USS *Cole* as it refueled in Aden, Yemen. Seventeen U.S. Navy sailors died in the blast, and the ship was nearly lost. Clinton wanted to launch a retaliatory strike against bin Laden, but a lack of intelligence about his location ruled out either a missile strike or a commando raid. "I was very frustrated," Clinton later wrote. "The enemy was very elusive, everyone was a potential target, our enormous arsenal was not a deterrent, and the openness and information technology of the modern world were being used against us." As president, Clinton's "biggest disappointment was not getting bin Laden."[39]

The most dramatic al-Qaeda strike against the United States occurred shortly after the end of Clinton's presidency. On September 11, 2001, nineteen al-Qaeda operatives simultaneously hijacked four U.S. airliners. Two of the planes were flown into the twin towers of the World Trade Center in New York City, causing both structures to collapse. A third plane crashed into the Pentagon near Washington, D.C., demolishing a wing of that building. The fourth plane, apparently destined to strike a target in Washington, crashed in a remote area of Pennsylvania after passengers, alerted to the unfolding events by cell-phone conversations with loved ones, stormed the cockpit in an effort to regain control of the aircraft. Killing some three thousand persons and deeply wounding the psyche of the American people, the 9/11 attacks were the most devastating enemy assault ever on the American homeland.[40]

The War on Terrorism and the War in Iraq, 2001–2005

The official U.S. response to the events of 9/11 was determined by President George W. Bush, George H. W. Bush's son, who had taken office in January 2001 after the closest and most contested presidential election since 1876. "We're at war," Bush told Vice President Richard Cheney, minutes after learning of the 9/11 attacks. "Somebody's going to pay." Sympathy from around the world buoyed the president. "In this tragic moment, when words seem so inadequate to express the shock people feel," *Le Monde* (Paris) declared, "the first thing that comes to mind is this: We are all Americans! We are all New Yorkers." NATO invoked its collective security proviso for the first time ever and sent warplanes to patrol the skies over North America. The UN Security Council condemned terrorism and called on states to eradicate it.[41]

The United States demolished the Taliban regime in Afghanistan within months of 9/11. On October 7, U.S. and allied forces launched devastating air strikes against al-Qaeda camps, airfields, and barracks. Some five hundred Special Forces and CIA paramilitary officers attacked Taliban strongholds in partnership with fighters of the indigenous Northern Alliance, which had long resisted Taliban authority. The Taliban collapsed in November, its remnants taking refuge in the southeastern mountains where they were subjected to continual air bombardment. The United Nations sponsored talks among Afghan factions in Bonn, Germany, leading to the signing on December 5 of an agreement to write a new constitution for the country, to appoint a transitional government, and to hold elections by 2004. In June 2002, the Grand Council of Afghanistan agreed on blueprints for a new government, and Hamid Karzai was appointed interim prime minister.[42]

Yet the U.S. victory in Afghanistan was not without its setbacks and limitations. In certain parts of the country, pro-Taliban and anti-American resistance continued despite U.S. operations to suppress it. Militants moved freely between the rugged, tribal borderlands of Afghanistan and Pakistan, regional warlords consolidated power at the expense of the Karzai government, and Osama bin Laden and Taliban leader Mullah Omar remained at large despite U.S. bounties on their heads. The country remained woefully underdeveloped and poor, and it experienced a nineteen-fold increase in illicit opium production in the year following the collapse of the Taliban. The United States belatedly enlisted the help of the United Nations in registering Afghan citizens to vote and holding a presidential election in October 2004. Karzai handily won the polling, although his victory provided him precious little stature in confronting the warlords, rebels, and opium traffickers who contested his authority.[43]

In addition to waging war in Afghanistan, Bush also led the United States into a controversial war in Iraq. The president and several of his top aides took office apparently convinced that they must break the debilitating stalemate with Iraq that had evolved through the 1990s. At his very first National Security Council meeting on January 30, 2001—months before 9/11—Bush revealed that he favored a goal of regime change in Baghdad in light of evidence that Hussein was building WMD. Vice President Cheney, according to his aides, had a "fever" about overthrowing Hussein. Secretary of Defense Donald Rumsfeld argued that enforcement of the no-fly zones was expensive as well as risky for the pilots who endured constant gunfire. Deputy Secretary of Defense Paul Wolfowitz advocated a military invasion of Iraq's southern oil fields to trigger a coup by Iraqi generals. Other officials argued that the international sanctions against Baghdad were difficult to maintain in the face of French and Russian pressure to ease them, and difficult to enforce in light of tricky questions about dual use technologies (such as hydraulic cylinders on dump trucks that could be retrofitted on missile launchers). By contrast, Secretary of State (and former chairman of the Joint Chiefs of Staff) Colin Powell cautioned that military operations would sour politically and urged a focus on strengthening the containment approach.[44]

The 9/11 attacks profoundly affected the Bush administration's approach toward Iraq. Despite a lack of evidence linking Iraq to 9/11, Wolfowitz argued that a link probably existed and that the American war in Afghanistan should be followed by an invasion of Iraq. Bush and Cheney seemed to conclude that the passivity of Clinton's approaches to Iraq and the limits of his responses to terrorism might have encouraged the 9/11 assault and that therefore more vigorous action was needed to send a political message to American adversaries. Intelligence reports that Pakistani scientists were supplying nuclear materials to Muslim states caused deep concern about an attack on the United States with a "dirty" bomb (a conventional explosive that distributed radioactive material) and thereby pushed the administration toward action. The CIA advised Bush that covert operations to oust Hussein would likely fail, given Hussein's rigorous security and ruthlessness against potential opponents. At about the same time the Pentagon staff prepared a detailed contingency plan for an invasion of Iraq, which made such a move a viable option for the president. Even though Iraq had nothing to do with 9/11, Bush stated in April 2002, he would act to prevent "a nation like Iraq, run by Saddam Hussein, to develop weapons of mass destruction, and then team up with terrorist organizations so they can blackmail the world."[45]

In 2002, Bush steadily built a public case for war against Iraq. In his State of the Union message on January 29, he called Iraq, Iran, and

North Korea an "axis of evil" deserving of extreme measures. In April, he told a journalist that "I made up my mind that Saddam needs to go." In an address at the U.S. Military Academy in May, the president declared a doctrine of preemptive war, asserting that "the war on terror will not be won on the defensive. We must take the battle to the enemy, disrupt his plans, and confront the worst threats before they emerge." In September, the White House released *The National Security Strategy of the United States*, a policy statement declaring that "the United States will, if necessary, act preemptively" against "a sufficient threat to our national security" and warning that the country would "make no distinction between terrorists and those who knowingly harbor or provide aid to them." In October, the president acknowledged that Iraq might not have WMD but stressed its effort to acquire them. "Facing clear evidence of peril," he intoned, "we cannot wait for the final proof, the smoking gun, that could come in the form of a mushroom cloud."[46]

The tone and substance of Bush's rhetoric stimulated considerable debate among Americans. Shell-shocked by 9/11, a broad cross-section of the public gave the president wide latitude. But dissenters argued that a war against Iraq would mislead the country down a perilous path. Even Brent Scowcroft, who served the first Bush presidency as national security adviser, noted that Saddam Hussein, a secular socialist with no record of terrorism, had no part in 9/11 and was unlikely to partner with a religious fanatic like bin Laden. Because the rest of the world opposed military operations in Iraq, moreover, the United States would need to fight alone. Vice President Cheney responded to such criticism in an address to a veterans group in late August. "There is no doubt that Saddam Hussein now has weapons of mass destruction," he warned, and "there is no doubt that he is amassing them to use against our friends, against our allies and against us."[47]

Undeterred by the criticism, Bush sold Congress on the case for war by stressing that such a war was winnable and necessary. "Saddam Hussein is a terrible guy who is teaming up with al Qaeda," the president told one group of legislators. "He tortures his own people and hates Israel." Alluding to Iraq's attempt to assassinate the first President Bush in 1993, the younger Bush told a member of Congress that Hussein "tried to kill my dad." Administration officials also argued that congressional endorsement of forceful action against Iraq would motivate the UN Security Council to take firm action against that country. By a 296–133 margin, the House approved a resolution on October 10 authorizing Bush to use force in Iraq "as he deemed to be necessary and appropriate." The Senate followed suit on the next day by a 77–23 vote.[48]

Bush also prompted the United Nations to impose firm measures against Iraq, although it remains unclear whether he sought to restore the inspections process of the 1990s or provide a pretext for war. In an address to the General Assembly on September 12, 2002, the president advised the United Nations to pass new resolutions to deal with Iraq or the United States would take action. In November, after weeks of effort, Powell convinced the Security Council unanimously to pass Resolution 1441, which found Iraq in "material breach" of previous UN resolutions, provided it "a final opportunity" to cooperate with inspections, and warned Iraq that "it will face serious consequences" if it defied the United Nations. France, Russia, and other states voted for the resolution on the understanding that it did not authorize military action.[49]

Bush allowed precious little time for Resolution 1441 to work. On November 25, former Swedish Foreign Minister Hans Blix led a team of one hundred UNMOVIC inspectors to Iraq. On December 7, Iraqi officials delivered forty-three binders of documents supposedly verifying that Iraq was free of WMD. While several Security Council powers favored taking time to examine these records and continue inspections, the Bush administration declared that the binders contained old records that revealed no new information. As John Keegan observes, UNMOVIC perhaps faced an impossible situation: proving a negative (that Iraq did not have WMD), on the basis of inspections of a sizeable country, governed by a dictator who lacked credibility, and under pressure of a very impatient U.S. government. On December 19, Bush declared that Iraq was in material breach of Resolution 1441.[50]

By late December, Bush steeled himself to launch a preemptive invasion of Iraq. On December 21, Director of Central Intelligence George Tenet assured him, using a basketball metaphor, that there was "slam dunk" evidence that Iraq harbored WMD. National Security Adviser Condoleezza Rice counseled the president that Iraq was stringing along UNMOVIC inspectors, that antiwar movements were forming in Europe and at home, that the UN Security Council consensus on Iraq was fragmenting, and that the United States could not sustain long term its incremental military buildup in the Middle East. Refusing to retreat and unable to delay, Bush decided to take the offensive.[51]

The Bush administration made its closing argument for war in early 2003. In his State of the Union message on January 28, the president explained that Iraq could not account for massive quantities of anthrax, botulinum toxin, sarin gas, and VX nerve agent that it had once possessed. He reported that British intelligence had indicated that Hussein had tried to purchase uranium in Africa (a charge that the CIA had disputed months earlier and that was later proven false). Even Secretary of State Powell overcame his reluctance about attacking Iraq. In an address to the United Nations on February 5, he summarized U.S. intelligence to argue that Hussein probably possessed WMD and had deceived UNMOVIC inspectors. When Hans Blix countered that UNMOVIC had found no smoking gun and that more inspections were needed, Powell retorted that Hussein had been given sufficient opportunity to come clean and deserved no more time.[52]

The United States moved to war in March. Bush considered asking the UN Security Council for a second resolution explicitly authorizing the use of force in light of Iraqi defiance of Resolution 1441. British Prime Minister Tony Blair, Bush's most supportive ally on the world stage, advocated such a move in light of a mounting antiwar movement among his people and within his own Labour Party. When it became clear, however, that France would veto a second resolution, Bush asserted that Resolution 1441 provided sufficient legal basis for offensive action. In a summit at Bermuda on March 16, he convinced Blair to go along. The next day, Bush issued an ultimatum to Saddam Hussein that he and his sons Odai and Qusai must leave Iraq within forty-eight hours or face the wrath of the American military. After Hussein defied the ultimatum, Bush summoned General Tommy Franks via video teleconference and declared: "For the sake of peace in the world and security for our country and the rest of the free world, and for the freedom of the Iraqi people, as of this moment I will give Secretary Rumsfeld the order necessary to execute Operation Iraqi Freedom. . . . May God bless the troops."[53]

Together with their British and Australian partners, U.S. forces made short work of Saddam Hussein's Iraq on the battlefield. In a twenty-one-day campaign starting on March 20, allied troops completely demolished and scattered the Iraqi army of some 400,000, occupied the country, destroyed the government, and drove Saddam into hiding (at a cost of 139 U.S. fatalities). The capture of Baghdad on April 9 and the toppling of towering statues of Hussein signaled the end of his regime. On May 1, Bush piloted a fighter plane to the carrier USS *Abraham Lincoln* near San Francisco and, standing beneath an enormous banner proclaiming "Mission Accomplished," delivered a rousing address and declared an end to major combat operations. U.S. soldiers found and killed Hussein's sons in a firefight on July 22. Hussein himself was captured on December 13, when a U.S. Army patrol discovered him hiding in a crude cellar on a farm near Tikrit. When soldiers lifted a trapdoor to find the fugitive dictator, he lifted his hands and declared, "I am the President of Iraq and I am ready to negotiate."[54]

In sharp contrast to the military destruction of Saddam Hussein's regime, however, the American occupation of Iraq was beset by serious problems. At a fundamental level, President Bush and Secretary of Defense Rumsfeld had apparently put little thought into the task of postwar reconstruction. "We predicted that everything was going to be swell," Undersecretary of Defense Douglas Feith told reporter James Fallows, "and we didn't plan for things not being swell." Rumsfeld confined the occupation force to some 140,000 U.S. soldiers, despite suggestions from respected military experts, including former Army Chief of Staff General Eric K. Shinseki, that more than 200,000 were needed to pacify the country of four million Kurds, ten million Sunni Muslims, and fifteen million Shi'a Muslims. Rumsfeld's decision to disband the Iraqi army and police force—in disregard of explicit warnings of the State Department, the CIA, various Pentagon offices, and other agencies—enabled looting and lawlessness to sweep the country in the days after Hussein's fall, with devastating effect on the country's business, medical, and cultural institutions, and it created a legion of idle, unemployed men, ripe for recruitment by an insurgency. Perhaps feeling triumphalist, the Bush administration also rejected calls for the United Nations to administer the occupation of Iraq. "We fought the war," an official told one journalist, "and, besides, the UN is not competent to handle a complex undertaking like Iraq." But the administration also showed limited competence, sending retired General Jay Garner to Baghdad on a futile quest to transfer sovereignty to Iraqis within ninety days.[55]

The Bush administration also faced trouble because it groomed Ahmed Chalabi, the exiled leader of the Iraqi National Congress, to stabilize postwar Iraq. Despite State Department and CIA skepticism about his credibility, Chalabi emerged under Pentagon sponsorship as Iraq's first postwar governor. Deputy Undersecretary of Defense William Luti called Chalabi the "George Washington of Iraq," and Chalabi sat in a place of honor near First Lady Laura Bush during the president's January 2004 State of the Union address. Less than three months later, however, U.S. forces helped Iraqi police raid Chalabi's office to search for evidence of criminal wrongdoing. Before long, State Department and CIA officials fed the media a portrait of Chalabi as a master con artist who had misled Pentagon neoconservatives with false intelligence about Saddam Hussein and lined his own pockets in the process.[56]

President Bush also lost credibility when U.S. officials scouring Iraq found no evidence that Saddam Hussein had possessed an arsenal of WMD, which had been the administration's most prominently articulated reason for invading the country. General Tommy Franks believed that U.S. forces had found "the equivalent of a dissembled pistol, lying on a table beside neatly arranged trays of bullets." But former UN inspector David Kay, appointed by the White House to scour Iraq for evidence of WMD, concluded in January 2004 that Hussein had abandoned his WMD years before the invasion and that Western intelligence agencies had been fooled by a mirage of deception, corruption, and mismanagement in Iraq's military-scientific complex. This verdict was confirmed in a 1,000-page report completed in October 2004 by Iraq Survey Group chief Charles A. Duelfer. Criticism of Bush's miscalculation was amplified by clear evidence that the president had grossly misrepresented intelligence when he charged in his 2003 State of the Union address that Iraq had attempted to acquire nuclear materials from Africa. Nor did anyone find convincing evidence of political connections between Hussein's regime and al-Qaeda.[57]

U.S. policy in Iraq also caused serious repercussions around the world. Bush's decision to wage a preemptive war over widespread international opposition fractured the NATO alliance and generated a surge in anti-Americanism in many countries, including formerly pro-U.S. Muslim states such as Indonesia and Nigeria. Many world leaders criticized American unilateralism, also manifest in the administration's withdrawal from the Anti-Ballistic Missile Treaty, its refusal to support the International Criminal Court, its retreat from the Kyoto Protocol and the Comprehensive Test Ban Treaty, and its refusal to heed the Geneva Conventions regulating treatment of prisoners, as a threat to the international order painstakingly constructed after World War II. As criticism mounted in the spring of 2004, photographs depicting the inhumane abuse of detainees by U.S. soldiers at Abu Ghraib Prison near Baghdad circulated around the world via television and the Internet, sparking a crescendo of anti-Americanism. The United States appeared, columnist Fareed Zakaria observed, as "an international outlaw in the eyes of much of the world."[58]

Critics also fretted that the occupation of Iraq undermined other U.S. foreign policy objectives. It diverted U.S. troops from the war in Afghanistan and the hunt for Osama bin Laden. It galvanized Islamic militants, provided a staging ground for terrorists to bloody the U.S. military, and thus rejuvenated an international terrorist network that had been on the run since the aftermath of 9/11. Major terrorist attacks in Spain,

Russia, and Britain, a foiled plot in the Philippines, and heightened security alerts in the United States encouraged the perception that the occupation of Iraq had stimulated anti-American rebellion worldwide. While Libya divested itself of WMD under the implicit threat of U.S. military action, Iran and North Korea accelerated their nuclear weapons programs, Pakistan teetered toward internal instability, the Israeli-Palestinian peace process screeched to a halt, and genocide in Sudan proceeded without notice. Homeland security reforms, some critics believed, were hobbled by the war in Iraq.[59]

Determined to silence the critics by building a stable democracy in Iraq, the Bush administration implemented an expensive program of state building. L. Paul Bremer, appointed head of the so-called Coalition Provisional Authority (CPA) in May 2003, managed a vast effort to rebuild Iraq's infrastructure, build a new police force, promote educational and social reform, jumpstart the economy, and generate a democratic potential and sense of nationhood in Iraq. The United States also secured UN Security Council Resolutions 1483, which legalized the occupation of Iraq and ended sanctions, and 1551, which recognized the CPA and urged progress toward constitutional government in Iraq. By the end of 2003, some thirty-five countries had sent troops to help the United States occupy and rebuild Iraq. By early 2005, U.S. personnel had rebuilt some 2,400 schools, medical clinics, and fire stations in Iraq.[60]

The United States also constructed a new Iraqi government. In July 2003, it appointed the Iraq Governing Council (IGC) and announced that it would transfer sovereignty to that body by June 30, 2004. In March 2004, the IGC signed an interim constitution and pledged to hold elections no later than January 2005 for a national assembly that would write a permanent constitution. On June 28 (two days ahead of deadline), the CPA passed control of the country to a regime headed by Ayad Allawi, a former Baathist and secular Shiite long eyed by U.S. and British intelligence agencies as a potential alternative to Hussein. Allawi immediately asserted his authority and collaborated with U.S. troops to crush pockets of armed resistance.[61]

Inside Iraq, however, stability and security proved elusive. Within months of the fall of Saddam Hussein, the U.S. military faced a mounting insurrection apparently perpetrated by Hussein loyalists and foreign infiltrators from more than two dozen states. U.S. soldiers were routinely killed and maimed by roadside bombs and sniper fire. By October 2003, terrorists bombed the UN, Iraqi police, and Red Cross headquarters in Baghdad as well as the Shrine of Imam Ali in Najaf. U.S. forces sought protection from attacks by confining themselves to sprawling bases near major cities, reducing the number of patrols and thereby ceding portions of the country to the insurgents. The rebels thus trained their fire on Iraqi Shiites, foreign contractors working for the United States, and members of the U.S.-trained Iraqi police force. By April 2004, forty-eight suicide bombers had killed more than seven hundred persons. Although the new police force proved unreliable and ineffective in suppressing the insurgency, more than eight hundred of its officers were killed in various attacks by May 2004.[62]

The transfer of authority to the Allawi government did little to staunch the bloodshed. In summer 2004, intense fighting raged in Najaf between U.S. Marines and the so-called Mahdi Army, a militia loyal to the radical cleric Moqtada al-Sadr. Although they inflicted hundreds of casualties, the Marines were unable to crush their opponents, and the fighting ended with a truce that enhanced al-Sadr's popular influence and reputation. By autumn, insurgents systematically kidnapped and executed hostages from various states cooperating with the U.S. occupation, escalated their attacks on U.S. soldiers, filled political vacuums left by the retraction of U.S. forces, and defied the authority of the Allawi government. In September 2004, the death toll among U.S. soldiers in Iraq surpassed one thousand personnel, including some 860 who died after the fall of Hussein in April 2003. By March 2005, more than fifteen hundred American soldiers had died in Iraq.[63]

Americans passionately debated the wisdom of invading Iraq. The war "was not worth it because of the costs involved and the lack of a threat," former assistant secretary of defense Lawrence Korb observed. "We now know that the other policy—sanctions and containment—was working. He [Hussein] was in a box." Craig R. Eisendrath and Melvin A. Goodman charged that "the Bush administration has undermined the foundations of American foreign policy, compromised the credibility of the White House, weakened the national security position of the United States, eroded civil liberties, and created greater chaos in the international arena." Rather than address the al-Qaeda threat with a sensible plan of homeland security, public relations among moderate Arabs, and a clear victory in Afghanistan, Richard A. Clarke, former counterterrorism expert under Presidents Clinton and Bush, added, "we went off on a tangent, off after Iraq, off on a path that weakened us and strengthened the next generation of al Qaedas. For even as we have been attriting the core al Qaeda organization, it has metastasized."[64]

Yet the war had many backers. "A regime of inspections, embargo, sanctions, no-fly zones and thousands of combat troops in Kuwait was an unstable equilibrium," conservative columnist Charles Krauthammer asserted. "The United States could have retreated and allowed Saddam Hussein free rein or it could have gone to war and removed him. . . . The president made the right choice, indeed the only choice." In campaigning for reelection in summer 2004, Bush portrayed the invasion as a means to safeguard the United States against attack by Iraqi-armed terrorists and, citing the "transformational power of liberty," predicted that a thriving democracy in Iraq would stimulate democracy across the Middle East.[65]

Two major developments in early 2005 buoyed President Bush and those who supported his policy. On January 30, eight million Iraqi Shi'a and Kurds, at substantial risk of retribution by insurgents, participated in national elections that determined membership of a 275-member Transitional National Assembly, which was sworn in amidst tight security on March 16. The assembly was charged with selecting a president and two vice presidents, who would choose a prime minister to govern the country during a transitional phase, and with writing a constitution and submitting it for popular approval by referendum in 2006. In addition, inklings of democracy appeared across the Middle East, as Saudi Arabia held municipal elections for the first time ever, Egypt agreed to schedule unprecedented secret-ballot, multi-party presidential elections, and Syria ended its military occupation of Lebanon. Pro-Bush voices observed that U.S. action in Iraq had sparked the trans-regional surge of democracy.[66]

Yet Bush's experiment with promoting democracy through military action continued to face major obstacles. Showing no sign of abating, the Iraqi insurgency continued to target U.S. troops and the elected government they protected. Dozens of U.S. soldiers and scores of Iraqi citizens and officials were killed in the weeks following the Iraqi elections. Syria's ruler Bashar Asad, who had succeeded his father in 2000, continued to meddle in Lebanon, where the radical Hizballah militia remained active. Only time would tell the legitimacy of Bush's vision of transforming and democratizing the Middle East.[67]

Conclusion

In American eyes, the Middle East became an increasingly dangerous region of the world during the 1990s and early 2000s. In addition to the Arab-Israeli conflict, the United States faced twin new threats in the aggressiveness of Saddam Hussein of Iraq and the rising tide of anti-American terrorism. Hussein had demonstrated his bellicosity by invading Kuwait in 1990, one decade after he invaded Iran, and in defying international sanctions, controls, and arms inspections procedures after he was forced to relinquish Kuwait. A new wave of terrorism, beginning with the first attack on the World Trade Center in 1993, sweeping through subsequent major attacks in Saudi Arabia, Kenya and Tanzania, and Yemen, and culminating in fury on 9/11, simultaneously instilled fear in the mind of America that additional catastrophic assaults would follow, perhaps involving weapons of mass destruction.

The administrations of George H. W. Bush, Bill Clinton, and George W. Bush approached these threats in unique ways. The elder Bush responded to the Iraqi invasion of Kuwait by knitting together a broad coalition of nations that, empowered with legal authority by the United Nations, waged a punishing but limited war of liberation that reached its stated goal of reversing Iraqi aggression while refraining from ousting Hussein. Clinton perpetuated Bush's policy of containing Hussein through enforcement of no-fly zones, economic sanctions, and international weapons inspections, backed by occasional military strikes on Iraqi targets. Clinton also simultaneously developed a thorough plan for dealing with terrorism through defensive and offensive operations. The events of 9/11 revealed the imperfection of his efforts.

The younger Bush made the fateful assumption that the twin threats posed by Saddam Hussein and the al-Qaeda terrorist network were linked. That conviction led him to initiate an invasion of Iraq designed to oust Hussein from power and prevent his weapons of mass destruction from reaching the hands of terrorists. Although the American military quickly dispensed with Hussein, it remained debatable whether the invasion reduced or increased the prospect of future terrorist attacks. Only time will tell the wisdom and propriety of American policy toward Iraq.

CHAPTER 8

CONCLUSION

T HE STORY OF AMERICAN POLICY IN the Middle East in the post–
World War II era is one of enormous growth of involvement and
power. Prior to 1941, the United States government practiced
passivity toward the region, and the country's involvement was limited to
oil development and cultural enterprises. World War II and the Cold War
awakened American officials to the importance of the region's oil resources, military bases, and other assets on the periphery of the Soviet
Union. That realization led American officials to accept increasing commitments to the stability and security of the region. By the turn of the
twenty-first century, the United States had identified vital interests in the
Middle East and developed the means to project its power throughout
the region. It was the dominant foreign power in the region.

The rising tide of American involvement in the Middle East can
be measured by the series of policy initiatives that embedded the U.S.
government in the region. The Truman Doctrine of 1947, the Middle
East Command concept of 1950–53, the Baghdad Pact of 1955, and the
Eisenhower Doctrine of 1957 underscored the importance the United
States attributed to the goal of protecting the region from Soviet communism. The Carter Doctrine of 1980—issued in the shadow of the Iranian
revolution and the Soviet invasion of Afghanistan—pledged the use of
military force to stop a Soviet thrust into the Persian Gulf region.
The Nixon Doctrine of 1969–74 and Ronald Reagan's strategic consensus aimed to achieve regional stability and security through part-
nerships with local states. The failures of both initiatives in practice
increased American resolve in the post–Cold War era to protect vital

American interests through unilateral action. Thus the stage was set for the two wars the United States launched against Iraq in 1991 and 2003.

As the United States became more deeply involved in the Middle East, it defined a general policy of promoting stability in the region. Preserving stability meant resisting the spread of Soviet influence into the region, preventing the success of radical revolutionary movements that would serve Soviet interests or otherwise undermine American concerns and defending vital Western interests such as access to the oil and military bases of the region. The quest for stability defined the broad American strategy in the Middle East during the Cold War and after.

In the late twentieth century, the United States experienced mixed success in its quest for stability in the Middle East. It denied the Soviets any enduring territorial gains in the region and it preserved good relations with local states that protected vital American interests. Yet the effort to contain the Soviet Union failed to prevent Soviet political inroads in various states in the region and occasionally increased the risk of triggering World War III.

American officials also faced difficulty in their quest to resist revolutionary change within the region. Mohammed Mossadgeh, Gamal Abdel Nasser, and Ayatollah Ruhollah Khomeini represented a class of Middle East leaders who sought decolonization, political independence, and national sovereignty and therefore resisted American influence as a manifestation of a discredited Western imperialism. U.S. officials resisted such challengers with a mixture of firmness and conciliation, using means as diverse as covert operations to overthrow Mossadegh in 1953, economic aid and political gestures to channel Nasser's energy into productive pursuits in the early 1960s, and indirect support of Iraqi power as a barrier against Iranian expansionism in the 1980s. The long struggle against revolutionary nationalism was marked by political setbacks, the erosion of assets, and forced readjustments of the American system in the region.

The Arab-Israeli conflict provided perpetual challenges to American diplomats. The conflict burst on the scene in the late 1940s, actually abetted by the Truman administration's efforts to reconcile competing security, political, and cultural interests. For some two decades thereafter, American officials favored peace in principle as part of their larger quest for stability, but refrained from promoting peace in order to avoid risks to the larger goal of anti-Soviet containment. The result of that passivity was a concentrated period of Arab-Israeli conflict (including the wars of 1956, 1967, and 1973 as well as the War of Attrition of 1969–70), rising animosity on all sides of the dispute, and the seepage of Soviet influence into certain Arab states.

These dynamics forced the United States to become more actively involved in peacemaking, with uneven results. Jimmy Carter scored a major success in brokering the Egyptian-Israeli peace treaty of 1979, but it was followed by, and perhaps helped cause, the Israeli invasion of Lebanon in 1982 and the start of the first Palestinian uprising in 1987. In the wake of the collapse of the Soviet Union and the liberation of Kuwait, the 1990s brought a new wave of peacemaking that resulted in a formal Israeli-Jordanian peace treaty and more stability than ever in Israeli relations with other Arab states. Yet the process of the 1990s fell apart short of a settlement between Israel and the Palestinian people over the questions of the territories occupied by Israel since 1967 and the prospects of establishing a State of Palestine. The violence of the early 2000s bore witness to the mistrust and impassioned feeling on both sides of the equation.

The United States also faced a mounting peril of terrorism in the late twentieth century. The Reagan administration addressed the threat with military means, most notably in the air raid against Libya in 1986. As the threat mounted in the 1990s—with the first major foreign terrorist attack targeting New York City in 1993—the Clinton administration responded by launching homeland security measures, bolstering law enforcement, and ordering limited military action. But the terrorist attacks continued, culminating in the catastrophe of September 11, 2001.

The Persian Gulf region also offered a series of complicated challenges to the United States. During the Iran-Iraq War of 1980–88, the United States indirectly assisted Iraqi efforts to contain revolutionary Iran before taking action to compel Tehran to accept a ceasefire. Saddam Hussein's subsequent invasion of Kuwait in 1990, however, drove a wedge between the United States and Iraq. In 1990–91, President George H. W. Bush led a multinational coalition to victory in the liberation of Kuwait and curtailment of Hussein's ability to make mischief. President Bill Clinton extended Bush's policy of containing Hussein.

In 2002–5, President George W. Bush conflated the threats of terrorism and Saddam Hussein. While fighting a war against al-Qaeda in Afghanistan, he also ordered a preemptive invasion of Iraq on the rationale of preventing Hussein from arming terrorists with weapons of mass destruction. The invasion successfully ousted Hussein but the occupation of Iraq caused serious problems for the United States.

Whether the Iraq War turns out as a victory or a defeat for the Bush administration, the United States will likely remain deeply involved in the Middle East for decades.

APPENDIX OF DOCUMENTS

Origins of the Cold War

1. U.S. OFFICIALS CLARIFY THE STRATEGIC IMPORTANCE OF IRAN, 1946

Source: U.S. Department of State, *Foreign Relations of the United States, 1946* (Washington: Government Printing Office, 1969), 7: 528-32.

From the beginning of the Cold War, U.S. officials considered the Middle East vital to the security of the United States. This calculation was based in part on the petroleum resources and military base facilities across the region, which American strategists desired to preserve for the Western world and to deny to the Soviet Union in times of peace or war. The following document, a memorandum by the State-War-Navy Coordinating Committee that excerpts a report by the Joint Chiefs of Staff, reveals the strategic importance that the Pentagon assigned to Iran.

TOP SECRET
SWN—4818   Washington, 12 October 1946

. . . 1. The Joint Chiefs of Staff consider that as a source of supply (oil) Iran is an area of major strategic interest to the United States. From the standpoint of defensive purposes the area offers opportunities to conduct delaying operations and/or operations to protect United States-controlled oil resources in Saudi Arabia. In order to continue any military capability for preventing a Soviet attack overrunning the whole Middle East including the Suez-Cairo Area, in the first rush, it is essential that there be maintained the maximum cushion of distance and difficult terrain features in the path of possible Soviet advances launched from the

Caucasus-Caspian area. Otherwise the entire Middle East might be over-run before sufficient defensive forces could be interposed. As to counter-offensive operations, the proximity of important Soviet industries, makes the importance of holding the Eastern Mediterranean-Middle Eastern area obvious. This is one of the few favorable areas for counteroffensive action. Quite aside from military counteroffensive action in the area, the oil resources of Iran and the Near and Middle East are very important and may be vital to decisive counteroffensive action from any area.

2. The Joint Chiefs of Staff consider that United States strategic interest in Iran is closely related to United States strategic interest in the Near and Middle East area as a whole as follows:

> . . . Loss of the Iraq and Saudi Arabia sources to the United States and her allies would mean that in case of war they would fight an oil-starved war. Conversely, de-nial of these sources to the USSR would force her to fight an oil-starved war. However, due to Russia's geo-graphic position, great land mass, and superior manpower potential, any lack of oil limiting air action by the United States and her allies or hampering their transportation ability or their war production would be of great advan-tage to the USSR. It is therefore to the strategic interest of the United States to keep Soviet influence and Soviet armed forces removed as far as possible from oil re-sources in Iran, Iraq, and the Near and Middle East . . .

2. SECRETARY OF STATE GEORGE MARSHALL UNDERSCORES THE STRATEGIC IMPORTANCE OF THE EASTERN MEDITERRANEAN, 1947

Source: U.S., Department of State, *Foreign Relations of the United States, 1947* (Washington: Government Printing Office, 1972), 5: 60–62.

Under the Truman Doctrine of 1947, the United States spent $400 million to help Greece suppress a communist insurrection and to bolster Turkey against Soviet pressures for concessions. To persuade Congress to allocate such funds, Secretary of State George C. Marshall, in a February 27, 1947, statement to members of Congress that is excerpted below, painted a grim picture of the *political conditions in the Eastern Mediterranean. President Harry S. Truman echoed Marshall's argument in an address to Congress on March 12 that launched the Truman Doctrine.*

A crisis of the utmost importance and urgency has arisen in Greece and to some extent in Turkey. This crisis has a direct and immediate relation to the security of the United States.

For the past ten days our representatives in Greece . . . have been warning us that economic collapse is imminent, that the morale of the Greek Army, already low, will be deeply shaken and that the integrity and independence of the country itself is threatened. What the Greek Government needs urgently are funds to meet the needs of the military and civilian population in foreign purchases and certain amounts of light military equipment in order to suppress the bandit groups, which under Communist leadership, are threatening the Government and the tranquility of the country. . . .

Our interest in Greece is by no means restricted to humanitarian or friendly impulses. If Greece should dissolve into civil war it is altogether probable that it would emerge as a communist state under Soviet control. Turkey would be surrounded and the Turkish situation, to which I shall refer in a moment, would in turn become still more critical. Soviet domination might thus extend over the entire Middle East to the borders of India. The effect of this upon Hungary, Austria, Italy and France cannot be overestimated. It is not alarmist to say that we are faced with the first crisis of a series which might extend Soviet domination to Europe, the Middle East and Asia.

There is no other power than the United States which can act to avert this crisis. . . .

The problem in Turkey is slightly different. The Russians, by conducting a war of nerves, have kept the entire Turkish Army mobilized with the resulting drain upon the economy of that country which it cannot long support under its present antiquated economic structure. It needs two things, financial assistance to increase its productiveness and some help to the end that its military forces may be rendered equally effective with fewer men. Here again only the United States can render effective help in view of the situation of Great Britain. Our military authorities are united in the view that the maintenance of the integrity of Turkey is essential to the entire independent structure of the eastern Mediterranean and the Middle East. . . .

Recognition of Israel

3. PRESIDENT HARRY TRUMAN AND ADVISERS DEBATE WHETHER TO RECOGNIZE THE JEWISH STATE, 1948

Source: U.S., Department of State, *Foreign Relations of the United States, 1948* (Washington: Government Printing Office, 1976), 5:972–76.

In the spring of 1948, Jewish leaders in Mandatory Palestine prepared to declare the independence of the State of Israel in the territory they controlled upon the withdrawal of British forces on May 15. American officials debated the pros and cons of recognizing the new state. After intensive discussions in Washington, like the one recounted below in a memorandum written by Secretary of State George C. Marshall, President Harry S. Truman decided to recognize Israel only minutes after its declaration of independence on May 15.

TOP SECRET

May 12, 1948

. . . The President said that he had called the meeting because he was seriously concerned as to what might happen in Palestine after May 15.

[Undersecretary of State] Mr. [Robert] Lovett gave a lengthy exposition of recent events bearing on the Palestine problem. . . .

I intervened at this juncture to recall what I had told Mr. [Moshe] Shertok [political representative of the Jewish Agency for Palestine] on May 8. I had stressed that it was extremely dangerous to base long-range policy on temporary military success. There was no doubt but that the Jewish army had gained such temporary success but there was no assurance whatever that in the long-range the tide might not turn against them. I told Mr. Shertok that they were taking a gamble. If the tide did turn adversely and they came running to us for help they should be placed clearly on notice now that there was no warrant to expect help from the United States, which had warned them of the grave risk which they were running. . . .

The President then invited [White House Special Counsel] Mr. Clark Clifford to make a statement. Mr. Clifford said that he had three main suggestions to offer, based upon consultation with colleagues of the White House staff.

Mr. Clifford said that he objected to the first article of our draft resolution which would place the General Assembly on record as reaffirming support of the efforts of the Security Council to secure a truce in Palestine. He said this reference was unrealistic since there had been no truce and probably would not be one. . . . Instead, the actual partition of Palestine had taken place "without the use of outside force".

Mr. Clifford's second point was strongly to urge the President to give prompt recognition to the Jewish State after the termination of the mandate on May 15. He said such a move should be taken quickly before the Soviet Union recognized the Jewish State. It would have distinct value in restoring the President's position for support of the partition of Palestine.

Mr. Clifford's third point was that the President, at his press conference on the following day, May 13, should make a statement of his intention to recognize the Jewish State, once the provision for democratic government outlined in the resolution of November 29, had been complied with, which he assumed would be the case. . . .

The rebuttal was made by Mr. Lovett. With regard to Mr. Clifford's reference to the article on truce, Mr. Lovett pointed out that the Security Council was still seized of this matter under its resolutions of April 1, April 17 and April 23. The United States in fact was a member of the Security Council's Truce Commission on Palestine. Surely the United States could not by its unilateral act get the Security Council to drop this matter and it would be most unbecoming, in light of our activities to secure a truce.

On the question of premature recognition, Mr. Lovett said that it would be highly injurious to the United Nations to announce the recognition of the Jewish State even before it had come into existence and while the General Assembly, which had been called into special session at the request of the United States, was still considering the question of the future government of Palestine. Furthermore, said Mr. Lovett, such a move would be injurious to the prestige of the President. It was a very transparent attempt to win the Jewish vote but, in Mr. Lovett's opinion, it would lose more votes than it would gain. Finally, to recognize the Jewish State prematurely would be buying a pig in a poke. How did we know what kind of Jewish State would be set up? At this stage Mr. Lovett read excerpts from a file of intelligence telegrams and reports regarding Soviet activity in sending Jews and Communist agents from Black Sea areas to Palestine.

Mr. Lovett also failed to see any particular urgency in the United States rushing to recognize the Jewish State prior to possible Soviet recognition.

I remarked to the President that, speaking objectively, I could not help but think that the suggestions made by Mr. Clifford were wrong. I thought that to adopt these suggestions would have precisely the opposite effect from that intended by Mr. Clifford. The transparent dodge to win a few votes would not in fact achieve this purpose. The great dignity of the office of the President would be seriously diminished. The counsel offered by Mr. Clifford was based on domestic political considerations, while the problem which confronted us was international. I said bluntly that if the President were to follow Mr. Clifford's advice and if in the elections I were to vote, I would vote against the President.

Mr. Lovett and I told the President that naturally after May 16 we would take another look at the situation in Palestine in light of the facts as they existed. Clearly the question of recognition would have to be gone into very carefully. A paper presenting the legal aspects of the problem had been prepared in the Department and would be promptly sent to Mr. Clifford.

The President initialed the draft resolution and the underlying position paper of May 11, and terminated the interview by saying that he was fully aware of the difficulties and dangers in the situation, to say nothing of the political risks involved which he, himself, would run.

Iranian Nationalism

4. AMBASSADOR LOY HENDERSON ASSESSES THE U.S. COUP IN IRAN, 1953

Source: U.S., Department of State, *Foreign Relations of the United States, 1952–1954* (Washington: Government Printing Office, 1989): 10: 759–60.

In August 1953, the Shah of Iran returned to power after the fall of Mohammed Mossadegh, a revolutionary nationalist challenger who had earlier gained the office of prime minister and forced the Shah to flee the country. Ample evidence confirms that American and British intelligence officers helped organize the coup against Mossadegh, conducted by pro-Shah military soldiers under the command of General Fazlollah Zahedi. The following document, part of a telegram sent by Ambassador to Iran Loy Henderson to the State Department, suggests that certain U.S. officials recognized the risk that American involvement in the coup might turn Iranian nationalism against the United States.

SECRET   NIACT [Night action]   TEHRAN, August 21, 1953

1. Unfortunately impression becoming rather widespread that in some way or other this Embassy or at least US Government has contributed with funds and technical assistance to over[throw] Mosadeq and establish Zahedi Government. Iranians unable believe any important political development can take place in country without foreigners being involved. Intensive propaganda in Tudeh [Iranian communist party] newspapers prior to their disappearance and over Soviet Radio that US Embassy working for Shah and Zahedi against Mosadeq has helped create this impression. Public, therefore, in general, inclined interpret various incidents or remarks as evidence American intervention. . . . Remarks by associates of Zahedi to effect Iran deeply indebted to Americans for success their efforts also being given deeper meaning than intended. . . .

2. For moment at least more praise than criticism heard from those who believe US involved in shift of government. Nevertheless we doing utmost discreetly to remove this impression because (a) it not in US interest over long run to be given credit for internal political developments in Iran even if those developments might be to Iran's advantage; (b) Zahedi's Government will be somewhat handicapped

if impression continues that it creature foreigners; (c) Zahedi's Government like all governments of Iran eventually will become unpopular and at that time US might be blamed for its existence. We do not believe, however, that it would serve any good purpose for Embassy to make formal denials.

3. . . . It might be useful, however, if spokesman for Department could find suitable occasion stress in factual way spontaneity of movement in Iran in favor of new Government. . . . We sincerely hope means can be found either through US Government channels or through private American news dissemination channels for American and world publics to understand that victory of Shah was result [of the] will [of the] Iranian people. Such comments . . . could be immediately useful here. . . .

5. IMAM KHOMEINI VOCALIZES IRANIAN NATIONALISM, 1964

Source: *Islamic Republic of Iran Broadcasting.* http://www.irib.ir/worldservice/imam/speech/16.htm (last accessed on September 13, 2004).

Returned to power in 1953, the Shah of Iran soon faced a resistance movement organized by a network of religious clerics. By the early 1960s, Imam Ruhollah Khomeini emerged as a leading voice of dissent against the Shah's secularism, his authoritarianism, his reliance on the United States for protection, and his granting to U.S. nationals certain privileges including legal immunity from Iranian law. Khomeini's "Speech Number Sixteen" of October 26, 1964, reprinted below, gave voice to his anti-Shah and anti-American fervor. The Shah attempted to repress such dissent, but the clerics under Khomeini's leadership ultimately prevailed by overthrowing him in 1979.

In the name of God, the Compassionate, the Merciful
We are from God and to Him is our return.
I cannot express the sorrow I feel in my heart. My heart is heavy. Since the day I heard of the latest developments affecting Iran, I have barely slept. I am profoundly disturbed. With sorrowful heart, I count the days until death shall come and deliver me. . . .

Our honour has been trampled underfoot; the dignity of Iran has been destroyed. The dignity of the Iranian army has been trampled underfoot!

They have taken a law to the Parliament according to which . . . all American military advisers, together with their families, technical and administrative officials, and servants—in short, anyone in any way connected to them—are to enjoy legal immunity with respect to any crime they may commit in Iran! If some American's servant, some American's cook, assassinates your *marja'-i taqlid* [literally, "model of imitation," denoting one of a class of advanced religious scholars in Shia Islam] in the middle of the bazaar, or runs over him, the Iranian police do not have the right to apprehend him! Iranian courts do not have the right to judge him! The dossier must be sent to America so that our masters there can decide what is to be done!

. . . The government shamelessly defended this scandalous measure. They have reduced the Iranian people to a level lower than that of an American dog. If someone runs over a dog belonging to an American, he will be prosecuted. Even if the Shah himself were to run over a dog belonging to an American, he would be prosecuted. But if an American cook runs over the Shah, or the *marja'* of Iran, or the highest official, no one will have the right to object.

Why?

Because they wanted a loan from America and America demanded this in return! This is apparently the case. A few days after this measure was approved, they requested a $200 million loan from America and America agreed to the request. It was stipulated that the sum of $200 million would be paid to the Iranian government over a period of five years, and that $300 million would be paid back to America over a period of ten years. Do you realise what this means? In return for this loan, America is to receive $100 million—or 800 million tumans—in interest! But in addition to this, Iran has sold itself to obtain these dollars! The government has sold our independence, reduced us to the level of a colony, and made the Muslim nation of Iran appear more lowly than savages in the eyes of the world! They have done this for the sake of a $200 million dollar loan for which they have to pay back $300 [million] dollars! . . .

Other countries imagine that it is the Iranian nation that has abased itself in this way. They do not know that it is the Iranian government, the Iranian Parliament—this Parliament which has nothing to do with the Iranian people. This is a Parliament elected at bayonet point, what does such a Parliament have to do with the people[?] The Iranian nation did not elect these deputies. Many of the high-ranking *'ulama* [religious scholars] and *maraji'* ordered a boycott of the elections, and the people obeyed them and did not vote. But then came the power of the bayonet, and these deputies were seated in the Parliament. . . .

O presidents and kings of the Muslim peoples! O Shah of Iran! Look at yourselves, look at us. Are we to be trampled underfoot by the boots of the Americans simply because we are a weak nation? Because we have no dollars? America is worse than Britain, Britain is worse than America and the Soviet Union is worse than both of them. Each one is worse than the other, each one is more abominable than the other. But today we are concerned with this malicious entity which is America. Let the American President know that in the eyes of the Iranian nation, he is the most repulsive member of the human race today because of the injustice he has imposed on our Muslim nation. Today, the Qur'an has become his enemy, the Iranian nation has become his enemy. Let the American government know that its name has been ruined and disgraced in Iran.

. . . All our troubles today are caused by this America. All our troubles today are caused by this Israel. Israel itself derives from America. These deputies and ministers derive from America. They have all been appointed by America. If they were not, then why don't they stand up and protest? . . .

The 'ulama must enlighten the people, and they in turn must raise their voices in protest to the Parliament and the government and ask, "Why did you do this? Why have you sold us? Are we your slaves that you sell us? We did not elect you to be our representatives, and even had we done so, you would forfeit your posts now on account of this act of treachery."

This is high treason! O God, they have committed treason against this country. O God, this government has committed treason against this country, against Islam, against the Qur'an. All the members of both houses who gave their agreement to this affair are traitors. . . .

We do not recognise this as a law. We do not recognise this Parliament as a true Parliament. We do not recognise this government as a true government. They are traitors, traitors to the people of Iran!

O God, remedy the affairs of the Muslims.

O God, bestow majesty on this sacred religion of Islam!

O God, destroy those individuals who are traitors to this land, who are traitors to Islam and to the Qur'an.

Aftermath of the 1967 Arab-Israeli War

6. PRESIDENT LYNDON JOHNSON'S ADMINISTRATION RECOGNIZES LIMITED U.S. OPTIONS, 1967

Source: U.S., Department of State, *Foreign Relations of the United States, 1964–1968* (Washington: Government Printing Office, 2004), 19:739–40.

The Six Day War of June 5–10, 1967 dramatically changed the political dynamics of the Arab-Israeli conflict. While achieving a stunning military victory against three adversaries, Israel occupied the West Bank (at the expense of Jordan), the Golan Heights (captured from Syria), and the Gaza Strip and the Sinai Peninsula (taken from Egypt). In the immediate aftermath of war, negotiations about the return of these occupied territories deadlocked as Israel declared that it would relent only as part of a comprehensive peace treaty, which the Arab powers refused to consider. On July 31, Special Consultant McGeorge Bundy alerted President Lyndon B. Johnson, in the memorandum excerpted below, that the mounting stalemate sharply limited American diplomatic options.

. . . 1. The Israeli position appears to be hardening as the Arabs still resist all direct negotiations. The Israelis have great confidence in their short-run political and military superiority. I think the evidence grows that they plan to keep not only all of Jerusalem but the Gaza Strip and the West Bank, too.

2. Unless the Arabs make a drastic change in their bargaining position, we have no practical way of opposing this Israeli position. We can insist on the principle of "withdrawal from danger" but as a practical matter the Israelis will continue to confront the Arabs—and us—with small accomplished facts (today they put in their currency in much of the occupied territory), and we will find it unwise to take any practical action in reply. When the Israelis come to us for major military supplies, we shall need to have serious talks, but I begin to think that our bargaining power even on this issue is not overwhelming. I think we can trade hard on such matters as nuclear policy and perhaps even get them to back off from the French missiles they have had on order, but as long as the Arabs are adamant, I doubt if we can or should make the Israeli view of Jerusalem or the West Bank into a federal case. We can't tell the Israelis to give things away to people who won't even bargain with them. We may well be heading toward a de facto settlement on the present cease-fire lines. . . .

We want it to be [Egyptian president Gamal Abdel] Nasser's fault, not ours, if the Israelis decide to stay where they are. . . .

In sum, I think the current short-run position should be one of quiet watchful waiting. . . .

7. ARAB GOVERNMENTS RESOLVE TO RESIST ISRAELI OCCUPATION, 1967

Source: Israel, Ministry of Foreign Affairs, http://www.mfa.gov.il/MFA/ Peace%20Process/Guide%20to%20the%20Peace%20Process/ The%20Khartoum%20Resolutions (last accessed March 10, 2005).

Arab statesmen gathered in Khartoum, Sudan, in August-September 1967 to formulate a pan-Arab front to contest Israel's territorial gains in the Six Day War. Deeply embittered by the military defeat suffered in June, these leaders adopted a resolution, printed below, indicating an uncompromising approach.

1 . The conference has affirmed the unity of Arab ranks, the unity of joint action and the need for coordination and for the elimination of all differences. The Kings, Presidents and representatives of the other Arab Heads of State at the conference have affirmed their countries' stand by and implementation of the Arab Solidarity Charter which was signed at the third Arab summit conference in Casablanca.

2. The conference has agreed on the need to consolidate all efforts to eliminate the effects of the aggression on the basis that the occupied lands are Arab lands and that the burden of regaining these lands falls on all the Arab States.

3. The Arab Heads of State have agreed to unite their political efforts at the international and diplomatic level to eliminate the effects of the aggression and to ensure the withdrawal of the aggressive Israeli forces from the Arab lands which have been occupied since the aggression of June 5. This will be done within the framework of the main principles by which the Arab States abide, namely, no peace with Israel, no recognition of Israel, no negotiations with it, and insistence on the rights of the Palestinian people in their own country.

4. The conference of Arab Ministers of Finance, Economy and Oil recommended that suspension of oil pumping be used as a weapon in the battle. However, after thoroughly studying the matter, the summit

conference has come to the conclusion that the oil pumping can itself be used as a positive weapon, since oil is an Arab resource which can be used to strengthen the economy of the Arab States directly affected by the aggression, so that these States will be able to stand firm in the battle. . . .

6. The participants have agreed on the need to adopt the necessary measures to strengthen military preparation to face all eventualities.

7. The conference has decided to expedite the elimination of foreign bases in the Arab States.

8. ISRAEL DETERMINED TO EXTEND OCCUPATION OF ARAB LANDS, 1967

Source: U.S., Department of State, *Foreign Relations of the United States, 1964–1968* (Washington: Government Printing Office, 2004), 19:1043–45.

In the face of Arab defiance, Israeli leaders hardened their position on the occupied territories during the summer and autumn of 1967. In a memorandum of November 17, printed below, Assistant Secretary of State Lucius D. Battle analyzed the shift in the Israeli perspective and noted an Israeli-American divergence on the territorial issue.

The attached telegram . . . , reporting the text of a resolution adopted by the Israeli Cabinet November 8, is the latest and presumably most authoritative statement of Israel's peace aims. Its particular significance lies in the explicit exclusion, in a formal GOI [Government of Israel] policy statement not intended for public consumption, of any settlement not arrived at through "direct negotiations" and formalized by "peace treaties."

Comparison of this Israeli position with earlier Israeli peace settlement objectives shows the evolution of Israel's position since the war. Specifically, the November 8 Israeli Cabinet resolution reflects a marked shift from Israel's earlier emphasis on the need for security from attack and acceptance by its neighbors to a pre-occupation with legalisms and an emphasis on the modalities of achieving such security and acceptance. In addition, freedom of passage for Israeli ships through the Suez Canal, which was not raised by the Israelis as a peace aim until some time after the end of the war, is prominently mentioned ahead of free passage through the Straits of Tiran, which was the immediate casus belli. Furthermore, paragraph 5 of the Israeli Cabinet resolution would appear to defer consideration of even a start toward solution of the refugee problem until after peace treaties are concluded.

The November 8 Israeli Cabinet resolution is in effect a prescription for "instant peace" entirely on Israel's terms. In our judgment it is patently unrealistic and a far cry from the goal recently described to [Israeli] Ambassador [Avraham] Harman by [Under Secretary of State] Gene Rostow. As Gene so eloquently put it, that goal as we see it is to devise arrangements binding on and accepted by the parties which, while safeguarding Israel's security, can create conditions that will transform the Middle Eastern environment over time into one in which true peace eventually becomes possible.

The effect of the latest Israeli formulation is two-fold. First, it will further limit [Israeli] Foreign Minister [Abba] Eban's flexibility in the UN context. Second, it gives the GOI's most formal stamp of approval . . . to a legally unassailable rationale for remaining in the occupied territories indefinitely. . . .

Israel's increasingly rigid emphasis on the modalities of a peace settlement is paralleled by expanding emphasis on the territorial elements of a settlement. . . . It has become clear over the past months that Israel envisages its future boundaries as including not only the entire city of Jerusalem but also a good slice of the Syrian Golan Heights (which lie outside Mandated Palestine) and the entire Gaza Strip (whose half million Arab Palestinian inhabitants can by no means be assumed to prefer a future under Israeli rule). In addition, there are strong emotional and historical pressures for Israeli retention of the West Bank or at least substantial portions thereof, even though the official GOI position remains that border adjustments in that area will be based only on security considerations (which implies that they would be minor). . . .

While the precise nature of Israel's minimum territorial demands remains unclear . . . , there is no doubt that Israel has come a long way from its position in June. On June 8, for example, Foreign Minister Eban told Ambassador [Arthur] Goldberg that Israel was not seeking territorial aggrandizement and had no colonial aspirations. On June 13, in a speech to military units in Sinai, Prime Minister [Levi] Eshkol said Israel had no intention of acquiring new territory as a result of the war.

We must, I think, assume that the Israeli Cabinet resolution of November 8 is not simply a bargaining position. Viewed in the context of growing Israeli territorial appetites, I find that resolution a profoundly

disturbing development. If Israel insists on pursuing the "direct negotiations" and "peace treaties" course to the exclusion of all others, then I
fear we do indeed face the prospect of permanent Israeli occupation of
the Arab territories now held.

There is, it seems to me, a growing gap between what we and the
Israelis mean when we speak of territorial "adjustments." . . . The en-
closed Israeli Cabinet resolution would appear to put Israel and us on
divergent courses.

9. UN SECURITY COUNCIL ADOPTS RESOLUTION 242 TO SETTLE OCCUPATION CONTROVERSY, 1967

Source: UN Security Council, http://www.un.org/Docs/sc/unsc_resolutions.
html (last accessed September 13, 2004).

*After a long debate on the Arab-Israeli situation, the UN Security Council unani-
mously passed Resolution 242 on November 22, 1967. Although intended to facilitate peacemaking, the resolution included two crucial ambiguities, providing that
Israel would withdraw from "territories" rather than "the territories" and failing to
specify whether Israeli withdrawal should precede or follow Arab recognition. These
ambiguities sharply limited the resolution's viability as a foundation for settlement.*

The Security Council,

Expressing its continuing concern with the grave situation in the
Middle East,

Emphasizing the inadmissibility of the acquisition of territory by
war and the need to work for a just and lasting peace in which every state
in the area can live in security,

Emphasizing further that all member states in their acceptance of
the Charter of the United Nations have undertaken a commitment to act
in accordance with Article 2 of the Charter,

1. *Affirms* that the fulfillment of Charter principles requires the
establishment of a just and lasting peace in the Middle East which should
include the application of both the following principles:

(i) Withdrawal of Israeli armed forces from territories of recent
conflict.

(ii) Termination of all claims or states of belligerency and respect for and acknowledgement of the sovereignty, territorial integrity and political independence of every state in the area and their right to live in peace within secure and recognized boundaries free from threats or acts of force.

2. *Affirms* further the necessity

(i) For guaranteeing freedom of navigation through international waterways in the area;

(ii) For achieving a just settlement of the refugee problem;

(iii) For guaranteeing the territorial inviolability and political independence of every state in the area through measures including the establishment of demilitarized zones. . . .

10. PALESTINIAN CHARTER CALLS FOR DESTRUCTION OF ISRAEL, 1968

Source: Palestine National Authority, http://www.pna.gov.ps/Government/gov/plo_charter.asp (last accessed March 5, 2005).

During the 1960s, Arab Palestinian nationalists became politically and militarily active, establishing the Palestine Liberation Organization in 1964 with the expressed purpose of destroying Israel. In the aftermath of the 1967 war, Palestinian leaders gradually secured recognition by Arab states as the legitimate representatives of the stateless Palestinian people. In July 1968, the Palestine National Council approved a National Charter, excerpted below, that called for the destruction of the State of Israel and the establishment of a State of Palestine through armed resistance.

Article 1: Palestine is the homeland of the Arab Palestinian people; it is an indivisible part of the Arab homeland, and the Palestinian people are an integral part of the Arab nation.

Article 2: Palestine, with the boundaries it had during the British Mandate, is an indivisible territorial unit.

Article 3: The Palestinian Arab people possess the legal right to their homeland and have the right to determine their destiny after achieving the liberation of their country in accordance with their wishes and entirely of their own accord and will.

Article 4: The Palestinian identity is a genuine, essential, and inherent characteristic; it is transmitted from parents to children. The Zionist occupation and the dispersal of the Palestinian Arab people, through the disasters which befell them, do not make them lose their Palestinian identity and their membership in the Palestinian community, nor do they negate them.

Article 5: The Palestinians are those Arab nationals who, until 1947, normally resided in Palestine regardless of whether they were evicted from it or have stayed there. . . .

Article 7: That there is a Palestinian community and that it has material, spiritual, and historical connection with Palestine are indisputable facts. It is a national duty to bring up individual Palestinians in an Arab revolutionary manner. All means of information and education must be adopted in order to acquaint the Palestinian with his country in the most profound manner, both spiritual and material, that is possible. He must be prepared for the armed struggle and ready to sacrifice his wealth and his life in order to win back his homeland and bring about its liberation. . . .

Article 9: Armed struggle is the only way to liberate Palestine. Thus it is the overall strategy, not merely a tactical phase. The Palestinian Arab people assert their absolute determination and firm resolution to continue their armed struggle and to work for an armed popular revolution for the liberation of their country and their return to it. They also assert their right to normal life in Palestine and to exercise their right to self-determination and sovereignty over it.

Article 10: Commando action constitutes the nucleus of the Palestinian popular liberation war. . . .

Article 15: . . . [T]he Arab nation must mobilize all its military, human, moral, and spiritual capabilities to participate actively with the Palestinian people in the liberation of Palestine. . . .

Article 19: The partition of Palestine in 1947 and the establishment of the state of Israel are entirely illegal, regardless of the passage of time, because they were contrary to the will of the Palestinian people and to their natural right in their homeland, and inconsistent with the principles embodied in the Charter of the United Nations; particularly the right to self-determination. . . .

Article 21: The Arab Palestinian people, expressing themselves by the armed Palestinian revolution, reject all solutions which are substitutes for the total liberation of Palestine and reject all proposals aiming at the liquidation of the Palestinian problem, or its internationalization.

Article 22: Zionism is a political movement organically associated with international imperialism and antagonistic to all action for liberation and to progressive movements in the world. It is racist and fanatic in its nature, aggressive, expansionist, and colonial in its aims, and fascist in its methods. Israel is the instrument of the Zionist movement, and geographical base for world imperialism placed strategically in the midst of the Arab homeland to combat the hopes of the Arab nation for liberation, unity, and progress. Israel is a constant source of threat vis-a-vis peace in the Middle East and the whole world. . . . [T]he liberation of Palestine will destroy the Zionist and imperialist presence and will contribute to the establishment of peace in the Middle East. . . .

The Strategic Importance of the Middle East in the 1970s–1980s

11. NATIONAL SECURITY ADVISER HENRY KISSINGER IDENTIFIES U.S. INTERESTS IN THE MIDDLE EAST, 1969

Source: U.S., Department of State, *Foreign Relations of the United States, 1969–1972* (Washington: Government Printing Office, 2003), 1:110–21.

In a broad survey of the political situation in the Middle East in October 1969, excerpted below, National Security Adviser Henry Kissinger cautioned President Richard Nixon that the Soviet Union had recently gained influence in the region by fomenting revolutionary movements that the United States found it difficult to resist.

. . . 1. As regards the Mid East, it is customary to think, to the exclusion of almost any other consideration, of the Arab/Israeli conflict. No doubt, the present Administration is engaged in a superhuman effort to make the two sides see reason and prevent a "fourth round," but in view of earlier US performances, it must be decidedly difficult for Arabs or Israelis to rely on anything but their own brute strength. A US role as an effective guarantor of any future compromise solution is simply not credible, because of our obvious past and present reluctance (with the one exception of Lebanon in 1958) to back up diplomatic agreements or political friendships with a US military presence.

2. Cynics used to believe that, because of the Jewish vote in the US, Washington would necessarily have to intervene in Israel's favor in any "real emergency." Actually, the historical record proves otherwise. In 1956, we turned against our French and British allies and our Israeli protégés and impelled the latter to evacuate the Sinai peninsula; while in 1967, when Nasser threatened war with remarkable frankness, we tried in every way to dissuade Tel Aviv from reacting to the Egyptian blockade of the Straits of Tiran by non-peaceful means. Israel then started military action on her own, strictly against our wish and will, and won so quickly and overwhelmingly that our readiness to come to its rescue no longer had to be tested. I do not, as you know, consider it an a priori US task and mission to protect Israel, but it so happens that in the eyes of the world that small Western enclave in a non-Western environment is considered our "client." . . .

3. Those Arab regimes, on the other hand, which have struggled to stay relatively pro-West can be even less trustful as regards our active help than the Israelis, since there is no Arab constituency in this country.

4. We have in the past been unable to protect the pro-US royal regime in Iraq. We did not help Saudi Arabia against the Nasser-supported Republican Yemen. We tolerated the establishment of a radically leftist, pro-Peking rather than pro-Moscow, Republic of South Yemen, when the British withdrew from Aden and the Aden Protectorates. We showed no interest, when the moderate government in the Sudan was overthrown by revolutionary radicals; and we obviously will do nothing, if after complete withdrawal of the British from the Persian Gulf area, the present rulers of the various Sheikdoms there should be thrown out by wild-eyed Arab nationalists with Marxist leanings. From the point of view of the moderate Arab leaders it must appear that friendship with the US does not offer protection and does not pay. . . .

5. Under the circumstances, even those Arabs who used to maintain a degree of friendship with the US cannot possibly place great trust in Washington's declarations of amity. It may be a paradox, but must nevertheless be understood, that, precisely because we have shown ourselves so peaceful and patient, so obviously unwilling to intervene with force anywhere or against anyone, it will now be virtually impossible for either Arab or Jew to see in the United States the great power that would actually protect one side against the other and maintain any agreed upon peaceful order by forceful means, should that prove necessary. . . .

6. It has widely been assumed that the USSR would restrain the Arabs, as we might restrain the Israelis, out of a fear of a direct US/USSR confrontation. It should be observed, however, that the . . . more the Soviets—looking at US actions and inactions around the world—become convinced that the US remains unbendingly resolved to negotiate rather than to confront, the smaller their incentive to restrain their clients; i.e., in the Mid East case, the Arabs.

12. PRESIDENT RICHARD NIXON EXPRESSES CONCERN WITH SOVIET INTRIGUE, 1970

Source: U.S., Department of State, http://www.state.gov/r/pa/ho/frus/nixon/i/20703.htm (last accessed February 23, 2005).

In a meeting with Republican leaders of Congress on February 17, 1970, President Richard M. Nixon expressed concern with Soviet expansion into the Middle East and suggested that he would support Israel on security rather than domestic political grounds. Nixon's remarks were recorded in a memorandum by Special Assistant Patrick Buchanan, excerpted below.

. . . Moving on to the Middle East, he [Nixon] said that many American politicians took it that it should be the basis of American foreign policy the simple question of whether or not Israel is to survive. That cannot be the basis of American foreign policy, he said. The interest of the US policy in the Middle East is designed to advance the United States interests primarily. Those interests involve vital stakes in the Mediterranean and Iran; they involve oil interests in the Arab world; they also are coincidental with the survival of Israel as a state. For one hard reason the Israelis are currently the strongest buffer against Soviet expansion in the entire region.

The President asked what the Soviet objectives in the Middle East were, and answered his own question. They want control of the Middle East; they want the oil it contains; they want a land bridge to Africa. Looking over the Middle East, the President said Tunis[ia] is too weak to matter. Morocco is distant, out on the Atlantic Coast, and you know what happened in Libya. Algeria, the UAR, Syria, Iraq, the Sudan are all either under great Soviet pressure or Soviet influence at this time. As for Spain, it has been relegated to outer darkness until [Francisco] Franco's death. Italy is paying now for the opening to the left of a few years back, which the President had opposed. We intend to see to it that Israel is not overrun for the reason that Israel is the current most effective stopper to the Mideast power of the Soviet Union. Our policy, said the President, will not be pleasing to some of our political friends. But it is not in Israel's interest for American policy to be one sided. Israel ought to make a deal when it is strong enough to whip anyone in the Middle East and will be strong enough for the next five years. The President said he indicated to Golda Meir when she was in the country that he had only gotten 8% of the Jewish vote and he was supporting the Israelis not for political reasons for the first time in recent history. He was supporting Israel because it was in the interest of the United States to do so. . . .

13. THE UNITED STATES AND ISRAEL FORM
A STRATEGIC PARTNERSHIP, 1981

Source: Israel, Ministry of Foreign Affairs, http://www.mfa.gov.il/mfa/
foreign+relations/israels+foreign+relations+since+1947/1981-1982/
77+memorandum+of+understanding+between+the+governm.htm (last accessed March 2, 2005).

President Ronald Reagan embraced Nixon's view of Israel as a strategic asset to the
United States. On November 30, 1981, the United States and Israel reached a
memorandum of understanding on strategic cooperation, which appears in part below.

PREAMBLE

This memorandum of understanding reaffirms the common
bonds of friendship between the United States and Israel and builds on
the mutual security relationship that exists between the two nations. The
parties recognize the need to enhance strategic cooperation to deter all
threats from the Soviet Union to the region. Noting the longstanding and
fruitful cooperation for mutual security that has developed between the
two countries, the parties have decided to establish a framework for continued consultation and cooperation to enhance their national security by
deterring such threats to the whole region.

The parties have reached the following agreements in order to
achieve the above aims.

ARTICLE I

United States-Israel strategic cooperation . . . is designed against
the threat to peace and security of the region caused by the Soviet Union
or Soviet-controlled forces from outside the region introduced into the
region. It has the following broad purposes:

A. To enable the parties to act cooperatively and in a timely manner to deal with the above-mentioned threat.

B. To provide each other with military assistance for operations
of their forces in the area that may be required to cope with this threat.

C. The strategic cooperation between the parties is not directed
at any state or group of states within the region. It is intended solely for
defensive purposes against the above-mentioned threat.

ARTICLE II

1. The fields in which strategic cooperation will be carried out to prevent the above-mentioned threat from endangering the security of the region include:

A. Military cooperation between the parties, as may be agreed by the parties.

B. Joint military exercise, including naval and air exercises in the Eastern Mediterranean Sea, as agreed upon by the parties.

C. Cooperation for the establishment and maintenance of joint readiness activities, as agreed upon by the parties.

D. Other areas within the basic scope and purpose of this agreement, as may be jointly agreed. . . .

Peace Process, 1978–

14. EGYPT AND ISRAEL REACH CAMP DAVID ACCORDS, 1978

Source: Jimmy Carter Library, http://www.jimmycarterlibrary.org/documents/
campdavid/accords.phtml (last accessed March 10, 2005).

*In September 1978, President Jimmy Carter nurtured the Egyptian-Israeli peace
process by hosting negotiations between Egyptian President Anwar Sadat and Israeli
Prime Minister Menachem Begin at Camp David. The meetings concluded with the
signing of two accords. One agreement, "A Framework for the Conclusion of a Peace
Treaty between Egypt and Israel" set the stage for the Egyptian-Israeli peace treaty of
March 1979. But the other accord, titled "A Framework for Peace in the Middle
East" and excerpted below, proved insufficient to achieve immediately the larger
goal of a regional peace.*

The Framework for Peace in the Middle East
    Muhammad Anwar al-Sadat, President of the Arab Republic of
Egypt, and Menachem Begin, Prime Minister of Israel, met with Jimmy
Carter, President of the United States of America, at Camp David from
September 5 to September 17, 1978, and have agreed on the following
framework for peace in the Middle East. They invite other parties to the
Arab-Israel conflict to adhere to it.

Preamble
    The search for peace in the Middle East must be guided by the
following:
    The agreed basis for a peaceful settlement of the conflict be-
tween Israel and its neighbors is United Nations Security Council Resolution 242, in all its parts.
    After four wars during 30 years, despite intensive human efforts,
the Middle East, which is the cradle of civilization and the birthplace of
three great religions, does not enjoy the blessings of peace. The people of
the Middle East yearn for peace so that the vast human and natural resources
of the region can be turned to the pursuits of peace and so that this area can
become a model for coexistence and cooperation among nations.
    The historic initiative of President Sadat in visiting Jerusalem
and the reception accorded to him by the parliament, government and
people of Israel, and the reciprocal visit of Prime Minister Begin to

Ismailia, the peace proposals made by both leaders, as well as the warm reception of these missions by the peoples of both countries, have created an unprecedented opportunity for peace which must not be lost if this generation and future generations are to be spared the tragedies of war. . . .

To achieve a relationship of peace . . . , future negotiations between Israel and any neighbor prepared to negotiate peace and security with it are necessary for the purpose of carrying out all the provisions and principles of Resolutions 242 and 338.

Peace requires respect for the sovereignty, territorial integrity and political independence of every state in the area and their right to live in peace within secure and recognized boundaries free from threats or acts of force. Progress toward that goal can accelerate movement toward a new era of reconciliation in the Middle East marked by cooperation in promoting economic development, in maintaining stability and in assuring security.

Security is enhanced by a relationship of peace and by cooperation between nations which enjoy normal relations. In addition, under the terms of peace treaties, the parties can, on the basis of reciprocity, agree to special security arrangements such as demilitarized zones, limited armaments areas, early warning stations, the presence of international forces, liaison, agreed measures for monitoring and other arrangements that they agree are useful.

Framework

Taking these factors into account, the parties are determined to reach a just, comprehensive, and durable settlement of the Middle East conflict through the conclusion of peace treaties based on Security Council resolutions 242 and 338 in all their parts. Their purpose is to achieve peace and good neighborly relations. They recognize that for peace to endure, it must involve all those who have been most deeply affected by the conflict. They therefore agree that this framework, as appropriate, is intended by them to constitute a basis for peace not only between Egypt and Israel, but also between Israel and each of its other neighbors which is prepared to negotiate peace with Israel on this basis. With that objective in mind, they have agreed to proceed as follows:

West Bank and Gaza

Egypt, Israel, Jordan and the representatives of the Palestinian people should participate in negotiations on the resolution of the Palestinian problem in all its aspects. To achieve that objective, negotiations relating to the West Bank and Gaza should proceed in three stages. . . .

Egypt-Israel

1. Egypt-Israel undertake not to resort to the threat or the use of force to settle disputes. Any disputes shall be settled by peaceful means in accordance with the provisions of Article 33 of the U.N. Charter.

2. In order to achieve peace between them, the parties agree to negotiate in good faith with a goal of concluding within three months from the signing of the Framework a peace treaty between them while inviting the other parties to the conflict to proceed simultaneously to negotiate and conclude similar peace treaties with a view [to] . . . achieving a comprehensive peace in the area. . . .

Associated Principles

1. Egypt and Israel state that the principles and provisions described below should apply to peace treaties between Israel and each of its neighbors—Egypt, Jordan, Syria and Lebanon.

2. Signatories shall establish among themselves relationships normal to states at peace with one another. . . . Steps to be taken in this respect include:

a. full recognition;

b. abolishing economic boycotts;

c. guaranteeing that under their jurisdiction the citizens of the other parties shall enjoy the protection of the due process of law.

3. Signatories should explore possibilities for economic development in the context of final peace treaties, with the objective of contributing to the atmosphere of peace, cooperation and friendship which is their common goal. . . .

6. The United Nations Security Council shall be requested to endorse the peace treaties and ensure that their provisions shall not be violated. . . .

15. PALESTINE DECLARES INDEPENDENCE, 1988

Source: Palestinian National Authority, http://www.pna.gov.ps/Government/gov/Declaration_of_Independence.asp (last accessed May 31, 2005).

Outside the Egyptian-Israeli dimension, the peace process launched at Camp David made no progress through the 1980s. Frustrated by the repressive features of Israeli military governance, Palestinians in the occupied territories launched a violent insurrection in December 1987. Under the leadership of Yasser Arafat, the Palestine National Council voted in November 1988 to approve UN Resolutions 242 and 338, to accept the UN partition plan of 1947 and thereby implicitly affirm the legitimacy of Israel, and to issue a Declaration of Independence, excerpted below.

In the name of God, the Compassionate, the Merciful

Palestine, the land of the three monotheistic faiths, is where the Palestinian Arab people was born, on which it grew, developed and excelled. Thus the Palestinian Arab people ensured for itself an everlasting union between itself, its land, and its history.

Resolute throughout that history, the Palestinian Arab people forged its national identity. . . .

Nourished by an unfolding series of civilizations and cultures, inspired by a heritage rich in variety and kind, the Palestinian Arab people added to its stature by consolidating a union between itself and its patrimonial Land. . . .

When in the course of modern times a new order of values was declared with norms and values fair for all, it was the Palestinian Arab people that had been excluded from the destiny of all other peoples by a hostile array of local and foreign powers. . . .

Despite the historical injustice inflicted on the Palestinian Arab people resulting in their dispersion and depriving them of their right to self-determination, following upon U.N. General Assembly Resolution 181 (1947), which partitioned Palestine into two states, one Arab, one Jewish, yet it is this Resolution that still provides those conditions of international legitimacy that ensure the right of the Palestinian Arab people to sovereignty.

By stages, the occupation of Palestine and parts of other Arab territories by Israeli forces, the willed dispossession and expulsion from their ancestral homes of the majority of Palestine's civilian inhabitants, was achieved by organized terror; those Palestinians who remained, as a vestige subjugated in its homeland, were persecuted and forced to endure the destruction of their national life. . . .

In Palestine and on its perimeters, in exile distant and near, the Palestinian Arab people never faltered and never abandoned its conviction in its rights of Return and independence. . . .

The massive national uprising, the intifada, now intensifying in cumulative scope and power on occupied Palestinian territories, as well as the unflinching resistance of the refugee camps outside the homeland, have elevated awareness of the Palestinian truth and right into still higher realms of comprehension and actuality. . . .

Whereas the Palestinian people reaffirms most definitively its inalienable rights in the land of its patrimony:

Now by virtue of natural, historical and legal rights, and the sacrifices of successive generations who gave of themselves in defense of the freedom and independence of their homeland;

In pursuance of Resolutions adopted by Arab Summit Conferences and relying on the authority bestowed by international legitimacy as embodied in the Resolutions of the United Nations Organization since 1947;

And in exercise by the Palestinian Arab people of its rights to self-determination, political independence and sovereignty over its territory,

The Palestine National Council, in the name of God, and in the name of the Palestinian Arab people, hereby proclaims the establishment of the State of Palestine on our Palestinian territory with its capital Jerusalem (Al-Quds Ash-Sharif).

The State of Palestine is the state of Palestinians wherever they may be. The state is for them to enjoy in it their collective national and cultural identity, theirs to pursue in it a complete equality of rights. In it will be safeguarded their political and religious convictions and their human dignity by means of a parliamentary democratic system of governance, itself based on freedom of expression and the freedom to form parties. The rights of minorities will duly be respected by the majority. . . .

The State of Palestine herewith declares that it believes in the settlement of regional and international disputes by peaceful means, in accordance with the U.N. Charter and resolutions. With prejudice to its natural right to defend its territorial integrity and independence, it therefore rejects the threat or use of force, violence and terrorism against its territorial integrity or political independence, as it also rejects their use against territorial integrity of other states.

Therefore, on this day unlike all others, November 15, 1988, as we stand at the threshold of a new dawn, in all honor and modesty we humbly bow to the sacred spirits of our fallen ones, Palestinian and Arab, by the purity of whose sacrifice for the homeland our sky has been illuminated and our Land given life. Our hearts are lifted up and irradiated by the light emanating from the much blessed intifada, from those who have endured and have fought the fight of the camps, of dispersion, of exile, from those who have borne the standard for freedom, our children, our aged, our youth, our prisoners, detainees and wounded, all those ties to our sacred soil are confirmed in camp, village, and town. We render special tribute to that brave Palestinian Woman, guardian of sustenance and Life, keeper of our people's perennial flame. To the souls of our sainted martyrs, the whole of our Palestinian Arab people that our struggle shall be continued until the occupation ends, and the foundation of our sovereignty and independence shall be fortified accordingly.

Therefore, we call upon our great people to rally to the banner of Palestine, to cherish and defend it, so that it may forever be the symbol of our freedom and dignity in that homeland, which is a homeland for the free, now and always.

In the name of God, the Compassionate, the Merciful. . . .

16. ISRAEL AND PLO DECLARE PRINCIPLES FOR PEACEMAKING, 1993

Source: U.S., Embassy in Tel Aviv, http://www.usembassy-israel.org.il/publish/peace/decprinc.htm (last accessed February 24, 2005).

One major factor in rejuvenating the Arab-Israeli peace process in the early 1990s was the negotiation of a Declaration of Principles by Israel and the PLO in 1993. Drafted during secret meetings in Oslo, the Declaration was officially approved on September 13 in a ceremony in Washington presided over by President William J. Clinton. The major parts of the Declaration appear below.

The Government of the State of Israel and the P.L.O. team . . . , representing the Palestinian people, agree that it is time to put an end to decades of confrontation and conflict, recognize their mutual legitimate and political rights, and strive to live in peaceful coexistence and mutual dignity and security and achieve a just, lasting and comprehensive peace settlement and historic reconciliation through the agreed political process. Accordingly, the two sides agree to the following principles:

ARTICLE I: AIM OF THE NEGOTIATIONS

The aim of the Israeli-Palestinian negotiations within the current Middle East peace process is, among other things, to establish a Palestinian Interim Self-Government Authority, the elected Council. . . . for the Palestinian people in the West Bank and the Gaza Strip, for a transitional period not exceeding five years, leading to a permanent settlement based on Security Council Resolutions 242 and 338.

It is understood that the interim arrangements are an integral part of the whole peace process and that the negotiations on the permanent status will lead to the implementation of Security Council Resolutions 242 and 338. . . .

ARTICLE III: ELECTIONS

1. In order that the Palestinian people in the West Bank and Gaza Strip may govern themselves according to democratic principles, direct, free and general political elections will be held for the Council under agreed supervision and international observation. . . .

ARTICLE IV: JURISDICTION

Jurisdiction of the Council will cover West Bank and Gaza Strip territory, except for issues that will be negotiated in the permanent status negotiations. The two sides view the West Bank and the Gaza Strip as a single territorial unit, whose integrity will be preserved during the interim period.

ARTICLE V: TRANSITIONAL PERIOD AND PERMANENT STATUS NEGOTIATIONS

1. The five-year transitional period will begin upon the withdrawal from the Gaza Strip and Jericho area.

2. Permanent status negotiations will commence as soon as possible, but not later than the beginning of the third year of the interim period, between the Government of Israel and the Palestinian people representatives.

3. It is understood that these negotiations shall cover remaining issues, including: Jerusalem, refugees, settlements, security arrangements, borders, relations and cooperation with other neighbors, and other issues of common interest.

4. The two parties agree that the outcome of the permanent

status negotiations should not be prejudiced or preempted by agreements reached for the interim period.

ARTICLE VI: PREPARATORY TRANSFER OF POWERS AND RESPONSIBILITIES

1. Upon the entry into force of this Declaration of Principles and the withdrawal from the Gaza Strip and the Jericho area, a transfer of authority from the Israeli military government and its Civil Administration to the authorised Palestinians for this task . . . will commence. This transfer of authority will be of a preparatory nature until the inauguration of the Council.

2. Immediately after the entry into force of this Declaration of Principles and the withdrawal from the Gaza Strip and Jericho area, with the view to promoting economic development in the West Bank and Gaza Strip, authority will be transferred to the Palestinians on the following spheres: education and culture, health, social welfare, direct taxation, and tourism. The Palestinian side will commence in building the Palestinian police force, as agreed upon. Pending the inauguration of the Council, the two parties may negotiate the transfer of additional powers and responsibilities, as agreed upon. . . .

ARTICLE VIII: PUBLIC ORDER AND SECURITY

In order to guarantee public order and internal security for the Palestinians of the West Bank and the Gaza Strip, the Council will establish a strong police force, while Israel will continue to carry the responsibility for defending against external threats, as well as the responsibility for overall security of Israelis for the purpose of safeguarding their internal security and public order. . . .

ARTICLE XIII: REDEPLOYMENT OF ISRAELI FORCES

1. After the entry into force of this Declaration of Principles, and not later than the eve of elections for the Council, a redeployment of Israeli military forces in the West Bank and the Gaza Strip will take place, in addition to withdrawal of Israeli forces carried out in accordance with Article XIV.

2. In redeploying its military forces, Israel will be guided by the principle that its military forces should be redeployed outside populated areas.

3. Further redeployments to specified locations will be gradually implemented commensurate with the assumption of responsibility for public order and internal security by the Palestinian police force pursuant to Article VIII above.

ARTICLE XIV: ISRAELI WITHDRAWAL FROM THE GAZA STRIP AND JERICHO AREA

Israel will withdraw from the Gaza Strip and Jericho area. . . .

17. PRESIDENT BILL CLINTON ISSUES STATEMENT UPON FAILURE OF PEACE TALKS, 2000

Source: U.S., Department of State, http://www.state.gov/www/regions/nea/ 000725_clinton_stmt.html (last accessed September 13, 2004).

Despite the progress of the early 1990s, the Israeli-Palestinian peace process collapsed in 2000 when Clinton proved unable, during a summit meeting at Camp David, to broker a final settlement between Israeli Prime Minister Ehud Barak and PLO Chairman Yasser Arafat. The following excerpt is taken from Clinton's public remarks at the conclusion of the conference on July 25, 2000.

. . . After 14 days of intensive negotiations between Israelis and Palestinians, I have concluded with regret that they will not be able to reach an agreement at this time. As I explained on the eve of the summit, success was far from guaranteed—given the historical, religious, political and emotional dimensions of the conflict.

Still, because the parties were not making progress on their own and the September deadline they set for themselves was fast approaching, I thought we had no choice. We can't afford to leave a single stone unturned in the search for a just, lasting and comprehensive peace.

Now, at Camp David, both sides engaged in comprehensive discussions that were really unprecedented because they dealt with the most sensitive issues dividing them; profound and complex questions that long had been considered off limits.

Under the operating rules that nothing is agreed until everything is agreed, they are, of course, not bound by any proposal discussed at the summit. However, while we did not get an agreement here, significant progress was made on the core issues. I want to express my appreciation to Prime Minister Barak, Chairman Arafat and their delegations for the efforts they undertook to reach an agreement.

Prime Minister Barak showed particular courage[,] vision, and an understanding of the historical importance of this moment. Chairman Arafat made it clear that he, too, remains committed to the path of peace. The trilateral statement we issued affirms both leaders' commitment to avoid violence or unilateral actions which will make peace more difficult and to keep the peace process going until it reaches a successful conclusion.

At the end of this summit, I am fully aware of the deep disappointment that will be felt on both sides. But it was essential for Israelis and Palestinians, finally, to begin to deal with the toughest decisions in the peace process. Only they can make those decisions, and they both pledged to make them, I say again, by mid-September.

Now, it's essential that they not lose hope, that they keep working for peace, they avoid any unilateral actions that would only make the hard task ahead more difficult. The statement the leaders have made today is encouraging in that regard.

Israelis and Palestinians are destined to live side by side, destined to have a common future. They have to decide what kind of future it will be. Though the differences that remain are deep, they have come a long way in the last seven years, and, notwithstanding the failure to reach an agreement, they made real headway in the last two weeks.

Now, the two parties must go home and reflect, both on what happened at Camp David and on what did not happen. For the sake of their children, they must rededicate themselves to the path of peace and find a way to resume their negotiations in the next few weeks. They've asked us to continue to help, and as always, we'll do our best. But the parties themselves, both of them, must be prepared to resolve profound questions of history, identity and national faith—as well as the future of sites that are holy to religious people all over the world who are part of the Islamic, Christian and Judaic traditions.

The children of Abraham, the descendants of Isaac and Ishmael can only be reconciled through courageous compromise. In the spirit of those who have already given their lives for peace and all Israelis, Palestinians, friends of peace in the Middle East and across the world, we long for peace and deserve a Holy Land that lives for the values of Judaism, Islam and Christianity. . . .

Gulf Wars

18. UN SECURITY COUNCIL CONDEMNS IRAQI AGGRESSION AGAINST KUWAIT, 1990

Source: UN Security Council, http://www.un.org/Docs/scres/1990/scres90.htm (last accessed September 13, 2004).

The United States reacted strongly to the Iraqi invasion of Kuwait in August 1990. President George H.W. Bush demanded the immediate withdrawal of Iraqi forces, imposed economic sanctions on Iraq, and encouraged other states to follow suit. Under U.S. leadership, the UN Security Council passed Resolution 660, which condemned the Iraqi aggression, demanded Iraqi withdrawal, and encouraged settlement of intra-Arab disputes through negotiations. Because Iraq remained in defiance of that and other resolutions, the Security Council followed up on November 29, 1990 by passing Resolution 678 (excerpted below), authorizing the use of military force to liberate Kuwait.

The Security Council,

. . . Noting that, despite all efforts by the United Nations, Iraq refuses to comply with its obligation to implement resolution 660 (1990) and . . . subsequent relevant resolutions, in flagrant contempt of the Security Council,

Mindful of its duties and responsibilities under the Charter of the United Nations for the maintenance and preservation of international peace and security,

Determined to secure full compliance with its decisions, . . .

1. Demands that Iraq comply fully with resolution 660 (1990) and all subsequent relevant resolutions, and decides, while maintaining all its decisions, to allow Iraq one final opportunity, as a pause of goodwill, to do so;

2. Authorizes Member States co-operating with the Government of Kuwait, unless Iraq on or before 15 January 1991 fully implements, as set forth in paragraph 1 above, the above-mentioned resolutions, to use all necessary means to uphold and implement resolution 660 (1990) and all subsequent relevant resolutions and to restore international peace and security in the area;

3. Requests all States to provide appropriate support for the actions undertaken in pursuance of paragraph 2 of the present resolution;

4. Requests the States concerned to keep the Security Council regularly informed on the progress of actions undertaken. . . .

5. Decides to remain seized of the matter.

19. UN SECURITY COUNCIL SAFEGUARDS AGAINST FUTURE IRAQI AGGRESSION, 1991

Source: UN Security Council, http://www.un.org/Docs/scres/1991/ scres91.htm (last accessed September 13, 2004).

Once the international coalition led by the United States drove Iraqi military forces from Kuwait in early 1991, the George H.W. Bush administration worked through the United Nations to establish safeguards against the renewal of hostilities by Iraq on other countries. On April 3, 1991, the United States encouraged the United Nations Security Council to approve Resolution 687, excerpted below.

The Security Council,

. . . 2. Demands that Iraq and Kuwait respect the inviolability of the international boundary . . . ;

3. Calls upon the Secretary-General to lend his assistance to make arrangements with Iraq and Kuwait to demarcate the boundary between Iraq and Kuwait, . . . ;

4. Decides to guarantee the inviolability of the above-mentioned international boundary and to take as appropriate all necessary measures to that end in accordance with the Charter of the United Nations. . . .

7. Invites Iraq to reaffirm unconditionally its obligations under the Geneva Protocol for the Prohibition of the Use in War of Asphyxiating, Poisonous or Other Gases, and of Bacteriological Methods of Warfare, signed at Geneva on 17 June 1925, and to ratify the Convention on the Prohibition of the Development, Production and Stockpiling of Bacteriological (Biological) and Toxin Weapons and on Their Destruction, of 10 April 1972;

8. Decides that Iraq shall unconditionally accept the destruction, removal, or rendering harmless, under international supervision, of:

(a) All chemical and biological weapons and all stocks of agents and all related subsystems and components and all research, development, support and manufacturing facilities;

(b) All ballistic missiles with a range greater than 150 kilometres and related major parts, and repair and production facilities;

9. Decides, for the implementation of paragraph 8 above, the following:

(a) Iraq shall submit to the Secretary-General . . . a declaration of the locations, amounts and types of all items specified in paragraph 8 and agree to urgent, on-site inspection as specified below;

(b) The Secretary-General . . . shall develop . . . a plan calling for the completion of the following acts within forty-five days of such approval:

(i) The forming of a Special Commission, which shall carry out immediate on-site inspection of Iraq's biological, chemical and missile capabilities, based on Iraq's declarations and the designation of any additional locations by the Special Commission itself;

(ii) The yielding by Iraq of possession to the Special Commission for destruction, removal or rendering harmless . . . of all items specified under paragraph 8 (a) above, . . . and the destruction by Iraq, under the supervision of the Special Commission, of all its missile capabilities, including launchers . . . ;

10. Decides that Iraq shall unconditionally undertake not to use, develop, construct or acquire any of the items specified in paragraphs 8 and 9 above and requests the Secretary-General . . . to develop a plan for the future ongoing monitoring and verification of Iraq's compliance with this paragraph . . . ;

11. Invites Iraq to reaffirm unconditionally its obligations under the Treaty on the Non-Proliferation of Nuclear Weapons of 1 July 1968;

12. Decides that Iraq shall unconditionally agree not to acquire or develop nuclear weapons or nuclear-weapons-usable material or any subsystems or components or any research, development, support or manufacturing facilities related to the above . . . ;

13. Requests the Director-General of the International Atomic Energy Agency . . . to carry out immediate on-site inspection of Iraq's nuclear capabilities . . . and to develop a plan . . . for the future ongoing monitoring and verification of Iraq's compliance with paragraph 12 above . . . ;

24. Decides that . . . all States shall continue to prevent the sale or supply, or the promotion or facilitation of such sale or supply, to Iraq by their nationals, or from their territories or using their flag vessels or aircraft, of:

(a) Arms and related materiel of all types . . . ;

32. Requires Iraq to inform the Security Council that it will not commit or support any act of international terrorism or allow any organization directed towards commission of such acts to operate within its territory and to condemn unequivocally and renounce all acts, methods and practices of terrorism. . . .

20. PRESIDENT GEORGE W. BUSH ISSUES AN ULTIMATUM TO IRAQI PRESIDENT SADDAM HUSSEIN, 2003

Source: U.S., The White House, http://www.whitehouse.gov/news/releases/2003/03/20030317-7.html (last accessed May 31, 2005).

Some twelve years after President George H.W. Bush took action to expel Iraqi forces from Kuwait, his son, President George W. Bush, decided to initiate hostilities against Iraq itself. The younger President Bush justified such an attack as a legitimate response to Saddam Hussein's defiance of UN resolutions and as a preemptive move against a prospective attack by Iraq, in alliance with international terrorists and using weapons of mass destruction. In an address to the world on March 17, 2003, excerpted below, Bush made his case for war and issued an ultimatum to Saddam Hussein. Three days later, Bush ordered American troops to invade Iraq.

My fellow citizens, events in Iraq have now reached the final days of decision. For more than a decade, the United States and other nations have pursued patient and honorable efforts to disarm the Iraqi regime without war. That regime pledged to reveal and destroy all its weapons of mass destruction as a condition for ending the Persian Gulf War in 1991.

Since then, the world has engaged in 12 years of diplomacy. We have passed more than a dozen resolutions in the United Nations Security Council. We have sent hundreds of weapons inspectors to oversee the disarmament of Iraq. Our good faith has not been returned.

The Iraqi regime has used diplomacy as a ploy to gain time and advantage. It has uniformly defied Security Council resolutions demanding full disarmament. Over the years, U.N. weapon inspectors have been threatened by Iraqi officials, electronically bugged, and systematically deceived. Peaceful efforts to disarm the Iraqi regime have failed again and again—because we are not dealing with peaceful men.

Intelligence gathered by this and other governments leaves no doubt that the Iraq regime continues to possess and conceal some of the most lethal weapons ever devised. This regime has already used weapons of mass destruction against Iraq's neighbors and against Iraq's people.

The regime has a history of reckless aggression in the Middle East. It has a deep hatred of America and our friends. And it has aided, trained and harbored terrorists, including operatives of al Qaeda.

The danger is clear: using chemical, biological or, one day, nuclear weapons, obtained with the help of Iraq, the terrorists could fulfill their stated ambitions and kill thousands or hundreds of thousands of innocent people in our country, or any other.

The United States and other nations did nothing to deserve or invite this threat. But we will do everything to defeat it. Instead of drifting along toward tragedy, we will set a course toward safety. Before the day of horror can come, before it is too late to act, this danger will be removed.

The United States of America has the sovereign authority to use force in assuring its own national security. That duty falls to me, as Commander-in-Chief, by the oath I have sworn, by the oath I will keep.

. . . Under [Security Council] Resolutions 678 and 687—both still in effect—the United States and our allies are authorized to use force in ridding Iraq of weapons of mass destruction. This is not a question of authority, it is a question of will.

. . . All the decades of deceit and cruelty have now reached an end. Saddam Hussein and his sons must leave Iraq within 48 hours. Their refusal to do so will result in military conflict, commenced at a time of our choosing. For their own safety, all foreign nationals—including journalists and inspectors—should leave Iraq immediately.

Many Iraqis can hear me tonight in a translated radio broadcast, and I have a message for them. If we must begin a military campaign, it will be directed against the lawless men who rule your country and not against you. As our coalition takes away their power, we will deliver the food and medicine you need. We will tear down the apparatus of terror and we will help you to build a new Iraq that is prosperous and free. In a free Iraq, there will be no more wars of aggression against your neighbors, no more poison factories, no more executions of dissidents, no more torture chambers and rape rooms. The tyrant will soon be gone. The day of your liberation is near. . . .

We are now acting because the risks of inaction would be far greater. In one year, or five years, the power of Iraq to inflict harm on all free nations would be multiplied many times over. With these capabilities, Saddam Hussein and his terrorist allies could choose the moment of deadly conflict when they are strongest. We choose to meet that threat now, where it arises, before it can appear suddenly in our skies and cities.

The cause of peace requires all free nations to recognize new and undeniable realities. In the 20th century, some chose to appease murderous dictators, whose threats were allowed to grow into genocide and global war. In this century, when evil men plot chemical, biological and nuclear terror, a policy of appeasement could bring destruction of a kind never before seen on this earth.

Terrorists and terror states do not reveal these threats with fair notice, in formal declarations—and responding to such enemies only after they have struck first is not self-defense, it is suicide. The security of the world requires disarming Saddam Hussein now . . . .

Free nations have a duty to defend our people by uniting against the violent. And tonight, as we have done before, America and our allies accept that responsibility.

Good night, and may God continue to bless America.

21. SENATOR EDWARD M. KENNEDY CRITICIZES PRESIDENT BUSH'S POLICY IN IRAQ, 2003

Source: Office of Edward M. Kennedy, http://kennedy.senate.gov/ index_low.html (last accessed May 31, 2005).

Veteran Democratic Senator Edward M. (Ted) Kennedy emerged as a prominent critic of the war in Iraq. In a speech to the School of Advanced International Studies of the Johns Hopkins University in Washington, D.C., on July 15, 2003, Kennedy articulated a detailed critique of President George Bush's war policy. The speech is excerpted below.

. . . Last fall, I came here to reaffirm my conviction that 9/11 had not nullified the long-standing basic principle that war should be the last resort, and to argue the case that America should not go to war against Iraq unless and until all other reasonable alternatives had been exhausted. Then—as now—I believed that the threat posed by Saddam Hussein was not serious enough or imminent enough to justify a rush to war, and that we were going to war under false pretenses. Then—as now—

I believed that war would distract from our broader war against terrorism and that we should not go to war with Iraq without the clear support of the international community. Then—as now—I believed that without a systematic re-examination, with dubious and even false rationalization, and without the informed consent of the American people, the Bush Administration was changing our long-standing foreign policy on preventive war to permit a pre-conceived determination to invade Iraq.

Supporters and opponents of the war alike were enormously proud of the way our troops performed in Operation Iraqi Freedom. The speed and success of their mission demonstrated the outstanding strength of the nation's armed forces. As a citizen of Massachusetts and a member of the Armed Services Committee in the Senate, it never ceases to amaze me how far we have come in the two centuries since the embattled farmers at Concord Bridge fired the shot heard around the world. . . .

It was a foregone conclusion that we would win the war. But pride goes before a fall, and the all-important question now is whether we can win the peace. In fact, we are at serious risk of losing it.

Our policy toward Iraq is adrift. Each day, our troops and their families are paying the price. Our clear national interest in the emergence of a peaceful, stable, democratic Iraq is being undermined.

On May 1, President Bush announced aboard the USS Abraham Lincoln that the United States and our allies had prevailed and that "major combat operations" in Iraq had ended. Not exactly. American troops in Iraq are now serving as police officers in a shooting gallery. In recent weeks, they've been subjected to 10 to 25 violent attacks a day by hostile fighters or forces.

In the 76 days that have passed since the President spoke, 81 more American troops have died. For the men and women of our armed forces who are dodging bullets in the streets and alleys of Baghdad, and other parts of Iraq, the battle is far from over. President Bush says of the attackers, "Bring 'em on." But how do you console a family by telling them that their son or daughter is a casualty of the post-war period?

The debate may go on for many months or even years about our intelligence failures before the war began. As we now know, despite the claim made in the State of the Union Address, Saddam was not purchasing uranium from Africa to build nuclear weapons.

Despite all the intelligence we were shown in the months leading up to war, despite the additional intelligence they said was there but could not be shared, we have yet to uncover any evidence that Iraq was stockpiling chemical or biological weapons. There was and is no evidence that

Saddam was conspiring with Al Qaeda. What was the imminent threat to the United States that required us to launch a preventive war in Iraq with very little international support? What was the imminent threat to the United States? It's a disgrace that the case for war seems to have been based on shoddy intelligence, hyped intelligence, and even false intelligence. All the evidence points to the conclusion that they put a spin on the intelligence and a spin on the truth. They have undermined America's prestige and credibility in the world—and undermined the trust that Americans should and must have in what their nation tells them. How many will doubt a future claim of danger even if it is real?

The failures of intelligence were bad enough. But the real failure of intelligence was our failure to understand Iraq.

There is no question that long before the war began, a serious issue was raised about the danger of winning the war and losing the peace. In fact, it was one of the principal arguments against going to war.

Before the war began . . . , Pentagon officials assured us on the Senate Armed Services Committee that firm plans were in place to secure and rebuild Iraq. But the reality is that the Administration had paper, but not a real plan—and precious little paper at that. We knew the post-war rebuilding of Iraq would be enormously difficult. Based on our experience in Bosnia, Kosovo, East Timor, and Afghanistan, we knew security could be a profound problem, and that there would be challenges from a restless population. We knew that building a national police force and a credible judicial system would be enormously complicated tasks. These are not new issues. But rather than learning lessons from the experiences in these four conflicts, the Administration was blinded by its own ideological bravado. It rushed ahead without planning for contingencies or raising even basic questions about likely events.

The foundation of our post war policy was built on a quicksand of false assumptions, and the result has been chaos for the Iraqi people, and continuing mortal danger for our troops. The truth, as my colleague Senator John Kerry starkly stated last week, is clearer with each passing day and each new casualty: "The Administration went to war without a thorough plan to win the peace."

The Pentagon assumed that we would be able to draw on thousands of Saddam's police force to protect security—but in the critical early weeks that followed the war, they were nowhere to be found, and too many of their officers turned out to be thugs and torturers.

The Pentagon assumed that the bulk of the Iraqi Armed Forces could be used to supplement our forces—but those soldiers did not join us.

The Pentagon assumed that some Iraqi exile leaders could return to Iraq to rally the population and lead the new government—but they were resented by the Iraqi people and the exiles were put on hold.

The Pentagon assumed that after a few hundred of Saddam's top advisers were removed from power, large numbers of local officials would remain to run the government—but the government crumbled.

The Pentagon assumed that Americans would be welcomed as liberators—but for some Iraqis we went from liberators to occupiers in a few short weeks. The dancing in the streets of some after the fall of the statue of Saddam was accompanied by an orgy of massive looting and chaos and was followed by growing frustration even from those who first saw us as liberators.

There was egg on the face of the Administration and its peace plan from Day One. Plan A was so obviously the wrong plan that General Garner, the man sent to oversee it, was abruptly replaced on Day 21, and Paul Bremer was rushed in to make up Plan B as he went along.

Today, Paul Bremer rules the country from Saddam's palace, while the Iraqi people sit in the dark without adequate water or electricity.

Hospital equipment and medical supplies have been stolen. Power grids in major cities are being sabotaged.

Cynicism and anger toward America is growing. Many Iraqis believe that we are unwilling—rather than unable—to restore basic services. They are losing faith and trust in our promise of a reconstructed, stable, democratic future. They fear that Saddam may still be alive.

Under fire from guerillas determined to see America fail, our soldiers are now performing police functions for which they have little training. They are building schools and hospitals—a task for which they are ill prepared. We are straining their endurance, and they want to know how long they will need to stay in Iraq. . . .

America won the war in Iraq, as we knew we would, but if our present policy continues, we may lose the peace. We must rise to the challenge of international co-operation. Saddam Hussein may no longer be in power, but the people of Iraq will not truly be liberated until they live in a secure country. And the war will not be over, no matter what is said on the deck of an aircraft carrier, until the fighting stops on the ground, democracy takes hold and the people of Iraq are able to govern themselves.

22. BUSH DEFENDS WAR POLICY DURING ACCEPTANCE SPEECH AT THE REPUBLICAN NATIONAL CONVENTION, 2004

Source: The White House, http://www.whitehouse.gov/news/releases/2004/09/20040902-2/. html (last accessed August 8, 2005).

In 2004, George W. Bush easily secured his party's nomination for reelection as President. In his September 2 acceptance speech at the Republican National Convention, Bush discussed several issues but devoted most of his attention to justifying the wars in Afghanistan and Iraq as essential steps in the defense of American liberty and security. Portions of his speech are printed below.

Mr. Chairman, delegates, fellow citizens: I am honored by your support, and I accept your nomination for President of the United States.

. . . Tonight I will tell you where I stand, what I believe, and where I will lead this country in the next four years.

. . . Four years ago, Afghanistan was the home base of al-Qaeda, Pakistan was a transit point for terrorist groups, Saudi Arabia was fertile ground for terrorist fundraising, Libya was secretly pursuing nuclear weapons, Iraq was a gathering threat, and al-Qaeda was largely unchallenged as it planned attacks. Today, the government of a free Afghanistan is fighting terror, Pakistan is capturing terrorist leaders, Saudi Arabia is making raids and arrests, Libya is dismantling its weapons programs, the army of a free Iraq is fighting for freedom, and more than three-quarters of al-Qaeda's key members and associates have been detained or killed. We have led, many have joined, and America and the world are safer.

This progress involved careful diplomacy, clear moral purpose, and some tough decisions. And the toughest came on Iraq. We knew Saddam Hussein's record of aggression and support for terror. We knew his long history of pursuing, even using, weapons of mass destruction. And we know that September the 11th requires our country to think differently: We must, and we will, confront threats to America before it is too late.

In Saddam Hussein, we saw a threat. . . . After more than a decade of diplomacy, we gave Saddam Hussein another chance, a final chance, to meet his responsibilities to the civilized world. He again refused, and I faced the kind of decision that comes only to the Oval Office—a decision no president would ask for, but must be prepared to make. Do I forget the lessons of September the 11th and take the word of a madman, or do I take action to defend our country? Faced with that choice, I will defend America every time.

Because we acted to defend our country, the murderous regimes of Saddam Hussein and the Taliban are history, more than 50 million people have been liberated, and democracy is coming to the broader Middle East. In Afghanistan, terrorists have done everything they can to intimidate people—yet more than 10 million citizens have registered to vote in the October presidential election—a resounding endorsement for democracy. Despite ongoing acts of violence, Iraq now has a strong Prime Minister, a national council, and national elections are scheduled for January. Our nation is standing with the people of Afghanistan and Iraq, because when America gives its word, America must keep its word.

As importantly, we are serving a vital and historic cause that will make our country safer. Free societies in the Middle East will be hopeful societies, which no longer feed resentments and breed violence for export. Free governments in the Middle East will fight terrorists instead of harboring them, and that helps us keep the peace. So our mission in Afghanistan and Iraq is clear: We will help new leaders to train their armies, and move toward elections, and get on the path of stability and democracy as quickly as possible. And then our troops will return home with the honor they have earned.

. . . Others understand the historic importance of our work. The terrorists know. They know that a vibrant, successful democracy at the heart of the Middle East will discredit their radical ideology of hate. They know that men and women with hope and purpose and dignity do not strap bombs on their bodies and kill the innocent. The terrorists are fighting freedom with all their cunning and cruelty because freedom is their greatest fear—and they should be afraid, because freedom is on the march.

I believe in the transformational power of liberty: The wisest use of American strength is to advance freedom. As the citizens of Afghanistan and Iraq seize the moment, their example will send a message of hope throughout a vital region. Palestinians will hear the message that democracy and reform are within their reach, and so is peace with our good friend, Israel. Young women across the Middle East will hear the message that their day of equality and justice is coming. Young men will hear the message that national progress and dignity are found in liberty, not tyranny and terror. Reformers, and political prisoners, and exiles will hear the message that their dream of freedom cannot be denied forever.

And as freedom advances—heart by heart, and nation by nation—America will be more secure and the world more peaceful.

    . . . I believe that America is called to lead the cause of freedom in a new century. I believe that millions in the Middle East plead in silence for their liberty. I believe that given the chance, they will embrace the most honorable form of government ever devised by man. I believe all these things because freedom is not America's gift to the world, it is the almighty God's gift to every man and woman in this world.

    This moment in the life of our country will be remembered. Generations will know if we kept our faith and kept our word. Generations will know if we seized this moment, and used it to build a future of safety and peace. The freedom of many, and the future security of our nation, now depend on us. And tonight, my fellow Americans, I ask you to stand with me. . . .

    God bless you, and may God continue to bless our great country.

NOTES

Chapter 1

1. Jardine quoted in Thomas A. Bryson, *Seeds of Mideast Crisis: The United States' Diplomatic Role in the Middle East during World War II* (Jefferson, NC: McFarland, 1981), 128. See also John A. DeNovo, *American Interests and Policies in the Middle East, 1900–1939* (Minneapolis: University of Minnesota Press, 1963), 114–27.

2. James A. Field, *From Gibraltar to the Middle East: America and the Mediterranean World, 1776–1882* (Chicago: Imprint Publications, 1991).

3. Phillip J. Baram, *The Department of State and the Middle East, 1919–1945* (Philadelphia: University of Pennsylvania Press, 1978), 49–57.

4. DeNovo, *American Interests*, 167–209; Daniel Yergin, *The Prize: The Epic Quest for Oil, Money, and Power* (New York: Simon & Schuster, 1991), 298–300.

5. Gerhard I. Weinberg, *A World at Arms: A Global History of World War II* (New York: Cambridge University Press, 1994), 348–63.

6. Weinberg, *World at Arms*, 224–32.

7. Peter L. Hahn, *The United States, Great Britain, and Egypt, 1945–1956: Strategy and Diplomacy in the Early Cold War* (Chapel Hill: University of North Carolina Press, 1991), 11–12, 15–16.

8. Louise L'Estrange Fawcett, *Iran and the Cold War: The Azerbaijan Crisis of 1946* (New York: Cambridge University Press, 1992), 108–22; Peter L. Hahn, *Caught in the Middle East: U.S. Policy toward the Arab-Israeli Conflict, 1945–1961* (Chapel Hill: University of North Carolina Press, 2004), 16 (quotation).

9. Baram, *Department of State*, 49–57.

10. Baram, *Department of State*, 124.

11. Fawcett, *Iran and the Cold War*, 93–107, 177–81; Mark J. Gasiorowski, *U.S. Foreign Policy and the Shah: Building a Client State in Iran* (Ithaca, NY: Cornell University Press, 1991), 45–47.

12. Arnold A. Offner, *Another Such Victory: President Truman and the Cold War, 1945–1953* (Stanford, CA: Stanford University Press, 2002), 84–86, 112–13, 167–73.

13. Melvyn P. Leffler, *A Preponderance of Power: National Security, the Truman Administration, and the Cold War* (Stanford, CA: Stanford University Press, 1992), 73–75, 125–27, 142–46.

14. Address by Truman, March 12, 1947, in *Documents of American Diplomacy from the American Revolution to the Present*, ed. Michael D. Gambone (Westport, CT: Greenwood Press, 2002), 305–308 (quotation 307); Offner, *Another Such Victory*, 199–209.

15. CIA, ORE 52, October 17, 1947, President's Secretary's File (PSF), Intelligence File, box 254, Harry S Truman Library (hereafter HSTL); State Department briefing book, January 10, 1950, David D. Lloyd Papers, HSTL. See also Yergin, *Prize*.

16. Caraway to Radford, March 20, 1956, CJCS Radford, box 16, 091 Palestine, Records of the Joint Chiefs of Staff, Record Group (RG) 218, National Archives (hereafter RG 218).

17. Hahn, *United States, Great Britain, and Egypt*, 23–28, 49–56, 58–62; David R. Devereux, *The Formulation of British Defence Policy towards the Middle East, 1948–56* (New York: St. Martin's Press, 1990); Michael Joseph Cohen, *Fighting World War III from the Middle East: Allied Contingency Plans, 1945–1954* (London: Frank Cass, 1997), 1–94.

18. U.S.-UK agreed minute, October 17, 1947, FO 800/476, Records of the Foreign Secretary's Office, Public Record Office (PRO), London; CIA, SR-13, September 27, 1949, PSF, Intelligence File, box 260, HSTL; State Department paper, n.d. [October 1952], Lot 57 D 298, box 3, General Records of the Department of State, RG 59, National Archives (hereafter RG 59).

19. State Department briefing book, January 10, 1950, David D. Lloyd Papers, HSTL.

20. State Department briefing book, January 10, 1950, David D. Lloyd Papers, HSTL. See also Robert D. Kaplan, *The Arabists: The Romance of an American Elite* (New York: Free Press, 1993).

21. Jones to Nitze, September 13, 1950, RG 59, Lot 64 D 563, box 14; Bruce to Truman, August 15, 1952, PSF, Subject File, box 181, HSTL. See also Pinkerton to Byrnes, May 29, 1946, RG 59, 711.90I.

22. Hahn, *Caught in the Middle East*, 16–17.

23. Childs to Marshall, December 27, 1948, CD 6–3–3, Records of the Secretary of Defense, RG 330, National Archives (hereafter RG 330); memorandum of conversation of meeting, n.d. [Mar. 23, 1950], White House Central File (Confidential), box 41, HSTL; memorandum of conversation by Department of Defense, December 17, 1951, in U.S. Department of State, *Foreign Relations of the United States, 1951* (Washington, DC: Government Printing Office, 1982), vol. 5, 1071–72 (hereafter *FRUS, 1951*).

24. Douglas Little, *American Orientalism: The United States and the Middle East since 1945* (Chapel Hill: University of North Carolina Press, 2002), 52–56.

25. Yergin, *Prize*, 445–49.

26. Memorandum by Sanger, November 14, 1949, RG 59, Lot 484, box 1. See also Hahn, *Caught in the Middle East*, 22.

27. JCS 1684/28, May 6, 1949, Maddocks to Army COS, April 8, 1949, P&O

091 Israel, Records of the Army Staff, Plans and Operations Division, RG 319, National Archives.

28. CIA, ORE 69–49, September 12, 1949, PSF: Subject, box 256, HSTL. See also Galia Golan, *Soviet Policies in the Middle East: From World War II to Gorbachev* (New York: Cambridge University Press, 1990), 1–10, 29–34, 40–43; Bruce Robellet Kuniholm, *Origins of the Cold War in the Near East: Great Power Conflict and Diplomacy in Iran, Turkey, and Greece* (Princeton, NJ: Princeton University Press, 1980), 303–431; Hashim Behbehani, *The Soviet Union and Arab Nationalism, 1917–1966* (New York: KPI, 1986), 104–14.

29. Talal Nizameddin, *Russia and the Middle East: Towards a New Foreign Policy* (New York: Linden Press, Simon & Schuster, 1984), 20–22; Golan, *Soviet Policies*, 1–10; Behbehani, *Soviet Union and Arab Nationalism*, 89–93.

30. Memorandum to Nixon, June 27, 1956, White House Office Files, Special Assistant Series, box 3, Dwight D. Eisenhower Library (hereafter DDEL). See also Hahn, *United States, Great Britain, and Egypt*, 191–93.

31. Memorandum by Gullion, February 25, 1953, RG 59, Lot 64 D 563, box 30. See also Hahn, *Caught in the Middle East*, 68–71.

32. Satterthwaite to Humelsine, February 4, 1949, RG 59, Lot 54 D 43, box 9.

33. Henderson to Acheson, September 28, 1945, RG 59, 711.90. See also Hahn, *Caught in the Middle East*, 148–50.

34. U.S.-U.K. agreed minute, October 17, 1947, FO 800/476. See also Hahn, *United States, Great Britain, and Egypt*, 74–77.

35. Text of Tripartite Declaration in a circular cable from Webb, May 20, 1950, U.S. Department of State, *FRUS, 1950* (Washington, DC: Government Printing Office, 1978), 5:167–68. See also Hahn, *Caught in the Middle East*, 74–75.

36. Bruce Robellet Kuniholm, "Turkey and the West since World War II," in *Turkey between East and West: New Challenges for a Rising Regional Power*, eds. Vojtech Mastny and R. Craig Nation (Boulder, CO: Westview, 1996), 45–51.

37. Hahn, *United States, Great Britain, and Egypt*, 109–28.

38. Hahn, *Caught in the Middle East*, 76–78.

39. State Department position paper, August 1, 1952, RG 59, 641.80; memorandum of conversation by Evans, November 6, 1952, Acheson Papers, box 67a, HSTL.

40. Minutes of meeting, July 9, 1953, U.S. Department of State, *FRUS, 1952–1954* (Washington, DC: Government Printing Office, 1986), 9:394–98.

41. Hahn, *United States, Great Britain, and Egypt*, 182–83.

42. Magnus Persson, *Great Britain, the United States, and the Security of the Middle East: The Formulation of the Baghdad Pact* (Lund: Lund University Press, 1998); Richard L. Jasse, "The Baghdad Pact: Cold War or Colonialism?" *Middle Eastern Studies* 27:1 (January 1991): 140–56; Ara Sanjian, "The Formulation of the Baghdad Pact," *Middle Eastern Studies* 33:2 (April 1997): 226–66; Elie Podeh, *The Quest for Hegemony in the Arab World: The Struggle over the Baghdad Pact* (New York: E. J. Brill, 1995).

43. Stevenson to Eden, January 17, 1955, FO 371/113608, JE1057/1, Political Correspondence of the Foreign Office, Public Record Office, London.

44. Hahn, *Caught in the Middle East*, 152–54.

45. Nigel John Ashton, *Eisenhower, Macmillan, and the Problem of Nasser: Anglo-American Relations and Arab Nationalism, 1955–59* (New York: St. Martin's Press, 1996), 192–93; Podeh, *Quest for Hegemony*, 237–41.

Chapter 2

1. Charles D. Smith, *Palestine and the Arab-Israeli Conflict* (New York: St. Martin's Press, 1988), 29–36; Avi Shlaim, *The Iron Wall: Israel and the Arab World* (New York: W. W. Norton, 2000), 1–27.

2. Smith, *Palestine*, 42–65; James L. Stokesbury, *A Short History of World War I* (New York: Morrow, 1981), 254–56.

3. Neil Caplan, *Palestine Jewry and the Arab Question, 1917–1925* (London, Frank Cass, 1978); Martin Kolinsky, *Law, Order, and Riots in Mandatory Palestine, 1928–35* (New York: St. Martin's Press, 1993); Michael Joseph Cohen, *Palestine to Israel: From Mandate to Independence* (London: Frank Cass, 1988), 1–49, 66–87; Mark A. Tessler, *A History of the Israeli-Palestinian Conflict* (Bloomington: Indiana University Press, 1994), 238–41.

4. Michael Joseph Cohen, *Palestine and the Great Powers, 1945–1948* (Princeton, NJ: Princeton University Press, 1982), 16–28.

5. Hahn, *Caught in the Middle East*, 23–26.

6. Hahn, *Caught in the Middle East*, 15–18; Frank W. Brecher, *Reluctant Ally: United States Foreign Policy toward the Jews from Wilson to Roosevelt* (New York: Green-wood Press, 1991).

7. Aaron Berman, *Nazism, the Jews, and American Zionism, 1933–1948* (Detroit: Wayne State University Press, 1990); David H. Shpiro, *From Philanthropy to Activism: The Political Transformation of American Zionism in the Holocaust Years, 1933–1945* (New York: Pergamon Press, 1994); Yaakov Ariel, *On Behalf of Israel: American Fundamentalist Attitudes toward Jews, Judaism, and Zionism, 1865–1945* (Brooklyn, NY: Carlson, 1991); Lester Irwin Vogel, *To See a Promised Land: Americans and the Holy Land in the Nineteenth Century* (University Park: Pennsylvania State University Press, 1993); Kenneth Ray Bain, *The March to Zion: United States Policy and the Founding of Israel* (College Station: Texas A&M University Press, 1979).

8. Hahn, *Caught in the Middle East*, 20–43.

9. Truman quoted in Alonzo L. Hamby, *Man of the People: A Life of Harry S Truman* (New York: Oxford University Press, 1995), 409. See also David G. McCullough, *Truman* (New York: Simon & Schuster, 1992), 596; Offner, *Another Such Victory*, 274–306.

10. Memorandum of conversation by Sanger, November 4, 1946, RG 59, Lot 57 D 298, box 10. See also Janice J. Terry, *Mistaken Identity: Arab Stereotypes in Popular Writing* (Washington, DC: American-Arab Affairs Council, 1985); Michael T. Benson, *Harry S Truman and the Founding of Israel* (Westport, CT: Praeger, 1997); Michael W. Suleiman, *The Arabs in the Mind of America*

(Brattleboro, VT: Amana Books, 1988); Kathleen Christison, *Perceptions of Palestine: Their Influence on U.S. Middle East Policy* (Berkeley: University of California Press, 1999).

11. Henderson to Lovett, November 24, 1947, *FRUS, 1947*, 5:1281–82. See also Bain, *March to Zion.*

12. Wooldridge to CNO, May 27, 1948, RG 330, 6–3–5. See also Cohen, *Palestine and the Great Powers*, 45–48.

13. Hahn, *Caught in the Middle East*, 44–63, 133–37; Peter Grose, *Israel in the Mind of America* (New York: Knopf, 1983), 228–30; Hamby, *Man of the People*, 269–70, 410.

14. Shlaim, *Iron Wall*, 34–41.

15. Hahn, *Caught in the Middle East*, 51–53.

16. Amitzur Ilan, *Bernadotte in Palestine, 1948: A Study in Contemporary Humanitarian Knight-Errantry* (Basingstoke, UK: Macmillan, 1989).

17. Hahn, *Caught in the Middle East*, 54–57.

18. Hahn, *Caught in the Middle East*, 57–59.

19. Itamar Rabinovich, *The Road Not Taken: Early Arab-Israeli Negotiations* (New York: Oxford University Press, 1991), 47–54; Shlaim, *Iron Wall*, 41–47.

20. Hahn, *Caught in the Middle East*, 86–132.

21. Layton to Radford, March 29, 1956, Whitman File: Administration Series, box 23, DDEL; memorandum by Dulles, June 1, 1953, RG 59, Lot 64 D 563, box 30. See also NSC 155/1, July 14, 1953, *FRUS, 1952–1954*, 9:399–406.

22. Unsigned policy paper, n.d. [c. November 1953], Whitman File: Administration Series. See also Hahn, *Caught in the Middle East*, 158–81.

23. Byroade to Dulles, November 22, 1954, RG 59, 684A.86. See also memorandum of conversation by Dulles, February 14, 1955, U.S. Department of State, *FRUS, 1955–1957* (Washington, DC: Government Printing Office, 1989), 14:53–54.

24. Murphy to Hoover, May 23, 1955, Dulles to Hoover, June 6, 1955, *FRUS, 1955–1957*, 14:199–205, 222–26.

25. Hahn, *Caught in the Middle East*, 182–86.

26. Hahn, *Caught in the Middle East*, 186–92.

27. Hahn, *United States, Great Britain, and Egypt*, 211–39; Steven Z. Freiberger, *Dawn over Suez: The Rise of American Power in the Middle East, 1953–1957* (Chicago: Ivan R. Dee, 1992), 159–209; Keith Kyle, *Suez* (New York: St. Martin's Press, 1991), 135–290.

28. Hahn, *Caught in the Middle East*, 195–98.

29. Minutes of NSC meeting, August 9, 1956, Whitman File, NSC Series, box 8.

30. Circular cable from JCS, October 17, 1956, RG 218, JCS Geographic File, 1954–1956, box 14, CCS 381 EMMEA (11–19–47); minutes of NSC meeting, October 26, 1956, Whitman File: NSC Series, box 8.

31. Avi Shlaim, "The Protocol of Sevres, 1956: Anatomy of a War Plot," *International Affairs* 73:3 (July 1997): 509–30.

32. Bulganin to Eisenhower, November 5, 1956, RG 59, 684A.86.

33. Memorandum of conversation by Goodpaster, November 5, 1956, Whitman File: Diary Series, box 19. See also Hahn, *Caught in the Middle East*, 200–207.

34. Hahn, *Caught in the Middle East*, 230–33.

35. Hahn, *Caught in the Middle East*, 235–60.

36. Memorandum of conversation by Jones, September 26, 1960, U.S. Department of State, *FRUS, 1958–1960* (Washington, DC: Government Printing Office, 1992), 13:600–607.

Chapter 3

1. Robert J. McMahon, "The Challenge of the Third World," in *Empire and Revolution: The United States and the Third World since 1945*, eds. Peter L. Hahn and Mary Ann Heiss (Columbus: Ohio State University Press, 2001), 1–7.

2. Richard J. Barnet, *Intervention and Revolution: The United States in the Third World* (New York: World, 1968), 13–91; Scott L. Bills, *Empire and Cold War: The Roots of U.S.–Third World Antagonism, 1945–47* (New York: St. Martin's Press, 1990), 151–74, 206–212; David D. Newsom, *The Imperial Mantle: The United States, Decolonization, and the Third World* (Bloomington: Indiana University Press, 2001), 44–47.

3. H. W. Brands, *Specter of Neutralism: The United States and the Emergence of the Third World, 1947–1960* (New York: Columbia University Press, 1989), 1–5; Gabriel Kolko, *Confronting the Third World: United States Foreign Policy, 1945–1980* (New York: Pantheon Books, 1988), 47–57.

4. Hahn, *Caught in the Middle East*, 290–91.

5. Mary Ann Heiss, *Empire and Nationhood: The United States, Great Britain, and Iranian Oil, 1950–1954* (New York: Columbia University Press, 1997), 45–64; Gasiorowski, *U.S. Foreign Policy and the Shah*, 62–67.

6. James F. Goode, *The United States and Iran: In the Shadow of Musaddiq* (New York: St. Martin's Press, 1997), 100–18.

7. Mary Ann Heiss, "Real Men Don't Wear Pajamas," in *Empire and Revolution: The United States and the Third World since 1945*, eds. Peter L. Hahn and Mary Ann Heiss (Columbus: Ohio State University Press, 2001), 178–94.

8. Gasiorowski, *U.S. Foreign Policy and the Shah*, 72–84; Goode, *United States*, 118–24.

9. George W. Stocking, *Middle East Oil: A Study in Political and Economic Controversy* (Nashville, TN: Vanderbilt University Press, 1970), 156–62; Heiss, *Empire and Nationhood*, 187–220.

10. Hahn, *United States, Great Britain, and Egypt*, 7–13.

11. Little, *American Orientalism*, 158–61.

12. Wadsworth quoted in Little, *American Orientalism*, 162.

13. Hahn, *United States, Great Britain, and Egypt*, 116–28.

14. Hahn, *United States, Great Britain, and Egypt*, 131–47.

15. Hahn, *United States, Great Britain, and Egypt*, 147–53.

16. Hahn, *United States, Great Britain, and Egypt*, 155–79; Hahn, *Caught in the Middle East*, 92–93.

17. Hahn, *United States, Great Britain, and Egypt*, 181–94; Ray Takeyh, *The Origins of the Eisenhower Doctrine: The U.S., Britain, and Nasser's Egypt, 1953–57*

(New York: St. Martin's Press, 2000), 26–104.

18. Hahn, *United States, Great Britain, and Egypt*, 194–206; Takeyh, *Origins of Eisenhower Doctrine*, 105–23.

19. Hahn, *Caught in the Middle East*, 194–209; Takeyh, *Origins of Eisenhower Doctrine*, 124–41.

20. Eisenhower to Dulles, December 12, 1956, Whitman File: Dulles-Herter Series, box 6.

21. Hahn, *Caught in the Middle East*, 224–28; Salim Yaqub, *Containing Arab Nationalism: The Eisenhower Doctrine and the Middle East* (Chapel Hill: University of North Carolina Press, 2004), 87–121.

22. Hahn, *Caught in the Middle East*, 236–38.

23. Douglas Little, "Cold War and Covert Action: The United States and Syria, 1945–1958," *Middle East Journal* 44:1 (Winter 1990): 69–75; Bonnie F. Saunders, *The United States and Arab Nationalism: The Syrian Case, 1953–1960* (Westport, CT: Praeger, 1996), 59–85; Ashton, *Problem of Nasser*, 122–49.

24. Hahn, *Caught in the Middle East*, 240–46.

25. Irene L. Gendzier, *Notes from the Minefield: United States Intervention in Lebanon and the Middle East, 1945–1958* (New York: Columbia University Press, 1997), 295–363.

26. Paper by Office of Naval Intelligence, February 6, 1957, RG 218, JCS Geographic File, box 7, CCS 092 Egypt (7-28-56).

27. Hahn, *Caught in the Middle East*, 266–69.

28. Memorandum of conversation by Corrigan, August 11, 1958, Whitman File: International Series, box 49. See also Matthew F. Holland, *America and Egypt: From Roosevelt to Eisenhower* (Westport, CT: Praeger, 1996), 147–63.

29. Reinhardt to Herter, July 5, 1960, *FRUS, 1958–1960*, 13:587–89; Hahn, *Caught in the Middle East*, 270–71; Holland, *America and Egypt*, 167–73 (quotation 168).

30. Warren Bass, *Support Any Friend: Kennedy's Middle East and the Making of the U.S.-Israel Alliance* (New York: Oxford University Press, 2003), 64–97; Douglas Little, "The Making of a Special Relationship: The United States and Israel, 1957–68," *International Journal of Middle East Studies* 25:4 (November 1993): 563–70.

31. Little, *American Orientalism*, 181–85; Bass, *Support Any Friend*, 98–143.

32. Douglas Little, "Nasser Delenda Est: Lyndon Johnson, the Arabs, and the 1967 Six-Day War," in *The Foreign Policies of Lyndon Johnson: Beyond Vietnam*, ed. H. W. Brands (College Station: Texas A&M University Press, 1999), 145–63 (quotation 152).

Chapter 4

1. Saunders to Rostow, June 24, 1966, U.S. Department of State, *FRUS, 1964–1968* (Washington, DC: Government Printing Office, 2000), 21:29–31.

2. Rusk to Johnson, January 16, 1964, *FRUS, 1964–1968*, 18:17–23; State Department paper, February 8, 1967, *FRUS, 1964–1968*, 21:39–41.

3. Saunders to Rostow, June 24, 1966, *FRUS, 1964–1968*, 21:29–31 (quotation); Douglas Little, "Choosing Sides: Lyndon Johnson and the Middle East," in *The Johnson Years: LBJ at Home and Abroad*, ed. Robert Divine (Lawrence: University Press of Kansas, 1987), 150–97.

4. Minutes of meeting, May 30, 1961, RG 130.23, 3294/8, Records of the Foreign Ministry, Israel State Archive, Jerusalem; Komer to Johnson, June 2, 1964, White House memorandum of conversation, June 1, 1964, National Security File (NSF), Coutry Files, box 142, Lyndon B. Johnson Library (hereafter LBJL); memorandum for the record by Komer, October 8, 1965, NSF, Name File, box 7, LBJL.

5. Komer to Johnson, May 28 and June 2, 1964, NSF, Country Files, box 142, LBJL (quotation); Komer to Bundy, n.d. [August 12, 1965], White House Central File (Confidential), box 9, LBJL.

6. Johnson to Hussein, January 2, 1964, Johnson to Faisal, June 15, 1964, *FRUS, 1964–1968*, 18:2–3; 21:444–45 (quotations); Little, "Choosing Sides," 151–61.

7. Bundy to Johnson, March 8, 1964, NSF, Memos to President: Bundy, box 1, LBJL; Saunders to Rostow, June 24, 1966, *FRUS, 1964–1968*, 21:29–31 (quotation); State Department background paper, July 26, 1966, NSF, Country Files, box 145, LBJL.

8. Saunders to Rostow, May 16, 1967, *FRUS, 1964–1968*, 21:41–48; Shlaim, *Iron Wall*, 228–36.

9. NSC, *History of Middle East Crisis*, volume 9, appendix P, box 20, NSF, 1, 5–13 (hereafter *NSCH*), LBJL.

10. Rostow to Johnson, May 17, 1967, Johnson to Eshkol, May 17, 1967, NSF, *NSCH*, vol. 1, box 17, LBJL; minutes of NSC meeting, May 24, 1967, NSF, NSC Meetings file, box 2, LBJL.

11. Johnson quoted in *NSCH*, 37, LBJL; minutes of NSC meeting, May 24, 1967, NSC Meetings file, box 2, NSF, LBJL; Rusk to Johnson, May 26, 1967, NSF, Country Files, box 142, LBJL.

12. Unsigned memorandum of conversation, May 26, 1967, NSF, *NSCH*, box 17, LBJL. See also Johnson to Eshkol, May 27, 1967, Eshkol to Johnson, May 30, 1967, NSF, *NSCH*, box 17, LBJL.

13. Minutes of NSC meeting, May 24, 1967, NSF, NSC Meetings file, box 2, LBJL.

14. Eshkol to Johnson, May 30, 1967, NSF, *NSCH*, vol. 2, box 17, LBJL; Rusk and McNamara to Johnson, May 30, 1967, *NSCH*, volume 3, box 18, LBJL. See also Shlaim, *Iron Wall*, 236–40.

15. Nolte to Rusk, May 26, 1967, Office File of White House Aides: George Christian, box 4, LBJL; Battle to Control Group, May 31, 1967, *NSCH*, 76; Wheeler to McNamara, June 2, 1967, *NSCH*, vol. 3, box 18, LBJL.

16. Smythe to Rusk, June 1, 1967, NSF, *NSCH*, vol. 14, box 22, LBJL (quotation); Rostow to Johnson, May 29, 1967, Hoopes to McNamara, June 2, 1967, *NSCH*, vol. 3, box 18, LBJL.

17. Memorandum for the record by Saunders, January 7, 1969 [June 7, 1967],

NSF, NSC Meetings, box 2, LBJL (quotation); Richard Bordeaux Parker, *The Politics of Miscalculation in the Middle East* (Bloomington: Indiana University Press, 1993), 114–22; William B. Quandt, *Peace Process: American Diplomacy and the Arab-Israeli Conflict since 1967* (Washington, DC: Brookings Institution, 1993), 25–48; Shlaim, *Iron Wall*, 241; Lyndon B. Johnson, *The Vantage Point: Perspectives of the Presidency, 1963–1969* (New York: Holt, Rinehart, and Winston, 1971), 287 (quotation); Peter L. Hahn, "An Ominous Moment: Lyndon Johnson and the Six Day War," in *Looking Back at LBJ: White House Politics in a New Light*, ed. Mitchell B. Lerner (Lawrence: University Press of Kansas, 2005), 78–100.

18. Eshkol to Johnson, June 5, 1967, *NSCH,* vol. 3, box 18, LBJL.

19. Circular cables from Rusk, June 5 and 7, 1967, NSF, *NSCH,* vol. 15, box 23, LBJL; CIA situation reports, June 6–10, 1967, CIA Records, Online Retrieval Infomation System (ORIS).

20. On the basis of the testimony of surviving crew members, writers such as James Ennes, Donald Neff, and Andrew Cockburn and Leslie Cockburn speculate that Israel attacked the ship to prevent the United States from detecting Israeli mobilization against Syrian forces in the Golan Heights and reporting such intelligence to the regime in Damascus, while James Bamford suggests that Israel acted to prevent detection of its mass killings of Egyptian prisoners of war in nearby Sinai. On the other hand, scholars such as David Schoenbaum and Michael B. Oren accept Israel's "honest error" argument. James M. Ennes, *Assault on the Liberty: The True Story of the Israeli Attack on an American Intelligence Ship* (New York: Random House, 1979); Donald Neff, *Warriors for Jerusalem: The Six Days That Changed the Middle East* (New York: Linden Press, Simon & Schuster, 1984), 246–75; Andrew Cockburn and Leslie Cockburn, *Dangerous Liaison: The Inside Story of the U.S.-Israeli Covert Relationship* (New York: HarperCollins, 1991), 152–53; James Bamford, *Body of Secrets: Anatomy of the Ultra-Secret National Security Agency* (New York: Doubleday, 2001), 185–239; David Schoenbaum, *The United States and the State of Israel* (New York: Oxford University Press, 1993), 157–59; Michael B. Oren, *Six Days of War: June 1967 and the Making of the Modern Middle East* (New York: Oxford University Press, 2002), 262–71. See also Richard B. Parker, ed., *The Six-Day War: A Retrospective* (Gainesville: University Press of Florida, 1996), 266–70.

21. Unsigned memorandum, June 9, 1967, *NSCH,* vol. 4, box 18, LBJL.

22. *NSCH,* 148 (quotation); memorandum for the record by Saunders, October 22, 1968 [June 10, 1967], NSC History, vol. 4, box 19, NSF, LBJL.

23. Kosygin to Johnson, June 10, 1967, *NSCH,* vol. 7, box 19, LBJL; unsigned memorandum of conversation, June 14, 1967, Diary Back-Up file, box 68, LBJL.

24. Rostow to Johnson, June 13, 1967, *NSCH,* vol. 5, box 18, (quotation); Panzer to Johnson, June 10, 1967, White House Central File, NS-D, box 193, LBJL.

25. Minutes of Cabinet meeting, November 1, 1967, Cabinet Papers, box 11, LBJL (quotation); Parker, *Politics of Miscalculation*, 127–29.

26. Smith, *Palestine*, 215–17; Parker, *Politics of Miscalculation*, 133–36.

27. Shlaim, *Iron Wall*, 289–98.

28. David A. Korn, *Stalemate: The War of Attrition and Great Power Diplomacy in the Middle East, 1967–1970* (Boulder, CO: Westview, 1992), 143–88; Parker, *Politics of Miscalculation*, 136–47.

29. Shlaim, *Iron Wall*, 289–98; Yaacov Bar-Siman-Tov, *The Israeli-Egyptian War of Attrition, 1967–1970: A Case Study of Limited Local War* (New York: Columbia University Press, 1980), 175–208;

30. Quandt, *Peace Process*, 94–111; Shlaim, *Iron Wall*, 298–301.

31. Quandt, *Peace Process*, 111–15

32. Shlaim, *Iron Wall*, 301–309.

33. Quandt, *Peace Process*, 116–33; Smith, *Palestine*, 222–24.

34. Shlaim, *Iron Wall*, 309–18; Quandt, *Peace Process*, 136–47.

35. Shlaim, *Iron Wall*, 318–24.

36. Walter Isaacson, *Kissinger: A Biography* (New York: Simon & Schuster, 1992), 512–24 (quotation 518); Quandt, *Peace Process*, 148–69.

37. Kenneth W. Stein, *Heroic Diplomacy: Sadat, Kissinger, Carter, Begin, and the Quest for Arab-Israeli Peace* (New York: Routledge, 1999), 80–90; Quandt, *Peace Process*, 169–71.

38. Stein, *Heroic Diplomacy*, 90–96; Quandt, *Peace Process*, 171–82 (quotation 173).

39. Isaacson, *Kissinger*, 537–38; Stephen E. Ambrose, *Rise to Globalism: American Foreign Policy, 1938–1980* (New York: Penguin Books, 1980), 281–82 (quotations).

40. Stein, *Heroic Diplomacy*, 97–162; Isaacson, *Kissinger*, 550–72 (quotation 572).

41. Stein, *Heroic Diplomacy*, 175–81; Quandt, *Peace Process*, 229–46.

42. Stein, *Heroic Diplomacy*, 187–98; Zbigniew Brzezinski, *Power and Principle: Memoirs of the National Security Advisor, 1977–1981* (New York: Farrar, Straus, Giroux, 1983), 84–110 (quotations 84, 97).

43. Itamar Rabinovich, *The War for Lebanon, 1970–1985* (Ithaca, NY: Cornell University Press, 1985), 34–59, 106–107; Smith, *Palestine*, 246–51.

44. Shlaim, *Iron Wall*, 347–63; Smith, *Palestine*, 251–54.

45. Shlaim, *Iron Wall*, 352–63.

46. Jimmy Carter, *Keeping Faith: Memoirs of a President* (New York: Bantam Books, 1982), 319–403; Brzezinski, *Power and Principle*, 252–78 (quotation 273); speech by Carter, September 18, 1978, in Gambone, *Documents of American Diplomacy*, 406–11 (quotation 407).

47. Quandt, *Peace Process*, 309–26; Cyrus R. Vance, *Hard Choices: Critical Years in America's Foreign Policy* (New York: Simon & Schuster, 1983), 245–52 (quotation 252); Brzezinski, *Power and Principle*, 278–88.

48. Shlaim, *Iron Wall*, 363–83; Smith, *Palestine*, 254–57.

49. Shlaim, *Iron Wall*, 384–400.

50. Smith, *Palestine*, 261–64.

51. Quandt, *Peace Process*, 340–41 (quotation 340); Shlaim, *Iron Wall*, 400–407;

Alexander M. Haig, *Caveat: Realism, Reagan, and Foreign Policy* (New York: Macmillan, 1984), 330–35.

52. Shlaim, *Iron Wall*, 407–12.

53. Shlaim, *Iron Wall*, 412–14; Ronald Reagan, *An American Life* (New York: Simon & Schuster, 1990), 360–62, 417–30.

54. Shlaim, *Iron Wall*, 412–17; Rabinovich, *War for Lebanon*, 143–45.

55. Address by Reagan, September 1, 1982, in Quandt, *Peace Process*, 476–83 (quotation 477); Reagan, *American Life*, 430–42; Smith, *Palestine*, 266–67.

56. Parker, *Politics of Miscalculation*, 181–88; Ian J. Bickerton and Carla L. Klausner, *A Concise History of the Arab-Israeli Conflict* (Englewood Cliffs, NJ: Prentice Hall, 1991), 222–23.

Chapter 5

1. James A. Bill, *The Eagle and the Lion: The Tragedy of American-Iranian Relations* (New Haven, CT: Yale University Press, 1988), 98–182; Barry M. Rubin, *Paved with Good Intentions: The American Experience and Iran* (New York: Oxford University Press, 1980), 91–123.

2. Richard W. Cottam, *Iran and the United States: A Cold War Case Study* (Pittsburgh: University of Pittsburgh Press, 1988), 110–54; Bill, *Eagle and Lion*, 183–214.

3. Rouhollah K. Ramazani, *The United States and Iran: The Patterns of Influence* (New York: Praeger, 1982), 72–99; Bill, *Eagle and Lion*, 156–92.

4. Gilles Kepel, *Jihad: The Trial of Political Islam*, trans. Anthony F. Roberts (Cambridge, MA: Harvard University Press, 2002), 23–42.

5. Bill, *Eagle and Lion*, 226–34 (quotation 233); Carter, *Keeping Faith*, 434; Robert A. Strong, *Working in the World: Jimmy Carter and the Making of American Foreign Policy* (Baton Rouge: Louisiana State University Press, 2000), 45–70.

6. Gary Sick, *All Fall Down: America's Tragic Encounter with Iran* (New York: Random House, 1985), 34–64; Bill, *Eagle and Lion*, 234–42.

7. Bill, *Eagle and Lion*, 243–60; Sick, *All Fall Down*, 68–129; Brzezinski, *Power and Principle*, 358–98.

8. Harold H. Saunders, "The Crisis Begins," in *American Hostages in Iran: The Conduct of a Crisis*, ed. Paul H. Kriesberg (New Haven, CT: Yale University Press, 1985), 35–60; Russell Leigh Moses, *Freeing the Hostages: Reexamining U.S. Iranian Negotiations and Soviet Policy, 1979–1981* (Pittsburgh: University of Pittsburgh Press, 1996), 1–9.

9. Bill, *Eagle and Lion*, 324–40 (quotation p. 324); Brzezinski, *Power and Principle*, 471–76.

10. Sick, *All Fall Down*, 186–205 (quotations 192, 205).

11. Vance, *Hard Choices*, 375–83, 398–409; Brzezinski, *Power and Principle*, 477–87; Harold H. Saunders, "Diplomacy and Pressure, November 1979–May 1980" in *American Hostages in Iran: The Conduct of a Crisis,* ed. Paul H. Kriesberg (New Haven: CT: Yale University Press, 1985), 72–143.

12. Strong, *Working in the World*, 238–59.

13. Sick, *All Fall Down*, 280–302 (quotation 299); Carter, *Keeping Faith*, 514–19 (quotation 514); Vance, *Hard Choices*, 409–13.

14. Carter, *Keeping Faith*, 524–44; Elizabeth Drew, *Portrait of an Election: The 1980 Presidential Campaign* (New York: Simon & Schuster, 1981), 36–48, 127–29, 179–80.

15. Sick, *All Fall Down*, 303–42; Carter, *Keeping Faith*, 590–95.

16. Gary Sick, *October Surprise: America's Hostages in Iran and the Election of Ronald Reagan* (New York: Random House, 1991) (quotations 12).

17. Peter W. Rodman, *More Precious than Peace: The Cold War and the Struggle for the Third World* (New York: Scribner's, 1994), 197–216.

18. Jimmy Carter, State of the Union address, January 1980, http://www.jimmycarterlibrary.org/documents/speeches/su80jec.phtml26 (last accessed August 26, 2004); Brzezinski, *Power and Principle*, 430–37, 443–50; Vance, *Hard Choices*, 389–95.

19. Ronald Reagan, State of the Union address, February 6, 1985, in Gambone, *Documents of American Diplomacy*, 441–42 (quotation 442); Rodman, *More Precious than Peace*, 259–81; Reagan, *American Life*, 552 (quotation).

20. Little, *American Orientalism*, 152–55; Rodman, *More Precious than Peace*, 324–49; James M. Scott, *Deciding to Intervene: The Reagan Doctrine and American Foreign Policy* (Durham, NC: Duke University Press, 1996), 46–73 (quotation 55).

21. Reagan, *American Life*, 407 (quotation); Quandt, *Peace Process*, 338–39.

22. Reagan, *American Life*, 410–16; Haig, *Caveat*, 167–93.

23. Agnes G. Korbani, *U.S. Intervention in Lebanon, 1958 and 1982* (New York: Praeger, 1991), 79–94.

24. George P. Shultz, *Turmoil and Triumph: My Years as Secretary of State* (New York: Scribner's, 1993), 196–234; Reagan, *American Life*, 436–67 (quotation 467).

25. Smith, *Palestine*, 270–73; Rabinovich, *War for Lebanon*, 186; Korbani, *U.S. Intervention*, 94–100.

26. John L. Esposito, *The Islamic Threat: Myth or Reality?* 3rd edition (New York: Oxford University Press, 1999), 128–42; Fouad Ajami, *The Arab Predicament: Arab Political Thought and Practice since 1967*, 2nd edition (New York: Cambridge, 1992), 8–28; Kepel, *Jihad*, 106–35; Michael Scott Doran, "Somebody Else's Civil War: Ideology, Rage, and the Assault on America," in *How Did This Happen? Terrorism and the New War*, eds. James F. Hoge and Gideon Rose (New York: Council on Foreign Relations, 2001), 40–43.

27. Paul R. Pillar, *Terrorism and U.S. Foreign Policy* (Washington, DC: Brookings Institution Press, 2001), 57–69; Bruce Hoffman, *Inside Terrorism* (New York: Columbia University Press, 1998), 67–155.

28. John K. Cooley, *Libyan Sandstorm* (New York: Holt, Rinehart, and Winston, 1982), 240–69; Brian L. Davis, *Qaddafi, Terrorism, and the Origins of the U.S. Attack on Libya* (New York: Praeger, 1990), 57–143; Reagan, *American Life*, 517–20 (quotation 518).

29. Reagan, *American Life*, 520 (quotation); Davis, *Qaddafi*, 143–71; Madeleine

Korbel Albright, *Madam Secretary*, with Bob Woodward (New York: Miramax Books, 2003), 328–31.

30. Dilip Hiro, *The Longest War: The Iran-Iraq Military Conflict* (London: Paladin, 1990), 7–212.

31. Bruce W. Jentleson, *With Friends Like These: Reagan, Bush, and Saddam, 1982–1990* (New York: W. W. Norton, 1994), 31–58 (quotation 58).

32. Reagan, *American Life*, 504–507; Shultz, *Turmoil and Triumph*, 783–859 (quotation 807).

33. Hiro, *Longest War*, 223–40.

34. Shaul Bakhash, *The Reign of the Ayatollahs: Iran and the Islamic Revolution* (New York: Basic Books, 1990), 270–74 (quotation 274); Hiro, *Longest War*, 241–50.

Chapter 6

1. Quandt, *Peace Process*, 344–50.

2. Quandt, *Peace Process*, 350–56.

3. Shlaim, *Iron Wall*, 424–39, 442–50; Quandt, *Peace Process*, 360–63.

4. Shlaim, *Iron Wall*, 450–54 (quotations 453, 451); Bickerton and Klausner, *Concise History*, 231.

5. Palestine National Council, "Palestinian Declaration of Independence," November 15, 1988, in Bickerton and Klausner, *Concise History*, 238–40; Shlaim, *Iron Wall*, 457–60.

6. Shlaim, *Iron Wall*, 454–67 (quotation 466).

7. Shultz, *Turmoil and Triumph*, 1016–34; Quandt, *Peace Process*, 364–67.

8. Shultz, *Turmoil and Triumph*, 1036–45 (quotation 1042).

9. Quandt, *Peace Process*, 385–92 (quotation 389); James A. Baker, *The Politics of Diplomacy: Revolution, War, and Peace, 1989–1992* (New York: Putnam, 1995), 115–32 (quotation 125).

10. Baker, *Politics of Diplomacy*, 115–32 (quotation 131); Quandt, *Peace Process*, 392–94.

11. Baker, *Politics of Diplomacy*, 412–29 (quotation 422); George Bush and Brent Scowcroft, *A World Transformed* (New York: Knopf, 1988), 547–48.

12. Baker, *Politics of Diplomacy*, 443–69, 487–512 (quotations 416, 512).

13. Quandt, *Peace Process*, 404–12; Shlaim, *Iron Wall*, 502–12.

14. Dennis Ross, *The Missing Peace: The Inside Story of the Fight for Middle East Peace* (New York: Farrar, Straus, and Giroux, 2004), 101–104; Israeli-PLO Declaration of Principles, September 13, 1993, in Bickerton and Klausner, *Concise History*, 274–79.

15. Statement by Clinton, September 13, 1993, in Bickerton and Klausner, *Concise History*, 270–72; Warren Christopher, *Chances of a Lifetime* (New York, Scribner, 2001), 194–204 (quotations 203–204); Bill Clinton, *My Life* (New York: Knopf, 2004), 541–45.

16. Christopher, *Chances of a Lifetime*, 211–16 (quotation 215); Clinton, *My Life*, 609–10, 625–26; address by Warren Christopher, October 24, 1994, in Warren Christopher, *In the Stream of History: Shaping Foreign Policy for a*

New Era (Stanford, CA: Stanford University Press, 1998), 195–202.

17. Ross, *Missing Peace*, 122–36, 188–93, 195–208; Christopher, *Chances of a Lifetime*, 205–208; Bickerton and Klausner, *Concise History*, 281–95.

18. Ross, *Missing Peace*, 126–28, 193–95, 209–15 (quotation 126); Bickerton and Klausner, *Concise History*, 281–91.

19. Christopher, *Chances of a Lifetime*, 216–24; Clinton, *My Life*, 626; Ross, *Missing Peace*, 137–63, 216–45.

20. Albright, *Madam Secretary*, 291–92 (quotation 292); Clinton, *My Life*, 747–48; Christopher, *In the Stream of History*, 497–504.

21. Clinton, *My Life*, 814–20 (quotation 820); Wye River Memorandum, October 23, 1998, in Bickerton and Klausner, *Concise History*, 344–48; Albright, *Madam Secretary*, 288–318; Ross, *Missing Peace*, 415–59.

22. Clinton, *My Life*, 832–33 (quotation 832); Bickerton and Klausner, *Concise History*, 317–29 (quotation 323).

23. Ross, *Missing Peace*, 650–711 (quotation 710); Clinton, *My Life*, 911–16 (quotation 915); Albright, *Madam Secretary*, 484–93.

24. Clinton, *My Life*, 925–26, 929, 935–38, 943–45 (quotations 937–38, 944–45); Ross, *Missing Peace*, 742–58 (quotations 757–58); Albright, *Madam Secretary*, 495–98.

25. Clinton, *My Life*, 883–88, 903–904 (quotation 886); Albright, *Madam Secretary*, 473–82 (quotation 481); Ross, *Missing Peace*, 536–90 (quotation 587).

26. Ross, *Missing Peace*, 509, 620–31 (quotation 626).

27. Albright, *Madam Secretary*, 494–95; Ross, *Missing Peace*, 725–33.

28. "Arabs Support Bush's Vision," June 4, 2003, http://www.dispatch.com/print_template.ph...y=dispatch/2003/early/2003/0604-00204.html (last accessed June 9, 2003); "Old Pessimism, New Hope," *Seattle Times*, June 30, 2003, A3; "Israel Attacks Islamic Jihad Base in Syria," October 5, 2003, http://www.usatoday.com/news/world/2003-10-05-israel-attack_x.htm (last accessed September 9, 2004); "Palestinian Forces Arrest Militant Leaders," *Columbus Dispatch*, February 6, 2005, A3.

29. "Israel Leaves Arafat Compound," September 30, 2002, http://www.cnn.com/2002/WORLD/meast/09/29/mideast/ (last accessed September 9, 2004); Bickerton and Klausner, *Concise History*, 343.

30. Colin L. Powell remarks to the press, May 21, 2001, http://www.state.gov/secretary/rm/2001/2965.htm (last accessed September 10, 2004). See also Powell interview with CBS News, March 10, 2002, http://www.state.gov/secretary/rm/2002/8704.htm (last accessed September 10, 2004); "Zinni: Both Sides Want End to 'Terrible Solution,'" March 15, 2002, http://www.cnn.com/2002/WORLD/meast/03/15/mideast/ (last accessed September 10, 2004); briefing by Colin L. Powell, March 29, 2002, www.state.gov/secretary/rm/2002/9067.htm (last accessed September 10, 2004).

31. Ron Suskind, *The Price of Loyalty: George W. Bush, the White House, and the Education of Paul O'Neill* (New York: Simon & Schuster, 2004), 70–72 (quotation 71); address by Bush, June 24, 2002, http://

www.whitehouse.gov/news/releases/2002/06/20020624-3.html (last accessed September 9, 2004).

32. Department of State, "A Performance-Based Roadmap to a Permanent Two-State Solution to the Israeli-Palestinian Conflict," April 30, 2003, http://www.state.gov/r/pa/prs/ps/2003/20062pf.htm (last accessed September 9, 2003).

33. "Arabs Support Bush's Vision," June 4, 2003, http:/www.dispatch.com/print_template.ph...y=dispatch/2003/early/2003/0604-00204.html (last accessed June 9, 2003); "Middle East Discussions Bear Fruit," June 5, 2003, http:/www.dispatch.com/print_template.ph...y=dispatch/2003/early/2003/0605-00200.html (last accessed June 9, 2003). See also Peter Slevin, "Bush Inserts U.S. as Arbiter in Middle East," *Washington Post*, June 6, 2003, A16.

34. Joshua Hammer, "Good Fences Make . . . " *Newsweek*, June 9, 2003, 32–33. See also Glenn Frankel, "Israelis Keep Stakes Planted at Outposts," June 6, 2003, *Washington Post*, A1, A16.

35. Hammer, "Good Fences Make . . ."; "Walling off the Peace," *Time*, December 22, 2003, 37–41; Fareed Zakaria, "For Sharon, an Unlikely Legacy," *Newsweek*, July 19, 2004, 39.

36. James Carney, "How Bush Got Religion," *Time*, June 16, 2003, 42–43; "Arafat Move Clouds Mideast Peace Summit," May 28, 2003, http://abcnews.go.com/wire/World/ap20030528_284.html (last accessed May 28, 2003); "Palestinian PM Withdraws Resignation," July 27, 2004, http:/www.cnn.com/2004/WORLD/meast/07/27/mideast/index.html (last accessed September 9, 2004); Matt Rees, "Two Lions Trying to Prevail," *Time*, November 8, 2004, 32–34.

37. "Can Hamas Be Defeated?" *Columbus Dispatch*, June 22, 2003; "Israel Starts Pulling Out of Gaza," *Seattle Times*, June 30, 2003, A1–A3; "16 Killed in Suicide Bombings on Buses in Israel," September 1, 2004, http://www.cnn.com/2004/WORLD/meast/08/31/mideast/index.html (last accessed September 9, 2004); "Israeli Missiles Injure 5 in Gaza," September 1, 2004, http://www.cnn.com/2004/WORLD/meast/09/01/mideast/index.html (last accessed September 9, 2004).

38. "Sharon Presents Plan for Gaza Withdrawal," August 31, 2004, http://www.cnn.com/2004/WORLD/meast/08/31/sharon.gaza/index.html (last accessed September 9, 2004); "Palestinian Forces Arrest Militant Leaders," *Columbus Dispatch*, February 6, 2005, A3; "Escaping Arafat's Shadow," *Time*, March 14, 2005.

39. "The End of Dreams," *Newsweek*, April 26, 2004; "Sharon Aide Says Goal of Gaza Plan is to Halt Road Map," *Washington Post*, October 7, 2004, A14, A28; "Meet the New Extremists," *Time*, November 8, 2004, 34; "Israel Reports More Progress in Talks with Palestinians," *Columbus Dispatch*, January 30, 2005, A3; "From the Shadows to Center Stage," *Time*, February 21, 2005, 26–27.

Chapter 7

1. Baker, *Politics of Diplomacy*, 261–67 (quotations 263–64); Bush and Scowcroft, *World Transformed*, 305–307.

2. Baker, *Politics of Diplomacy*, 267–71 (quotation 268); Jentleson, *With Friends Like These*, 154–56 (quotation 155); Bush and Scowcroft, *World Transformed*, 307–308.

3. Michael T. Klare, *Rogue States and Nuclear Outlaws: America's Search for a New Foreign Policy* (New York: Hill and Wang, 1995), 33–4, 38–41; Peter L. Hahn, "Grand Strategy," in *U.S. Foreign Policy after the Cold War*, eds. Randall B. Ripley and James M. Lindsay (Pittsburgh: University of Pittsburgh Press, 1997), 200–12.

4. Baker, *Politics of Diplomacy*, 271–74 (quotation 271); Majid Khadduri and Edmund Ghareeb, *War in the Gulf, 1990–91: The Iraq-Kuwait Conflict and its Implications* (New York: Oxford University Press, 1997), 79–88.

5. Bush and Scowcroft, *World Transformed*, 309–13; Lawrence Freedman and Efraim Karsh, *The Gulf Conflict 1990–1991: Diplomacy and War in the New World Order* (Princeton, NJ: Princeton University Press, 1993), 42–61; Iraqi transcript of meeting, July 25, 1990, in *The Gulf War Reader: History, Documents, Opinions*, eds. Micah L. Sifry and Christopher Cerf (New York: Times Books, 1991), 122–33.

6. Glenn Frankel, "How Lines in the Sand in 1922 Sketched the Invasion of 1990," *Washington Post National Weekly Edition*, September 10–16, 1990, 16 (quotation); Bush and Scowcroft, *World Transformed*, 335; Michael A. Palmer, *Guardians of the Gulf: A History of America's Expanding Role in the Persian Gulf, 1833–1992* (New York: Free Press, 1992), 163–74.

7. Bush and Scowcroft, *World Transformed*, 313–24.

8. John Robert Greene, *The Presidency of George Bush* (Lawrence: University Press of Kansas, 2000), 116–17, 124–25 (quotations 117, 125); Bush and Scowcroft, *World Transformed*, 324–48 (quotation 333).

9. Baker, *Politics of Diplomacy*, 325–28, 355–65 (quotations 327, 363); Colin L. Powell, *My American Journey* (New York: Random House, 1995), 475–89; Bush and Scowcroft, *World Transformed*, 377–83, 442–49.

10. Bush and Scowcroft, *World Transformed*, 461; Baker, *Politics of Diplomacy*, 382–95; Freedman and Karsh, *Gulf Conflict*, 299–330.

11. Powell, *My American Journey*, 511–12 (quotation 511); Bush and Scowcroft, *World Transformed*, 451–57 (quotation 453); Baker, *Politics of Diplomacy*, 385–90 (quotation 388); Freedman and Karsh, *Gulf Conflict*, 331–41.

12. Bush and Scowcroft, *World Transformed*, 460–61, 468–77 (quotation 472); Baker, *Politics of Diplomacy*, 396–410.

13. Bush and Scowcroft, *World Transformed*, 477–79 (quotation 478); Palmer, *Guardians of the Gulf*, 224–27.

14. Bush and Scowcroft, *World Transformed*, 478–87; Freedman and Karsh, *Gulf Conflict*, 386–409.

15. Bush and Scowcroft, *World Transformed*, 464; Baker, *Politics of Diplomacy*, 435–38 (quotations 436, 435).

16. Bush and Scowcroft, *World Transformed*, 488–92 (quotation 489); Powell, *My American Journey*, 524–28 (quotation 527); Baker, *Politics of Diplomacy*, 438–42.
17. Albright, *Madam Secretary*, 272–76 (quotation 276); Clinton, *My Life*, 472.
18. Bob Woodward, *Plan of Attack* (New York: Simon and Schuster, 2004), 9–10.
19. Christopher, *In the Stream of History*, 193–94 (quotation 194); address by Warren Christopher, October 24, 1994, *In the Stream of History*, 195–202 (quotation 201); Clinton, *My Life*, 525–26, 624, 728; Christopher, *Chances of a Lifetime*, 232–35.
20. UN Security Council Resolution 687, April 8, 1991, www.un.org/docs/scres/1991/scres91.htm (last accessed September 13, 2004); Clinton, *My Life*, 669–70; Albright, *Madam Secretary*, 272–76.
21. Albright, *Madam Secretary*, 275–80.
22. Albright, *Madam Secretary*, 280–83.
23. Clinton, *My Life*, 833–34 (quotation 833); Albright, *Madam Secretary*, 283–87.
24. Albright, *Madam Secretary*, 283–87 (quotation 287); Woodward, *Plan of Attack*, 9–10.
25. UN Security Council Resolution 1284, December 17, 1999, ods-dds-ny.un.org/doc/UNDOC/GEN/N99/396/09/PDF/N9939609.pdf?OpenElement (last accessed September 20, 2004); John Keegan, *The Iraq War* (New York: Knopf, 2004), 110–11.
26. Peter L. Bergen, *Holy War, Inc.: Inside the Secret World of Osama Bin Laden* (New York: Free Press, 2001), 24–40; Pillar, *Terrorism*, 30–31, 47–50; National Commission on Terrorist Attacks upon the United States, *The 9/11 Commission Report: Final Report of the National Commission on Terrorist Attacks upon the United States* (New York: W. W. Norton, 2004), 49–55.
27. Doran, "Somebody Else's Civil War," 33–52; Kepel, *Jihad*, 5–20.
28. Kepel, *Jihad*, 136–84; Pillar, *Terrorism*, 42–46; Hoffman, *Inside Terrorism*, 95–100; Esposito, *Islamic Threat*, 171–86.
29. Kepel, *Jihad*, 237–98; Albright, *Madam Secretary*, 319–26.
30. Pillar, *Terrorism*, 46–47, 53–55, 62; Kepel, *Jihad*, 222–36.
31. Kepel, *Jihad*, 313–20.
32. Doran, "Somebody Else's Civil War," 31–39 (quotation 36); Bergen, *Holy War, Inc.*, 63–105 (quotation 94); Kepel, *Jihad*, 317–20 (quotation 320).
33. Fawaz A. Gerges, *America and Political Islam: Clash of Cultures or Clash of Interests?* (New York: Cambridge University Press, 1999), 78–85 (quotation 79).
34. Clinton, *My Life*, 497, 651–52, 675; Hoffman, *Inside Terrorism*, 92–93, 199–204.
35. Clinton, *My Life*, 702, 705, 717–18, 788–90 (quotation 705); address by Warren Christopher, May 21, 1996, *In the Stream of History*, 444–51.
36. Christopher, *Chances of a Lifetime*, 225–32; Clinton, *My Life*, 797–98, 804 (quotation); *9/11 Commission Report*, 59–70.
37. Albright, *Madam Secretary*, 361–62, 368–75; Bergen, *Holy War, Inc.*, 105–26.

38. Clinton, *My Life*, 798 (quotation), 803–805; Albright, *Madam Secretary*, 364–68.

39. Clinton, *My Life*, 891, 925–26, 935 (quotations 925–26, 935); Albright, *Madam Secretary*, 375–76.

40. *9/11 Commission Report*, 1–46, 339–40.

41. *9/11 Commission Report*, 38–40 (quotation 39); *Le Monde*, September 12, 2001, http://www.worldpress.org/1101we_are_all_americans.htm (last accessed October 1, 2004).

42. Tommy Franks, *American Soldier*, with Malcolm McConnelly (New York: Regan Books, 2004), 283–317; Bob Woodward, *Bush at War* (New York: Simon & Schuster, 2002), 312–16; Craig R. Eisendrath and Melvin A. Goodman, *Bush League Diplomacy: How the Neoconservatives Are Putting the World at Risk* (Amherst, NY: Prometheus Books, 2004), 37–45, 222.

43. Nicholas D. Kristof, "Afghanistan's Once-Hopeful Future is Sinking into Culture of Narco-Terrorism," *Columbus Dispatch*, November 18, 2003; "The Hunt Heats Up," *Newsweek*, March 15, 2004, 46–48; Fareed Zakaria, "Warlords, Drugs, and Votes," *Newsweek*, August 9, 2004, 39; "Afghan Candidates Drop out of Election after Ink Snafu," *Columbus Dispatch*, October 10, 2004, A1–A2.

44. Woodward, *Plan of Attack*, 4, 12–23 (quotation 4); Suskind, *Price of Loyalty*, 70–75, 84–86.

45. *9/11 Commission Report*, 334–38; Woodward, *Plan of Attack*, 24–74, 119–20 (quotation 120).

46. Woodward, *Plan of Attack*, 84–95, 119–20, 132, 194–202 (quotations 119, 132, 202); Eisendrath and Goodman, *Bush League Diplomacy*, 134 (quotation).

47. Woodward, *Plan of Attack*, 159–66 (quotation 164).

48. Woodward, *Plan of Attack*, 185–91, 203–204 (quotations 187–188).

49. UN Resolution 1441, November 8, 2002, in *The Iraq War Reader: History, Documents, Opinions*, eds. Micah L. Sifry and Christopher Cerf (New York: Touchstone Books, 2003), 648–52; Woodward, *Plan of Attack*, 180–85, 220–27.

50. Keegan, *Iraq War*, 111–14.

51. Woodward, *Plan of Attack*, 247–54 (quotation 249).

52. Woodward, *Plan of Attack*, 294–95, 308–18.

53. Woodward, *Plan of Attack*, 346–79; Keegan, *Iraq War*, 114–20; Franks, *American Soldier*, 431 (quotation).

54. Keegan, *Iraq War*, 1–7, 127–203 (quotation 4); Eisendrath and Goodman, *Bush League Diplomacy*, 61–62; "'Ladies and Gentlemen, We Got Him,'" *Time*, December 22, 2003, 15–19.

55. Eisendrath and Goodman, *Bush League Diplomacy*, 62–64; "Refereeing in Hell," *Newsweek*, January 19, 2004, 36–37; Fareed Zakaria, "In Iraq, It's Time for Some Smarts," *Newsweek*, March 1, 2004, 39 (quotation); Fallows, "Blind into Baghdad" (quotation).

56. Eisendrath and Goodman, *Bush League Diplomacy*, 63 (quotation); "Bush's

Mr. Wrong," *Newsweek*, May 31, 2004, 22–32.

57. Franks, *American Soldier*, 546–48 (quotation 547); "A Question of Trust," *Time*, July 21, 2003, 22–26; "What Went Wrong," *Newsweek*, February 9, 2004, 24–31; "U.S. 'Almost All Wrong' on Inspections," *Washington Post*, October 7, 2004, A1, A34; Eisendrath and Goodman, *Bush League Diplomacy*, 69–70, 110–14; Richard A. Clarke, *Against All Enemies: Inside America's War on Terror* (New York: Free Press, 2004), 264–71.

58. "Abu Ghraib and Beyond," *Newsweek*, May 17, 2004, 32–38; Fareed Zakaria, "The Price of Arrogance," *Newsweek*, May 17, 2004, 39 (quotation); "Welcome to the Real World," *Newsweek*, June 23, 2004, 28–35; Eisendrath and Goodman, *Bush League Diplomacy*, 65–69, 94–96; Melvyn P. Leffler, "Think Again: Bush's Foreign Policy," *Foreign Policy* 144 (September/ October 2004): 22–27.

59. Eisendrath and Goodman, *Bush League Diplomacy*, 71–72, 77–94; "The Despot and his Demons," *Newsweek*, January 12, 2004, 32–33, "Has the War Made Us Safer?" *Newsweek*, April 12, 2004, 24–28; Clarke, *Against All Enemies*, 247–62.

60. Keegan, *Iraq War*, 210–13; "Racing the Clock in Iraq," *Newsweek*, February 9, 2004, 32–38; "Despite Insurgency, U.S. Has Significant Successes," *Columbus Dispatch*, January 30, 2005.

61. "Iraq's New S.O.B.," *Newsweek*, July 26, 2004, 36–37; "Taunts, Traps, and Tests," *Newsweek*, August 23, 2004, 32–33.

62. "Al-Qaeda's New Home," *Time*, September 15, 2003, 60–61; "Rough Justice in Iraq," *Newsweek*, May 10, 2004, 26–30; "The Dark Road Ahead," *Newsweek*, April 12, 2004, 28–34; "We Are Your Martyrs," *Newsweek*, April 19, 2004, 36–41; "A Deadly Face-Off," *Newsweek*, April 26, 2004, 30–33; "Iraq's Repairman," *Newsweek*, July 5, 2004, 22–30.

63. "Taunts, Traps, and Tests," 32–33; "It's Worse than You Think," *Newsweek*, September 20, 2004, 30–33; "Developments in Iraq," *Columbus Dispatch*, March 27, 2005, A3.

64. Korb quoted in "Justification for War Still Hotly Debated," *Columbus Dispatch*, March 19, 2004, A10; Eisendrath and Goodman, *Bush League Diplomacy*, 219–20; Clarke, *Against All Enemies*, 286–87.

65. Charles Krauthammer, "President Made the Best of Two Choices," *Columbus Dispatch*, January 30, 2004; Bush, acceptance speech at Republican National Convention, August 2004, http://www.gopconvention. com/ cgi-data/speeches/files/v46q7t4op60p0109d9b8i8373 arhnn0r.shtml (last accessed September 13, 2004).

66. "A Vote for Hope," *Time*, February 14, 2005, 33–35; "When History Turns a Corner," *Time*, March 14, 2005, 20–25; "Iraqi Predicts Accord on Government in Days," *Columbus Dispatch*, March 27, 2005, A3.

67. "Hizballah's Herald," *Time*, March 21, 2005, 48; "U.S. Military Deaths in War with Iraq from January to February 2005," http://abcnews.go.com/US/ story?id=385553 (last accessed June 9, 2005).

BIBLIOGRAPHY

Published Primary Sources

Gambone, Michael D., ed. *Documents of American Diplomacy from the American Revolution to the Present*. Westport, CT: Greenwood Press, 2002.

National Commission on Terrorist Attacks upon the United States. *The 9/11 Commission Report: Final Report of the National Commission on Terrorist Attacks upon the United States*. New York: W. W. Norton, 2004.

Sifry, Micah L. and Christopher Cerf, eds. *The Gulf War Reader: History, Documents, Opinions*. New York: Times Books, 1991.

———. *The Iraq War Reader: History, Documents, Opinions*. New York: Touchstone Books, 2003.

U.S. Department of State. *Foreign Relations of the United States, 1947*. Vol. 5. Washington, DC: U.S. Government Printing Office, 1972.

———. *Foreign Relations of the United States, 1950*. Vol. 5. Washington, DC: U.S. Government Printing Office, 1978.

———. *Foreign Relations of the United States, 1951*. Vol. 5. Washington, DC: U.S. Government Printing Office, 1982.

———. *Foreign Relations of the United States, 1952–1954*. Vol. 9. Washington, DC: U.S. Government Printing Office, 1986.

———. *Foreign Relations of the United States, 1955–1957*. Vol. 14. Washington, DC: U.S. Government Printing Office, 1989.

———. *Foreign Relations of the United States, 1958–1960*. Vol. 13. Washington, DC: U.S. Government Printing Office, 1992.

———. *Foreign Relations of the United States, 1964–1968*. Vol. 18. Washington, DC: U.S. Government Printing Office, 2000.

———. *Foreign Relations of the United States, 1964–1968*. Vol. 21. Washington, DC: U.S. Government Printing Office, 2000.

Secondary Materials

Ajami, Fouad. *The Arab Predicament: Arab Political Thought and Practice since 1967.* 2nd ed. New York: Cambridge University Press, 1992.

Albright, Madeleine Korbel. *Madam Secretary.* With Bob Woodward. New York: Miramax Books, 2003.

Ambrose, Stephen E. *Rise to Globalism: American Foreign Policy, 1938–1980.* New York: Penguin Books, 1980.

Ariel, Yaakov S. *On Behalf of Israel: American Fundamentalist Attitudes toward Jews, Judaism, and Zionism, 1865–1945.* Brooklyn, NY: Carlson, 1991.

Ashton, Nigel John. *Eisenhower, Macmillan, and the Problem of Nasser: Anglo-American Relations and Arab Nationalism, 1955–59.* New York: St. Martin's Press, 1996.

Bain, Kenneth Ray. *The March to Zion: United States Policy and the Founding of Israel.* College Station: Texas A&M University Press, 1979.

Baker, James A. *The Politics of Diplomacy: Revolution, War, and Peace, 1989–1992.* New York: Putnam, 1995.

Bakhash, Shaul. *The Reign of the Ayatollahs: Iran and the Islamic Revolution.* New York: Basic Books, 1990.

Bamford, James. *Body of Secrets: Anatomy of the Ultra-Secret National Security Agency.* New York: Doubleday, 2001.

Baram, Phillip J. *The Department of State and the Middle East, 1919–1945.* Philadelphia: University of Pennsylvania Press, 1978.

Barnet, Richard J. *Intervention and Revolution: The United States in the Third World.* New York: World, 1968.

Bar-Siman-Tov, Yaacov. *The Israeli-Egyptian War of Attrition, 1967–1970: A Case-Study of Limited Local War.* New York: Columbia University Press, 1980.

Bass, Warren. *Support Any Friend: Kennedy's Middle East and the Making of the U.S.-Israel Alliance.* New York: Oxford University Press, 2003.

Behbehani, Hashim. *The Soviet Union and Arab Nationalism, 1917–1966.* New York: KPI, 1986.

Benson, Michael T. *Harry S Truman and the Founding of Israel.* Westport, CT: Praeger, 1997.

Bergen, Peter L. *Holy War, Inc.: Inside the Secret World of Osama Bin Laden.* New York: Free Press, 2001.

Berman, Aaron. *Nazism, the Jews, and American Zionism, 1933–1948*. Detroit, MI: Wayne State University Press, 1990.

Bickerton, Ian J., and Carla L. Klausner. *A Concise History of the Arab-Israeli Conflict*. Englewood Cliffs, NJ: Prentice Hall, 1991.

Bill, James A. *The Eagle and the Lion: The Tragedy of American-Iranian Relations*. New Haven, CT: Yale University Press, 1988.

Bills, Scott L. *Empire and Cold War: The Roots of U.S.–Third World Antagonism, 1945–47*. New York: St. Martin's Press, 1990.

Brands, H. W. *Specter of Neutralism: The United States and the Emergence of the Third World, 1947–1960*. New York: Columbia University Press, 1989.

Brecher, Frank W. *Reluctant Ally: United States Foreign Policy toward the Jews from Wilson to Roosevelt*. New York: Greenwood Press, 1991.

Bryson, Thomas A. *Seeds of Mideast Crisis: The United States Diplomatic Role in the Middle East during World War II*. Jefferson, NC: McFarland, 1981.

Brzezinski, Zbigniew. *Power and Principle: Memoirs of the National Security Advisor, 1977–1981*. New York: Farrar, Straus, and Giroux, 1983.

Bush, George and Brent Scowcroft. *A World Transformed*. New York: Knopf, 1988.

Caplan, Neil. *Palestine Jewry and the Arab Question, 1917–1925*. London: Frank Cass, 1978.

Carter, Jimmy. *Keeping Faith: Memoirs of a President*. New York: Bantam Books, 1982.

Christison, Kathleen. *Perceptions of Palestine: Their Influence on U.S. Middle East Policy*. Berkeley: University of California Press, 1999.

Christopher, Warren. *Chances of a Lifetime*. New York: Scribner, 2001.

———. *In the Stream of History: Shaping Foreign Policy for a New Era*. Stanford, CA: Stanford University Press, 1998.

Clarke, Richard A. *Against All Enemies: Inside America's War on Terror*. New York: Free Press, 2004.

Clinton, Bill. *My Life*. New York: Knopf, 2004.

Cockburn, Andrew and Leslie Cockburn. *Dangerous Liaison: The Inside Story of the U.S.-Israeli Covert Relationship*. New York: Harper Collins, 1991.

Cohen, Michael Joseph. *Fighting World War III from the Middle East: Allied*

Contingency Plans, 1945–1954. London: Frank Cass, 1997.

——. *Palestine and the Great Powers, 1945–1948.* Princeton, NJ: Princeton University Press, 1982.

——. *Palestine to Israel: From Mandate to Independence.* London: Frank Cass, 1988.

Cooley, John K. *Libyan Sandstorm.* New York: Holt, Rinehart, and Winston, 1982.

Cottam, Richard W. *Iran and the United States: A Cold War Case Study.* Pittsburgh: University of Pittsburgh Press, 1988.

Davis, Brian L. *Qaddafi, Terrorism, and the Origins of the U.S. Attack on Libya.* Westport, CT: Praeger, 1990.

DeNovo, John A. *American Interests and Policies in the Middle East, 1900–1939.* Minneapolis: University of Minnesota Press, 1963.

Devereux, David R. *The Formulation of British Defence Policy towards the Middle East, 1948–56.* New York: St. Martin's Press, 1990.

Doran, Michael Scott. "Somebody Else's Civil War: Ideology, Rage, and the Assault on America." In *How Did This Happen? Terrorism and the New War,* edited by James F. Hoge and Gideon Rose, 31–52. New York: Council on Foreign Relations, 2001.

Drew, Elizabeth. *Portrait of an Election: The 1980 Presidential Campaign.* New York: Simon & Schuster, 1981.

Eisendrath, Craig R., and Melvin A. Goodman. *Bush League Diplomacy: How the Neoconservatives Are Putting the World at Risk.* Amherst, NY: Prometheus Books, 2004.

Ennes, James M. *Assault on the Liberty: The True Story of the Israeli Attack on an American Intelligence Ship.* New York: Random House, 1979.

Esposito, John L. *The Islamic Threat: Myth or Reality?* 3rd ed. New York: Oxford University Press, 1999.

Fallows, James. "Bush's Lost Year." *Atlantic Monthly* 294, no. 3 (October 2004): 68–84.

Fawcett, Louise L'Estrange. *Iran and the Cold War: The Azerbaijan Crisis of 1946.* New York: Cambridge University Press, 1992.

Field, James A. *From Gibraltar to the Middle East: America and the Mediterranean World, 1776–1882.* Chicago: Imprint Publications, 1991.

Franks, Tommy. *American Soldier.* With Malcom McConnelly. New York: Regan Books, 2004.

Freedman, Lawrence, and Efraim Karsh. *The Gulf Conflict 1990–1991: Diplomacy and War in the New World Order.* Princeton, NJ: Princeton University Press, 1993.

Freiberger, Steven Z. *Dawn over Suez: The Rise of American Power in the Middle East, 1953–1957.* Chicago: Ivan R. Dee, 1992.

Gasiorowski, Mark J. *U.S. Foreign Policy and the Shah: Building a Client State in Iran.* Ithaca, NY: Cornell University Press, 1991.

Gendzier, Irene L. *Notes from the Minefield: United States Intervention in Lebanon and the Middle East, 1945–1958.* New York: Columbia University Press, 1997.

Gerges, Fawaz A. *America and Political Islam: Clash of Cultures or Clash of Interests?* New York: Cambridge University Press, 1999.

Golan, Galia. *Soviet Policies in the Middle East: From World War II to Gorbachev.* New York: Cambridge University Press, 1990.

Goode, James F. *The United States and Iran: In the Shadow of Musaddiq.* New York: St. Martin's Press, 1997.

Greene, John Robert. *The Presidency of George Bush.* Lawrence: University Press of Kansas, 2000.

Grose, Peter. *Israel in the Mind of America.* New York: Knopf, 1983.

Hahn, Peter L. *Caught in the Middle East: U.S. Policy toward the Arab-Israeli Conflict, 1945–1961.* Chapel Hill: University of North Carolina Press, 2004.

———. "Grand Strategy," in *U.S. Foreign Policy after the Cold War*, edited by Randall B. Ripley and James M. Lindsay, 185–214. Pittsburgh: University of Pittsburgh Press, 1997.

———. "An Ominous Moment: Lyndon Johnson and the Six Day War." In *Looking Back at LBJ: White House Politics in a New Light*, edited by Mitchell B. Lerner, 78–100. Lawrence: University Press of Kansas, 2005.

———. *The United States, Great Britain, and Egypt, 1945–1956: Strategy and Diplomacy in the Early Cold War.* Chapel Hill: University of North Carolina Press, 1991.

Haig, Alexander M. *Caveat: Realism, Reagan, and Foreign Policy.* New York: Macmillan, 1984.

Hamby, Alonzo L. *Man of the People: A Life of Harry S Truman.* New York: Oxford University Press, 1995.

Heiss, Mary Ann. *Empire and Nationhood: The United States, Great Britain, and Iranian Oil, 1950–1954.* New York: Columbia University Press, 1997.

———. "Real Men Don't Wear Pajamas." In *Empire and Revolution: The United States and the Third World since 1945*, edited by Peter L. Hahn and Mary Ann Heiss, 178–94. Columbus: Ohio State University Press, 2001.

Hiro, Dilip. *The Longest War: The Iran-Iraq Military Conflict.* London: Paladin, 1990.

Hoffman, Bruce. *Inside Terrorism.* New York: Columbia University Press, 1998.

Holland, Matthew F. *America and Egypt: From Roosevelt to Eisenhower.* Westport, CT: Praeger, 1996.

Ilan, Amitzur. *Bernadotte in Palestine, 1948: A Study in Contemporary Humanitarian Knight-Errantry.* Basingstoke: Macmillan, 1989.

Isaacson, Walter. *Kissinger: A Biography.* New York: Simon & Schuster, 1992.

Jasse, Richard L. "The Baghdad Pact: Cold War or Colonialism?" *Middle Eastern Studies* 27:1 (January 1991): 140–56.

Jentleson, Bruce W. *With Friends Like These: Reagan, Bush, and Saddam, 1982–1990.* New York: W.W. Norton, 1994.

Johnson, Lyndon B. *The Vantage Point: Perspectives of the Presidency, 1963–1969.* New York: Holt, Rinehart, and Winston, 1971.

Kaplan, Robert D. *The Arabists: The Romance of an American Elite.* New York: Free Press, 1993.

Keegan, John. *The Iraq War.* New York: Knopf, 2004.

Kepel, Gilles. *Jihad: The Trail of Political Islam.* Translated by Anthony F. Roberts. Cambridge: Harvard University Press, 2002.

Khadduri, Majid, and Edmund Ghareeb. *War in the Gulf, 1990–91: The Iraq-Kuwait Conflict and its Implications.* New York: Oxford University Press, 1997.

Klare, Michael T. *Rogue States and Nuclear Outlaws: America's Search for a New Foreign Policy.* New York: Hill and Wang, 1995.

Kolinsky, Martin. *Law, Order, and Riots in Mandatory Palestine, 1928–35.* New York: St. Martin's Press, 1993.

Kolko, Gabriel. *Confronting the Third World: United States Foreign Policy, 1945–*

1980. New York: Pantheon Books, 1988.

Korbani, Agnes G. *U.S. Intervention in Lebanon, 1958 and 1982.* New York: Praeger, 1991.

Korn, David A. *Stalemate: The War of Attrition and Great Power Diplomacy in the Middle East, 1967–1970.* Boulder, CO: Westview, 1992.

Kuniholm, Bruce Robellet. *The Origins of the Cold War in the Near East: Great Power Conflict and Diplomacy in Iran, Turkey, and Greece.* Princeton, NJ: Princeton University Press, 1980.

———. "Turkey and the West since World War II." In *Turkey between East and West: New Challenges for a Rising Regional Power,* edited by Vojtech Mastny and R. Craig Nation, 45–70. Boulder, CO: Westview, 1996.

Kyle, Keith. *Suez.* New York: St. Martin's Press, 1991.

Leffler, Melvyn P. *A Preponderance of Power: National Security, the Truman Administration, and the Cold War.* Stanford, CA: Stanford University Press, 1992.

———. "Think Again: Bush's Foreign Policy." *Foreign Policy* 144 (September/October 2004): 22–27.

Little, Douglas. *American Orientalism: The United States and the Middle East since 1945.* Chapel Hill: University of North Carolina Press, 2002.

———. "Choosing Sides: Lyndon Johnson and the Middle East." In *The Johnson Years: LBJ at Home and Abroad,* edited by Robert Divine, 150–97. Lawrence: University Press of Kansas, 1987.

———. "Cold War and Covert Action: The United States and Syria, 1945–1958." *Middle East Journal* 44, no. 1 (Winter 1990): 51–75.

———. "The Making of a Special Relationship: The United States and Israel, 1957–68." *International Journal of Middle East Studies* 25, no. 4 (November 1993): 563–585.

———. "Nasser Delenda Est: Lyndon Johnson, the Arabs, and the 1967 Six-Day War." In *The Foreign Policies of Lyndon Johnson: Beyond Vietnam,* edited by H. W. Brands, 145–67. College Station: Texas A&M University Press, 1999.

McCullough, David G. *Truman.* New York: Simon & Schuster, 1992.

McMahon, Robert J. "The Challenge of the Third World." In *Empire and Revolution: The United States and the Third World since 1945,* edited by Peter L. Hahn and Mary Ann Heiss, 1–14. Columbus: Ohio State

University Press, 2001.

Moses, Russell Leigh. *Freeing the Hostages: Reexamining U.S.-Iranian Negotiations and Soviet Policy, 1979–1981.* Pittsburgh: University of Pittsburgh Press, 1996.

Neff, Donald. *Warriors for Jerusalem: The Six Days That Changed the Middle East.* New York: Linden Press, Simon & Schuster, 1984.

Newsom, David D. *The Imperial Mantle: The United States, Decolonization, and the Third World.* Bloomington: Indiana University Press, 2001.

Nizameddin, Talal. *Russia and the Middle East: Towards a New Foreign Policy.* New York: St. Martin's Press, 1999.

Offner, Arnold A. *Another Such Victory: President Truman and the Cold War, 1945–1953.* Stanford, CA: Stanford University Press, 2002.

Oren, Michael B. *Six Days of War: June 1967 and the Making of the Modern Middle East.* New York: Oxford University Press, 2002.

Palmer, Michael A. *Guardians of the Gulf: A History of America's Expanding Role in the Persian Gulf, 1833–1992.* New York: Free Press, 1992.

Parker, Richard Bordeaux. *The Politics of Miscalculation in the Middle East.* Bloomington: Indiana University Press, 1993.

———, ed. *The Six-Day War: A Retrospective.* Gainesville: University Press of Florida, 1996.

Persson, Magnus. *Great Britain, the United States, and the Security of the Middle East: The Formulation of the Baghdad Pact.* Lund: Lund University Press, 1998.

Pillar, Paul R. *Terrorism and U.S. Foreign Policy.* Washington, DC: Brookings Institution Press, 2001.

Podeh, Elie. *The Quest for Hegemony in the Arab World: The Struggle over the Baghdad Pact.* New York: E. J. Brill, 1995.

Powell, Colin L. *My American Journey.* New York: Random House, 1995.

Quandt, William B. *Peace Process: American Diplomacy and the Arab-Israeli Conflict since 1967.* Washington, DC: Brookings Institution, 1993.

Rabinovich, Itamar. *The Road Not Taken: Early Arab-Israeli Negotiations.* New York: Oxford University Press, 1991.

———. *The War for Lebanon, 1970–1985.* Ithaca, NY: Cornell University Press, 1985.

Ramazani, Rouhollah K. *The United States and Iran: The Patterns of Influence.* New York: Praeger, 1982.

Reagan, Ronald. *An American Life.* New York: Simon & Schuster, 1990.

Rodman, Peter W. *More Precious than Peace: The Cold War and the Struggle for the Third World.* New York: Scribner's, 1994.

Ross, Dennis. *The Missing Peace: The Inside Story of the Fight for Middle East Peace.* New York: Farrar, Straus, and Giroux, 2004.

Rubin, Barry M. *Paved with Good Intentions: The American Experience and Iran.* New York: Oxford University Press, 1980.

Sanjian, Ara. "The Formulation of the Baghdad Pact," *Middle Eastern Studies* 33:2 (April 1997): 226–66.

Saunders, Bonnie F. *The United States and Arab Nationalism: The Syrian Case, 1953–1960.* Westport, CT: Praeger, 1996.

Saunders, Harold H. "The Crisis Begins." In *American Hostages in Iran: The Conduct of a Crisis*, edited by Paul H. Kriesberg, 35–71. New Haven, CT: Yale University Press, 1985.

———. "Diplomacy and Pressure, November 1979–May 1980." In *American Hostages in Iran: The Conduct of a Crisis*, edited by Paul H. Kriesberg, 72–143. New Haven, CT: Yale University Press, 1985.

Schoenbaum, David. *The United States and the State of Israel.* New York: Oxford University Press, 1993.

Scott, James M. *Deciding to Intervene: The Reagan Doctrine and American Foreign Policy.* Durham: Duke University Press, 1996.

Shlaim, Avi. *The Iron Wall: Israel and the Arab World.* New York: W.W. Norton, 2000.

———. "The Protocol of Sevres, 1956: Anatomy of a War Plot." *International Affairs* 73, no. 3 (July 1997): 509–530.

Shpiro, David H. *From Philanthropy to Activism: The Political Transformation of American Zionism in the Holocaust Years, 1933–1945.* New York: Pergamon Press, 1994.

Shultz, George P. *Turmoil and Triumph: My Years as Secretary of State.* New York: Scribner's, 1993.

Sick, Gary. *All Fall Down: America's Tragic Encounter with Iran.* New York: Random House, 1985.

———. *October Surprise: America's Hostages in Iran and the Election of Ronald Reagan.* New York: Random House, 1991.

Smith, Charles D. *Palestine and the Arab-Israeli Conflict.* New York: St. Martin's Press, 1988.

Stein, Kenneth W. *Heroic Diplomacy: Sadat, Kissinger, Carter, Begin, and the Quest for Arab-Israeli Peace.* New York: Routledge, 1999.

Stocking, George W. *Middle East Oil: A Study in Political and Economic Controversy.* Nashville: Vanderbilt University Press, 1970.

Stokesbury, James L. *A Short History of World War I.* New York: Morrow, 1981.

Strong, Robert A. *Working in the World: Jimmy Carter and the Making of American Foreign Policy.* Baton Rouge: Louisiana State University Press, 2000.

Suleiman, Michael W. *The Arabs in the Mind of America.* Brattleboro: Amana Books, 1988.

Suskind, Ron. *The Price of Loyalty: George W. Bush, the White House, and the Education of Paul O'Neill.* New York: Simon & Schuster, 2004.

Takeyh, Ray. *The Origins of the Eisenhower Doctrine: The U.S., Britain, and Nasser's Egypt, 1953–57.* New York: St. Martin's Press, 2000.

Terry, Janice J. *Mistaken Identity: Arab Stereotypes in Popular Writing.* Washington, DC: American-Arab Affairs Council, 1985.

Tessler, Mark A. *A History of the Israeli-Palestinian Conflict.* Bloomington: Indiana University Press, 1994.

Vance, Cyrus R. *Hard Choices: Critical Years in America's Foreign Policy.* New York: Simon & Schuster, 1983.

Vogel, Lester Irwin. *To See a Promised Land: Americans and the Holy Land in the Nineteenth Century.* University Park: Pennsylvania State University Press, 1993.

Weinberg, Gerhard I. *A World at Arms: A Global History of World War II.* New York: Cambridge University Press, 1994.

Woodward, Bob. *Bush at War.* New York: Simon & Schuster, 2002.

———. *Plan of Attack.* New York: Simon & Schuster, 2004.

Yaqub, Salim. *Containing Arab Nationalism: The Eisenhower Doctrine and the Middle East.* Chapel Hill: University of North Carolina Press, 2004.

Yergin, Daniel. *The Prize: The Epic Quest for Oil, Money, and Power.* New York: Simon & Schuster, 1991.

INDEX

213

ABOUT THE AUTHOR

PETER L. HAHN is professor of history at Ohio State University and executive director of the Society for Historians of American Foreign Relations. He is the author of *Caught in the Middle East: U.S. Policy Toward the Arab-Israeli Conflict, 1945-1961* (2004) and *The United States, Great Britain, and Egypt, 1945-1956: Strategy and Diplomacy in the Early Cold War* (1991), and co-editor (with Mary Ann Heiss) of *Empire and Revolution: The United States and the Third World Since 1945* (2001). Hahn held a Fulbright Senior Research Fellowship in Jerusalem in 1995 and he received the Stuart L. Bernath Lecture Prize in 1997.